Northwest
OREGON

BEST SHORT HIKES in™ Northwest OREGON

RHONDA & GEORGE OSTERTAG

THE MOUNTAINEERS BOOKS

Published by
The Mountaineers Books
1001 SW Klickitat Way, Suite 201
Seattle, WA 98134

© 2003 by Rhonda and George Ostertag

First edition, 2003

Project Editor: Laura Slavik
Editor: Paula Thurman
Acquiring Editor: Cassandra Conyers
Cover and Book Design: The Mountaineers Books
Layout: Jennifer LaRock Shontz
Mapmaker: George Ostertag
Photographer: All photos by George Ostertag

Cover photograph: *Olallie Lake Scenic Area, Mount Hood National Forest*
Frontispiece: *McKenzie Wild and Scenic River, Willamette National Forest*

Library of Congress Cataloging-in-Publication Data

Ostertag, Rhonda, 1957-
  Best short hikes in Northwest Oregon / Rhonda Ostertag and George
Ostertag.— 1st ed.
      p. cm.
  Includes bibliographical references and index.
   ISBN 0-89886-880-7 (pbk.)
   1. Hiking—Oregon—Guidebooks. 2. Trails—Oregon—Guidebooks. 3.
Oregon—Guidebooks. I. Ostertag, George, 1957- II. Title.
  GV199.42.O7 O845 2003
  796.52'09795—dc21
                                                  2002152805

CONTENTS

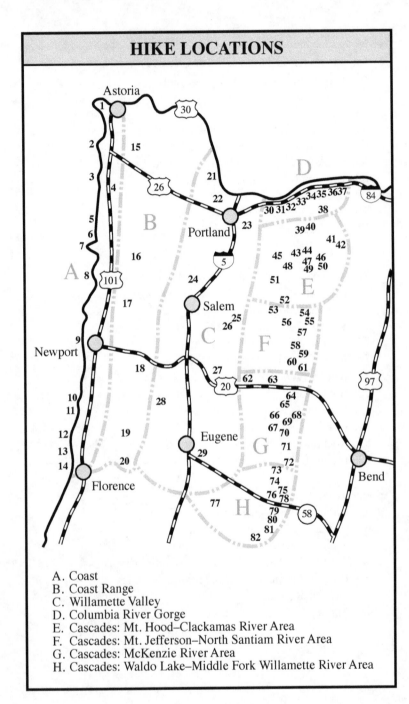

HIKE LOCATIONS

A. Coast
B. Coast Range
C. Willamette Valley
D. Columbia River Gorge
E. Cascades: Mt. Hood–Clackamas River Area
F. Cascades: Mt. Jefferson–North Santiam River Area
G. Cascades: McKenzie River Area
H. Cascades: Waldo Lake–Middle Fork Willamette River Area

MAP LEGEND

Interstate	(95)	Town	◯
U.S. Highway	(101)	Wetland	☩
State or County Road	(2)	Campground	▲
Forest Service Road	7745	Picnic Area	⛱
Paved Road	▬▬▬▬	Dam	▬
Gravel Road	══════	Bridge	‿
Unimproved Road	=======	Building	∎
Trailhead/Parking	Ⓟ	Summit	▲ 2,477 ft
Described Trail	∿∿∿	Mine/Quarry	⚒
Alternate Trail	∿∿∿	Viewpoint	⊙
Creek/Waterfall	∿∿∿	Point of Interest	★
River	﹏﹏	Boat Launch	🛶
Body of Water	⬭	Lookout Tower	🏛
Spring	℘	Lighthouse	🗼

INTRODUCTION

This book of *Best Short Hikes* gathers the preeminent trail offerings in northwest Oregon from the Pacific Coast to the Cascade crest and encompasses the attractions of the Coast Range, Willamette Valley, and Columbia River Gorge National Scenic Area. With a focus on the best, the book brings together old favorites and lesser-known trails. Oregon's northwest quadrant bursts with diversity—wilderness realms, wildlife areas, volcanic and glacial legacies, old-growth forests, idyllic valley niches, and untrammeled coast. Not bad for a bunch of short hikes!

That's all great, you might think, but are these trails right for you? You bet they are—even if you don't consider yourself a hiker. Whether you are new to the outdoors or a one-time backpacker who has hung up the boots and compass, this book is for you. Families, RVers, sightseers, and followers of Audubon; little legs and old legs; and the stressed out, pooped out, and those who just want to get out will find suitable trails.

There is a growing group of outdoor enthusiasts who, like you, are interested in short outings that can be accomplished in anywhere from a fraction of an hour to a part of a day's time and don't require a lot of planning. This book is packed with a variety of these outings, and what's really great is you probably already have what you need to hit the trail.

A number of hikes are located off commonly taken through-routes, off scenic driving routes, near campgrounds, or by popular attractions, so you can make the most of your time in an area. Others are off the beaten track, fulfilling the need for escape. Several of the trails package neatly together or link up with other trails, allowing for the plotting of longer outings. A few offer a bit more challenge for when you want that sense of accomplishment at the end of the day.

The assembled trails generally keep within an 8-mile round trip limit, with more than half less than 5 miles round trip. With a range of trail difficulty, this book can mature with you. As your hiking skills grow or as your little ones grow up, you can pick out trails of increasing difficulty. Some trails are barrier-free, so no one has to be left behind. The splendor of the outdoors should be available to all.

What we like best about the shorter trail lengths is they allow for time for enjoying the passage and discoveries along the way. Sometimes the passage turns out to be the best part—nature is filled with

Indigo Lake and Sawtooth Mountain, Cascade Lakes Recreation Area, Willamette National Forest

wonder and surprise. After all, hiking is not a race and you are not required to reach the destination. Remember, your time on the trail should free you from pressure, not add to it.

With such trail highlights in this collection as sleepy and racing rivers, tumbling and graceful waterfalls, mountain lakes, summit lookouts, wildflower meadows, record-setting trees, history, and solitude, what are you waiting for? Pick an attraction (a trail) and go for it. You, too, can be a happy wanderer.

HOW TO USE THIS BOOK

The organization is kept simple. The book is divided by geographic provinces, Coast, Coast Range, Willamette Valley, Columbia River Gorge, and Cascades, with the Cascades subdivided into four areas by the major river divides: Clackamas, North Santiam, McKenzie, and Middle Fork Willamette.

A heading to each write-up supplies the decision-making essentials about a trail (features, length, elevation change, difficulty, season, and maps, with an information line showing the agency to contact, permit or fee requirements, and trail user advice). We do not provide estimated hiking times because you best know your ability and how you like to walk—pokey, briskly, or somewhere in between. From the distance, elevation, and difficulty listing, you can pretty well judge the time it will take to finish the trail. Usually, you will want to factor in added time for enjoying the lake, view, or catching your breath, especially when the trail is rough or has a hefty elevation change. Weather conditions can also affect trail time. Muddy, wet trails require more time and effort.

The first paragraph of each hike write-up summarizes the trail's character, rewards, and special features; the second paragraph gives the directions. The remainder of the text briefly describes each trail's progress, noting landmarks, worthy features, and junctions.

The ratings of *easy*, *moderate*, and *difficult* are subjective. Basically, an easy trail is short (3 miles round trip or less), features generally mild ups and downs with no more than 200 feet of elevation change, and has a good walkable or wheelchair-accessible surface. Obstacles are few and minor. Moderate trails have a top distance of 5 miles and can have as much as 1,000 feet of elevation change. The path may be narrower or rockier with some obstacles, which may include unassisted stream crossings either atop rocks or by wading. Difficult trails exceed 5 miles in length and typically have an elevation change greater than 1,000 feet. They can be rugged, steep, and challenging and may be inappropriate for young children or people with impaired health.

Remember, these are just guiding principles based on fair weather conditions and routine maintenance of the trail. Off-season hiking between maintenance periods can be more difficult. Trails can also change over time: re-routes, the loss or addition of bridges, erosion, and more can alter difficulty and/or course. Weather is another overriding condition. Frost, snow, and wet conditions can bump an easy-rated trail up to a difficult rating. Heat, too, can influence the perception of effort. Because each reader brings a different set of skills, experience, and health to the mix, get to know your own limits and that of your hiking party to best assess the trail's appropriateness for you.

MAPS

Typically recommended maps include basic national forest maps, site maps/brochures, and topographic maps, commonly referred to as topos. Topographic maps show the elevation contours so you can gauge the total climb or descent. The tighter the contour line spacing, the steeper the terrain. Topos may be produced by the U.S. Geological Survey (USGS), private business, or the U.S. Forest Service (USFS), which has a selection of maps with topographic detail. You can purchase maps at most outdoor stores and at USFS offices.

Boardwalk along Lost Creek Nature Trail, Mount Hood National Forest

So what's the difference between the USGS maps and the basic national forest maps of the USFS?

USGS maps cover a more focused area, showing the elevation and providing information about the steepness of the terrain, vegetation, stream crossings, and guiding landmarks. Because they are dated, though, they may not even show the trail or all of the necessary roads to reach the trailhead. Newer, privately produced maps based on the USGS information are often better, updated, and easier to read, but you are still likely to need a road map.

USFS maps show the big picture and are typically a better source for getting you to the trailhead. These maps show the roads and road surfaces, the maintained trails (at the time of the map making), land ownership, campgrounds, waterways, and major landmarks. Although the basic national forest maps do not have topo lines, many of the USFS wilderness area maps now do.

Although sometimes stocked at the site, trail brochures are best requested from the appropriate supervising agency before visiting. State park maps should be requested from the actual state park or from the Oregon State Parks headquarters in Salem. Other site maps should be requested from the agency listed in the information line of the trail summary.

For many of the short hikes described in this book, the simple line map shown in the brochure or in the text will be adequate to guide you. Although as your urge to explore takes you out on longer, more complicated trails, knowing about the other maps, how to read them, and how to use them with a compass is invaluable.

READING A COMPASS

Because the compass locates magnetic north and maps are based on a true north orientation, you'll need to adjust your compass to reflect the declination (the difference between magnetic north and true north) in order to properly read maps. For Oregon the mean declination is about 20 degrees east. For specific locales, it may vary one or two degrees; search the bottom border of the map for the precise declination. To adjust the compass, put the hot end of the needle on the declination mark, by either rotating the compass or rotating the dial. The north symbol on the dial will now show true north. Rotate the map, matching its north arrow to that of the adjusted compass. You can now properly read the map, identifying landmarks, headings, and trail progress. Who knows? If you become really good at it, you might add orienteering to your pastimes.

PASSES AND PERMITS

A day-use fee is charged at many state parks; come prepared to pay and have a supply of one-dollar bills for the mechanical fee collection sites, which are common. If you frequent the parks, the annual pass is a worthwhile purchase, providing no-fuss entry. A parking pass is also required at Sauvie Island Wildlife Area, with day and annual passes available.

At most U.S. Forest Service trailheads, the Northwest Forest Pass is now required. These are available on a daily or annual basis and are sold at ranger offices and select area outdoor outlets. Again, if you spend quite a bit of time on forest service lands, the annual pass is convenient, saving you both money and time. Annual passes also allow for spur-of-the-moment trip planning—a big plus. Although many trailheads have self-service fee stations, others do not, so before driving a long way into the trailhead, buy your pass in advance.

The most complicated part about the program is that not all trailheads require a Northwest Forest Pass. One suggestion is to check the web page listed in Appendix B to see which trailheads currently need Northwest Forest Passes or call the appropriate ranger district.

Wilderness permits are typically supplied at the wilderness entry registration site. While in the wilderness, completed permits are required to be in the hiking party's possession at all times. Again, because trailhead supplies can run out, you may want to obtain a permit, along with the forest pass, at a USFS ranger office before driving to the trailhead.

WHAT WILL YOU NEED?

First and foremost, you will need a good pair of well-fitting, comfortable hiking boots or supportive walking shoes that have a heavy rubber sole for gripping the trail surface and a construction that provides protection for toes and ankles. Street shoes are inadequate. If your feet hurt, you cannot enjoy the trail or its attractions. Because even a sidewalk crack in the city can steal your balance or cause you to turn an ankle, proper footwear is a must. If you are hiking with young ones, be sure they, too, have on good protective shoes, not some flimsy sneakers.

Food and Water

Water is the most important item to carry and be sure to bring plenty. Even light exercise can dehydrate you, and sometimes the merit of the attraction will cause you to linger longer than anticipated. It is always best to bring water from home because even developed sources can have problems such as a broken pipe or a failed water safety test. A plastic bota slings easily over the shoulder, and even most fanny packs have water-bottle pockets.

Wildwood National Recreation Trail, Forest Park

Food or snacks are also a good idea because you will be expending energy. Since the Northwest is known for its rain, repackaging food in water-resistant zip-seal plastic bags ensures what you pack will stay usable. Nobody wants to reach into a pack full of squished, soggy food, let alone eat the gooey mess. Zipper bags also allow you to save any uneaten portions for later. Remember all wrappers, peels, and shells must be packed out. If you do not throw it around the living room to biodegrade, do not throw it in the wild.

Proper Map for Trail or Park

Although short trails may be free of puzzling junctions, it remains a good idea to carry the map(s) that show both the trail and the driving route to the trailhead. These maps can help you confirm that you are on track, identify the panorama, read the terrain, discern progress, and plot alternatives. The trail summary lists the most useful maps for the trip.

Extras

Depending on trail length, time, and season, the amount of gear needed or desired will vary. A good-quality fanny pack or a day pack with reinforced straps and side pockets for water bottles will help ease the transport of selected items. Even for most short hikes, something for warmth and a first-aid packet with antiseptic, bandages, and aspirin are important to carry. Placing a whistle in your child's pack can help speed your reunion if you become separated.

Identification guidebooks, binoculars, and cameras can enhance the trip. Sunscreen, lip balm, raingear, woolen hats, and gloves are seasonal considerations. The appendixes at the back of the book include other suggestions you might consider. Not all items will apply to all trips, but the suggestions should help guide you through packing decisions. You may have your own list of indispensable items.

ACTING RESPONSIBLY IN THE WILD

When you enter the outdoors—the wild—you enter an unspoken pact to keep it clean, beautiful, and safe for the next trail traveler and for future generations. Hiking is a privilege that should not be abused.

Trash and Waste

In the outdoors, the standing policy is pack it in, pack it out. There are no exceptions.

Cigarette butts, gum and candy wrappers, cans, bottles, and disposable diapers—all must be packed out. If you are unwilling to do this, you should remain at home.

For human waste, use the provided toilet facilities wherever possible. When there are no toilets, use a trowel to dig a cat hole 6 to 8 inches deep and at least 200 feet from trails and water. Then, bury the waste well with soil, rocks, leaves, and limbs. Tissue should be packed out in a zip-seal bag to where it can be properly disposed. It is a good idea to carry antibacterial solution or towelettes for proper sanitation.

Dogs

Even good-tempered, well-mannered dogs cause problems in the wild, scaring wildlife merely by their scent and tearing up vegetation as they romp. Where pets are allowed, heed the leash laws and keep the animal controlled at all times, not just when other people are present.

Courtesy

Because more and more people are seeking the sanctuary of the great outdoors, hikers need to be thoughtful in their conduct. Preserve the quiet, keep to the trails, and leave no trace that you have passed this way. (To familiarize yourself with the principles of no-trace travel, go to the Leave No Trace website listed in Appendix B.)

SAFETY

By entering the wild, you assume some degree of risk. Although this book attempts to caution you to dangers, point out confusing junctions, and warn of seasonal risks, trails and roads can change, nature is unpredictable, and only you know your capabilities and limitations. Exercise common sense.

The following tips will also help keep you safe:

- Notify a responsible party of the intended destination and time of your return before departing for the trail. Then, be sure to notify them again of your safe return. This notification procedure insures someone can initiate a search, if you don't check in.
- Before striking out on the trail, have a game plan for what to do should you become separated. This is especially important when hiking with children. Confusion can quickly grow to panic. The plan may be as simple as hug a tree. Specify who will conduct the search and who will stay put. Everyone, even tiny ones, should carry at least a sweater, water, snack, and a whistle.
- When straying from the trail or proceeding on an uncertain path, make a note of where you are, how you got there, and which route you are now taking. If straying to a lakeshore or other attraction, take a moment to note where you arrived as well. This will allow you to easily backtrack to the trail. Do not wander too far or too long timewise off-trail or on an unknown trail, certainly no farther than you can safely backtrack.
- Be alert while in the wild. Learn which plants, insects, and animals pose a threat, where they occur, and how to avoid them.

Identification books, interpretive trails, and area naturalists are all good information sources.

▪ Come prepared with safe drinking water or some form of treatment (purification tablets or water purification systems that strain

Forest trail stairway, McDowell Creek Falls County Park

out both harmful organisms and debris). Wild sources must always be treated. Don't let the clarity fool you. The microorganism *Giardia* exists even in pristine-looking waters and causes extreme intestinal distress.

▪ Drink plenty of water—hiking demands it. If you feel thirsty, you have waited too long. This is no time to be stingy; drink often and heartily. Dehydration and heat exhaustion can cause fatigue, headaches, kidney stones, and worse. Remember, you will require more fluids than if you were simply sitting at a desk or changing channels.

▪ Pay attention to the weather and exercise good judgment about starting out, turning back, or seeking appropriate shelter. Being caught on an open peak or standing beneath a lone-standing tree in a lightning storm is dangerous. Be sure to pack something warm, as well as rainwear (when appropriate). Hypothermia does not need sub-zero temperatures to strike. For their weight, wool hats perform a great service in retaining body heat. If you plan and pack for the emergency, quite likely it will never happen.

▪ Know first-aid and carry a supply of the basic items needed for treatment. If anyone suffers from allergies or other medical conditions that might require onsite treatment, be sure to carry the needed medications.

▪ Pack responsibly. Shortcuts intended to save weight can have bad consequences.

▪ Learn to trust your instincts. If you are questioning a situation, there is probably a good reason.

▪ Even though a trail is described in the book, conditions can change over time making the trail unhikeable or dangerous.

While this information will get you started, good instructional books on outdoor skills, etiquette, and safety are readily available at local libraries and outdoor outlets and can provide you with more information. Classes and lectures can also increase your appreciation for and safety in the outdoors. Even outdoor veterans can benefit from a refresher.

Prescribed outdoor skills are continuing to evolve to meet the demands of increased visitorship and reflect environmental awareness. Some of your old scouting skills may be outdated, so take a few minutes to brush up on the latest skills.

A NOTE ABOUT SAFETY

Safety is an important concern in all outdoor activities. No guidebook can alert you to every hazard or anticipate the limitations of every reader. Therefore, the descriptions of roads, trails, routes, and natural features in this book are not representations that a particular place or excursion will be safe for your party. When you follow any of the routes described in this book, you assume responsibility for your own safety. Under normal conditions, such excursions require the usual attention to traffic, road and trail conditions, weather, terrain, the capabilities of your party, and other factors. Because many of the lands in this book are subject to shifts in funding and/or management policies, conditions may have changed since this book was written that make your use of some of these routes unwise. Always check for current conditions, obey posted private property signs, and avoid confrontations with property owners or managers. Keeping informed on current conditions and exercising common sense are the keys to a safe, enjoyable outing.

—*The Mountaineers Books*

COAST

The Oregon coast is an extraordinary retreat beloved by state residents and visitors alike. It encompasses long, uninterrupted sandy strands, rugged headlands, windswept dunes, and picturesque offshore rocks, juxtaposed with inland forests and pastoral valleys. Coastal waterfalls and productive bays and estuaries expand the discovery. It is a place of gulls, bald eagles, and migrating gray whales, along with colonies of nesting seabirds. Harbor seals and sea lions offer delightful encounters. Farther inland, deer, elk, and perhaps spawning salmon will halt you in your tracks.

This prized shoreline also boasts a romantic and proud history, punctuated by tales of lighthouses, ghosts, shipwrecks, and buried treasure. Wandering the coastal reaches, hikers will come upon places viewed by Captain James Cook, Captain Robert Gray, and the Corps of Discovery led by Meriwether Lewis and William Clark.

Old-growth and second-growth forests of impressive Sitka spruce or Douglas fir–hemlock, coastal meadows, thickets of salal, sandstone cliffs, and dunegrass habitats are among the realms explored. Oregon is blessed with great accessible beaches and shores the entire length of its coast. The ones included in this section capture the magic and launch the discovery.

Spring and fall are generally the finest times to stroll the beach. In summer, the valley heat creates a temperature inversion that pulls in the cool coastal fog and produces windy beach conditions. (Bring jackets and windbreakers.) For such times, though, you need only drive a few miles inland to reclaim the sun and milder conditions; headlands, peaks, and coastal streams are among the options for discovery. Winters along the beach find exciting conditions with storm fronts rolling in one after the other. Although brief, the breaks between storms are absolutely beautiful.

Collectors return home with shell fragments, shell fossils, agates, driftwood, and perhaps a true treasure—a glass float. Each winter, several of Oregon's coastal communities hide highly decorative artist-blown

Footprints on South Jetty Beach, Oregon Dunes National Recreation Area

glass floats along the beaches for combers to find. Be sure to observe any local restrictions on the collecting of natural items.

What you should know, if you go: The coastal strands are ideal for walking, but beware of the notorious sneaker waves that unexpectedly pulse into the shore at irregular speed and volume. Also, keep off and away from drift logs during incoming tides. The incoming water can lift, shift, and toss logs as easily as toothpicks, making them both dangerous and deadly. Be sure to carry or at least study the appropriate tide table before starting out on your beach walk and allow ample time for a safe return before the incoming tide. Remember: cliffs can prohibit escape, so don't dally near them when the tide is encroaching.

When strolling the tops of coastal cliffs, keep well back from the edge. The vegetation can give a sense of land where there is none, and it is often slippery from mist, fog, or rain. Besides that, these cliffs are tall, vertical, and unforgiving of the misstep. Rein in pets and youngsters. The coastal cliffs are no place for tomfoolery.

1. COFFENBURY LAKE

Features	▪	Attractive coastal lake, birdwatching
Distance	▪	2.4-mile loop
Elevation change	▪	Minimal
Difficulty	▪	Easy
Season	▪	Year-round, quieter for birding after Labor Day
Map	▪	Fort Stevens State Park map
Information	▪	Oregon State Parks; day-use fee

A good route for beginners, casual hikers, young families, and nature lovers, this trail hugs the perimeter of Coffenbury Lake, within Fort Stevens State Park (a former military reservation) outside of Hammond. This long, narrow 50-acre freshwater lake offers an engaging stroll tucked away from the elements of Oregon's northernmost coastal beach. The hike simultaneously explores two environments: the towering Sitka spruce and pine of the stabilized dune and the shoreline habitat of twisted alders and teeming rushes. Birding and nature study are popular pursuits; bring binoculars.

From US 101, 2.7 miles south of the US 101–US 30 junction in Astoria; 9 miles north of Seaside, turn west off US 101 onto Harbor Drive/Highway 104 toward Warrenton, Hammond, and Fort Stevens

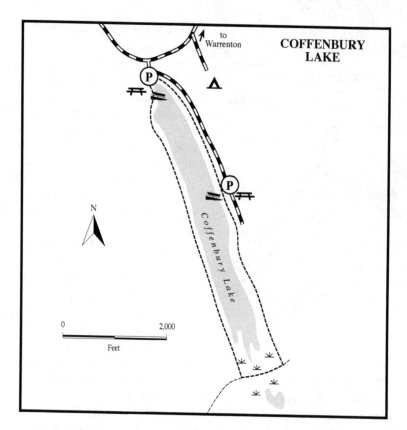

State Park. Then follow the well-marked route south and west along DeLaura Beach Lane/Ridge Road, reaching the campground entrance in 4.5 miles. Turn left and proceed 0.5 mile to Coffenbury Lake's northern day-use area.

Begin the hike heading west across the lawn above the beach area to enter the shoreline forest near a wooden post for counterclockwise

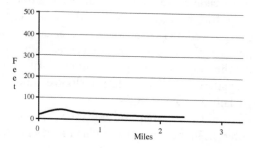

Coffenbury Lake, Fort Stevens State Park

travel. Ignore footprints streaking up the dune. On this perimeter tour of Coffenbury Lake, picnic areas at the start and part way around offer seasonal amenities, including a chance to take a swim or perhaps rent a paddle boat for new perspectives. The lake fills a sliver depression in the dunes, reaching a maximum depth of only 9 feet. It invites with a shimmery blackness and wonderful reflections.

The dune-reclaiming temperate rainforest shapes a lovely rim and travel aisle. On the west shore the trail passes through a scenic arbor of cascara and shows a modest roll before entering a more open stretch along the marshy southern end of the lake. The trail then meets a jeep road (1.1 miles). Turn left, tracing the jeep road across the causeway, which presents Coffenbury Lake to the left and a textured, snag-dotted marsh to the right. A passing beaver may capture attention. Shy of 1.2 miles, turn left off the jeep trail to travel the east shore of Coffenbury Lake.

The shrubs and trees, estuary, and open water habitats draw a host of birds. We were treated to the rare sight of an immature bald eagle striking a heron in flight. The lake is periodically stocked with rainbow trout or steelhead. Wading birds, ospreys, kingfishers, and bald eagles seemingly endorse the action.

Nearing the eastside day-use area (1.6 miles), the trail abandons its forest sojourn to traverse a grassy shore and pass below the developed park. Beaver-gnawed sticks may float to shore. Continuing north along the lake perimeter, pick up a fragmented paved path at the forest edge. It advances the loop, extending frequent cross-lake views. Following the paved path to its end, complete the loop coming out at the northern lake parking area at 2.4 miles.

Tip: Between mid-December and mid-March, when the bald eagles feed on fish runs in the Lower Columbia River, sightings of the regal bird are more likely. Clatsop Spit and Trestle Bay near Swash Lake are other popular birding sites in the area.

2. TILLAMOOK HEAD

Features ■	Picturesque headland, coastal panoramas, historic gun bunkers
Distance ■	5.4 miles round trip to Clarks Point of View
Elevation change ■	1,000 feet
Difficulty ■	Difficult
Season ■	Year-round
Map ■	Ecola State Park map
Information ■	Oregon State Parks; day-use fee

The date January 7, 1806, in William Clark's journal describes Tillamook Head—its nearly perpendicular sides, cloud cap, fine view, and the hand-to-root difficulty of the climb. Today's hikers can revel in the same wild splendor but find a much easier ascent on a developed national recreation trail (NRT). While traversing the richly forested headland, gather both history and viewpoints. The selected hike concludes at Clarks Point of View, but hikers who arranged for a shuttle pick-up may walk the NRT to its end in Seaside. Views stretch to Cape Disappointment in Washington and include the mouth of the Columbia River, Seaside, and the offshore 1880s-built Tillamook Lighthouse, now abandoned to sea lions and the will of the sea. Interpretive signs about the Lewis and Clark Expedition and forest ecology dot the way.

To travel this part of the Oregon Coast Trail, at the north end of Cannon Beach, turn west off US 101, following signs to Ecola State Park, and go to Indian Beach parking. For an optional 6-mile shuttle hike north, find the northern terminus at the south end of Seaside:

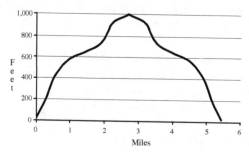

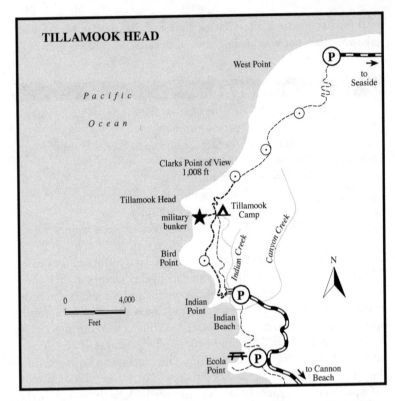

From South Holladay (US 101), turn west onto Avenue U, crossing the Necanicum River. Turn left onto Edgewood, which becomes Sunset Boulevard and ends at the trailhead.

Descend from Indian Beach parking, hiking north to travel the historic Indian route across the headland that brought Clark from the saltworks in Seaside to this site in quest of a rumored beached whale. In Chinook Indian, *ekoli* means whale, hence the park name. The harvested blubber and oil were crucial to the Lewis and Clark expedition's return east. Indian Beach is an inviting strand cupping a large cove. A side trip to it finds shell mounds, evidence of early Indian occupancy.

Cross Indian Creek and ascend the headland, briefly gaining beach overlooks. Travel in switchback-fashion through dense coastal thicket, a Sitka spruce forest close to the ocean cliffs, and fern meadow marked by large alders. A choked hemlock–spruce forest precedes Tillamook Camp and the junction at 1.6 miles. Tillamook Camp is an open-area hiker camp with covered tables and a pit toilet. A detour west from here leads to a World War II gun-encampment bunker. West of the bunker find an open vista of Tillamook Rock and Lighthouse coupled with the black sandy beach below and the offshore rocks where seabirds nest.

From Tillamook Camp, continue north toward Seaside. Much of the headland trek is through rainforest of dense Sitka spruce, western hemlock, and alder, including old-growth trees 6 to 8 feet thick and 200 feet tall. Woodland and coastal wildflowers dot the understory. Roosevelt elk may be seen.

At 2.7 miles reach the 60-foot detour to Clarks Point of View— the standout vista on the trek. It presents a long-distance view to the north and the vast ocean sweep. Additional views follow, with Tillamook Head View at 3.6 miles, signaling an alternative turnaround spot if you have added energy but didn't arrange a shuttle.

Round-trippers, turn around and backtrack. At Tillamook Camp, though, you may choose to descend the service jeep track through forest to Indian Beach parking. It remains inland from the coastal cliffs and offers a fast walk downhill if daylight is waning.

Through-trail (shuttle) hikers have another mile of scattered views, passing through forest and salmonberry-alder settings. Between 4.8 and 5.4 miles, find switchbacks. Marshy areas can dot the route even in early summer; plank walkways are being installed over wetter spots.

Indian Beach, Ecola State Park

The northern extent of the trek is through Elmer Feldenheimer Forest Preserve. At 6 miles emerge at Sunset Boulevard.

OF SPECIAL INTEREST

At nearby Fort Clatsop, now a national memorial, Lewis and Clark and the Corps of Discovery passed the soggy winter of 1805–1806. There they tended to survival and prepared for the return trip east. A replica fort, small museum, and summer living history demonstrations unfold the tale of their great odyssey. Reach Fort Clatsop National Memorial off US 101 between Astoria and Seaside.

3. CAPE FALCON

Features	▪	Stirring coastal vantage, old- and second-growth Sitka spruce
Distance	▪	4.5 miles round trip
Elevation change	▪	100 feet
Difficulty	▪	Moderate, with difficult—even dangerous—sections when wet
Season	▪	Year-round
Map	▪	Oswald West State Park brochure
Information	▪	Oregon State Parks; no fee for trail use, walk-in fee campground

Within 2,474-acre Oswald West State Park, this trail (part of the greater Oregon Coast Trail) wraps its way north along the folded headland of Cape Falcon to reach a western plateau for wild coastal views and heart-pounding coastline images. Discover Neahkahnie Mountain, Cape Meares, Smuggler Cove, and the cliffs of Cape Falcon. From this vantage 200 feet above the sea, visitors can discover the spouts of gray whales (December through June), passing pelagic birds, or a soaring bald eagle, but be cautious along the cliffs and closely watch any little ones.

Find the Cape Falcon trailhead west off US 101 on the north side of the Short Sand Creek bridge, 13.7 miles south of the US 101–US 26 junction. Parking is open 6:00 A.M. to 10:00 P.M. You will find additional parking 0.1 mile farther south at the park's walk-in campground on the west side of US 101 or at the picnicking/day-use lot across from it. Restrooms are located at the latter and within the campground, which sits in a magical setting of old-growth Sitka spruce.

Short Sand Beach Sitka spruce sunset, Oswald West State Park

Hike west briefly strolling among old-growth Sitka spruce; a magnificent monarch sits next to the trailhead. Lovely old nurse stumps, interspersed hemlocks, and showers of sword fern add to viewing. Moss, deer fern, and sugar-scoop decorate the trail sides. As the trail traverses the steep ravine slope of Short Sand Creek, second growth replaces the big trees.

After a slow steady descent reach the 0.4-mile junction, where Short Sand Beach is reached to the left. The Cape Falcon Trail heads right, continuing its rolling journey across the forest slope of this broad sculpted cape. Side drainages can hold soggy passage; elsewhere, sections of choked forest turn daylight into darkness. Wrens flit among the understory shrubs and tangle.

At 0.8 mile, look for the hollow shell of an enormous stump along with its tumbled colossus; both sit trailside. The size suggests a mythological explanation. By midway, teasing coastal glimpses urge you forward. This part of the hike joins the crash of the waves with the dark, moody beauty of a tight Sitka spruce forest. At 2 miles

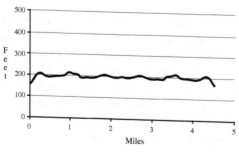

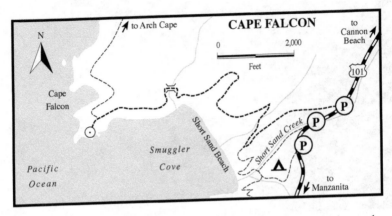

come to a trail fork. Spur left to roam Cape Falcon peninsula; to the right continues the Oregon Coast Trail to Arch Cape.

The cape spur dead-ends at the coastal rim in 0.1 mile, with tracked spurs branching right to wriggle up through the otherwise impenetrable, wind-clipped coastal thicket of salal and wild rose. On the slope, the salal can reach 7 feet high. Atop the plateau, trampled paths weave through a lower thicket to present various coastal vantages. Over-the-shoulder glances find Neahkahnie Mountain. Below to the south, view Smuggler Cove where Short Sand and Necarney Creeks merge and meet the sea. Cape Meares sits farther south. To the north is another picturesque cove cupped by impressive plunging cliffs. A charged excitement engulfs visitors like the ocean mist.

When roaming the plateau for vistas, travel safer interior paths where possible, and be wary whenever approaching the rim to better views. The rim is unstable, and its cloak of heavy vegetation is deceptive—the edge may come sooner than you think. Be especially cautious when conditions are wet. Return as you came or stroll farther north glimpsing the rugged north side of Cape Falcon.

OF SPECIAL INTEREST

Oregon enjoys unprecedented beach access and much of the credit goes to the man for whom Oswald West State Park was named. In 1913, forward-thinking Governor Oswald West had the state's beaches declared public highways. This measure insured the beaches would remain public. The result is long natural strands and coastal shores interrupted only by the rivers and large creeks breaking through to the ocean. Numerous waysides and parks supply easy beach access along the entire length of the Oregon coast.

4. NEAHKAHNIE MOUNTAIN

Features ■	Summit vantage, panoramic views, gray whale watching
Distance ■	3 miles round trip
Elevation change ■	1,100 feet
Difficulty ■	Moderate
Season ■	Year-round, but crown may be in clouds
Map ■	USGS Nehalem 7.5'
Information ■	Oregon State Parks

One translation of Neahkahnie is "abode of the deities," which seems appropriate once you claim the summit (elevation 1,631 feet). From here, you can survey the Nehalem River flood plain, Nehalem Bay, the beach and coastal communities to the south, the coast and forest of Oswald West State Park, and the ceaseless ridges of the Coast Range. Clear-day views span south to Cape Foulweather and north up the Washington coast. Wild rose, foxglove, goatsbeard, wild onions, and thimbleberry bring seasonal color to the mountain. In spring, the pink coast fawn lily adds its beauty.

To access this peak in Oswald West State Park, turn east off US 101, 2.2 miles south of the parking for Oswald West's walk-in campground (16 miles south of the US 101–US 26 junction). When coming from the south, it's 1.2 miles north of the exit for Neahkahnie Beach, north of Manzanita. A cedar trail post and green-and-white hiker sign mark the turn. Follow the gravel access road 0.4 mile to find the limited turnouts for trail parking; the marked trail is on the left.

Tracing part of an old Indian trail, this trail switchbacks up the mountain's brushy south slope with its dotting of red alder and spruce. Local Native Americans regularly burned Neah-Kah-Nie to keep the area viable for browse and hunting. Deer and a herd of Roosevelt elk

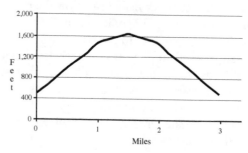

Neahkahnie Beach from Neahkahnie Mountain, Oswald West State Park

still frequent the vicinity. Almost immediately views open up of the shoreline, bay, and beach community. At 0.5 mile, the trail takes a couple of quick switchbacks, touring an area of larger trees and varied ground cover. Eventually, full stands of Sitka spruce steal views.

Atop the ridge near a switching station at 1 mile, follow the signed route for the Oregon Coast Trail toward Short Sand Beach. The summit is 0.5 mile ahead, the westernmost of three skyline knobs. The trail traverses Neahkahnie's north flank just below the ridge, passing through second-growth spruce. Where it cuts up over the ridge just behind the summit knob, spur over to the view. On a clear day from December through June, the lofty post serves whalewatchers. Some 20,000 gray whales pass along the Oregon coast in their migration between Alaska and the warm waters off Baja. During World War II, the Coast Guard used this site to watch for invaders.

Return as you came. The Oregon Coast Trail descends to cross US 101 to reach Short Sand Beach.

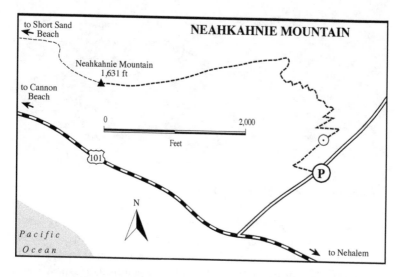

NEAHKAHNIE MOUNTAIN

OF SPECIAL INTEREST

Native American oral history has it that a 1700s Spanish galleon shipwrecked near the base of Neahkahnie Mountain. Even more intriguing, this is where the marooned sailors supposedly buried their treasure. Past beachcomber findings of strange letters on semiburied stones and beeswax candles, known to be among the cargo, have fanned treasure-seekers' hopes.

5. BAYOCEAN PENINSULA

Features ▪	Wild beach, bay shore, excellent birding
Distance ▪	Up to 7 miles round trip or a 7.4-mile loop
Elevation change ▪	Minimal
Difficulty ▪	Easy to difficult (depending on length of selected walk)
Season ▪	Year-round (when blustery, bay side is preferable)
Maps ▪	None
Information ▪	Tillamook County Parks

Ideal for all family members, Bayocean Peninsula rolls out a dual attraction of a pristine, natural sandy beach and a bay-shore bike-pedestrian way that can be united for a loop. The spit separates Tillamook Bay from the Pacific Ocean and is a national estuary

Horseback riders on beach, Bayocean Peninsula

project. In the early 1900s, the peninsula supported the bustling beach resort of Bayocean, which ultimately was swallowed by the sea in the 1950s. Now nature reigns supreme. Birding is outstanding with Tillamook Bay, the ocean beach, the surf, the peninsula's Cape Meares Lake, and dense inland vegetation and seasonal wetlands creating habitat; bring binoculars.

From US 101 in Tillamook, turn west on Third Street/Netarts Highway for Three Capes, go 1.8 miles, and turn north on Bayocean Road. Continue 5 miles, skirting the bay to reach the one-way loop road out to Bayocean Peninsula on the right. Follow the lower road 0.9-mile north to the gate and day-use parking; the dike road holds the exit. Chemical toilets are available at the trailhead, May through September.

For the *beach walk*, round the gate taking the initial open aisle west. This sandy track passes through a canyon of even-height scotchbroom, shorepine, and Sitka spruce. Traverse the rolling dune plain to descend a seaward dune to the beach at 0.4 mile. Because horseback riding is popular along the beach, deep hoof prints may be encountered on the dune crossing. Once on the beach, turn north but

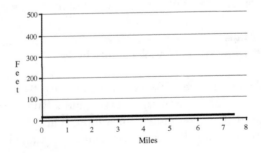

first take a moment to memorize where you came out to speed your return. Look for signs and other clues.

A wonderful coastal stroll stretches to the tip of the spit and South Jetty; looks south find Cape Meares and Three Arch Rocks. Grass-capped dunes with a tall conifer hill at 2 miles abut the beach. Width of the strand varies with tide and season. Along the upper beach, find loose sands, scattered drift logs, and tide-carried whatnots; the lower beach is compressed for easy walking.

Gulls, shorebirds, cormorants, and scoters are commonplace; bald eagle, tufted puffin, or peregrine falcon bring an added thrill. At 3.5 miles, reach Kincheloe Point and the rocky tongue of South Jetty. It captures a broad fan of clean sand, ideal for sunning. Across the inlet water is North Jetty, which sped the demise of the resort. The riprap bank of the jetty channel appeals to anglers. Seals and sleek-headed sea lions frequent the bay.

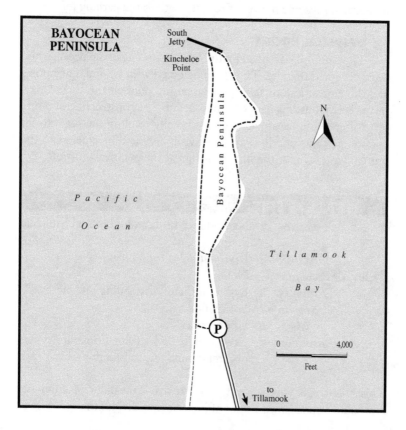

For the *bay hike*, round the gate and follow the fire lane north along Tillamook Bay—a large scalloped open-water. Bay views characterize the start, with the Coast Range cutting a ragged eastern skyline and Garibaldi to the north. An abrupt bank, a ring of rocks and logs, and a muddy beach at low tides separate the trail from the bay. Spy ducks, loons, grebes, great blue herons, kingfishers, curlews, eagles, and ospreys. Towhees scratch in the ground cover of the inland woods. Farther along, conifer and alder sometimes block bay views. At 0.8 mile, round a second gate. At 3 miles, end at the monument rock indicating "South Jetty–Tillamook Bay and Bar." It serves as a convenient turnaround landmark and pit toilets are nearby.

If a *loop hike* is on your agenda, it is best to take the beach leg first to avoid searching for the return over the dune. The 0.9-mile link travels the grassy plain behind the riprap bank of the bay channel. On the bay side of the peninsula, meet up with the bay shore fire-lane trail near the monument rock and hike the fire lane south to the parking lot.

OF SPECIAL INTEREST

The peninsula is named for the 1907 resort city of Bayocean, which once occupied this site. The city blossomed with a hotel, bungalows, and the largest indoor saltwater swimming pool on the West Coast, but its bright bustling days were numbered. The construction of North Jetty altered the ocean currents, eventually sending the sea into the community, washing it away. Most visitors would be clueless to this human past, save for the historical sign at the peninsula turnoff.

6. NETARTS SPIT

Features	Natural spit, birding, harbor seal haul-out at tip
Distance	Up to 10 miles round trip
Elevation change	None
Difficulty	Easy to difficult, depending on length
Season	Year-round
Maps	Unnecessary
Information	Oregon State Parks; Cape Lookout day-use or campground fee, consult tide table

This hike treats you to a singularly relaxing meander of mind and foot. The 5-mile sandy finger of Netarts Spit divides the rich fishery

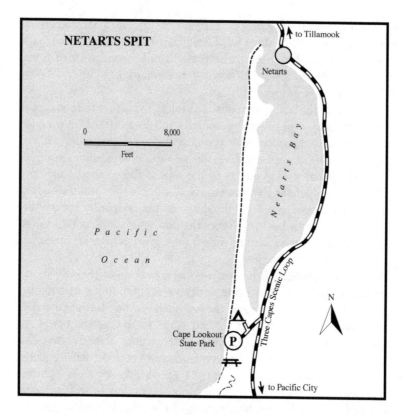

of Netarts Bay from the open ocean, while the beach rolls out the perfect way to get to know it. On this northbound journey, find continuous views of Cape Meares and Three Arch Rocks National Wildlife Refuge—that is unless fog enfolds the scene. Attractive vegetated rolling dunes divide the beach from Netarts Bay, which hosts more than 150 bird species. If you get as far as the tip of the spit, travel quietly because harbor seals haul-out to bask on the bay side.

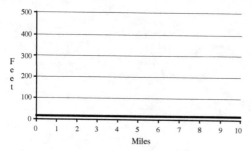

From US 101 in Tillamook, turn west on Third Street/Netarts Highway and follow signs for Three Capes Scenic Loop and Cape Lookout State Park. Reach the park 12 miles southwest of town. Locate the beach access below the developed park at either the day-use area or the campground.

Once on the beach, turn north traveling the broad, uninterrupted sandy strand, journeying away from the 400-foot cliffs of Cape Lookout. Your initial strides carry you past the developed park, with its wind-shaped Sitka spruce. Oceanscapes and coastal dunes complement the journey. Digressions to the tops of the seaward dunes add overlooks of Netarts Bay, the vegetated middle spit, and the coastal mountains to the east, while holding out the possibility for wildlife sightings. A rocky base reinforces the dunes for the first 1.25 miles, replaced by a natural scatter of drift logs. During high seas be especially watchful of these logs.

Having left behind the beach-going crowd, enjoy the wild strand stretched out before you. Long, serial waves lap to shore, with deposited shell fragments recording the last tideline. Shorebirds gather and disperse, feeding in the just-washed sands. Crab pots and buoys are other discoveries. Seasonally, great concentrations of sand crabs cause the beach sands to ripple and give stomachaches to the feeding gulls.

By 2.5 miles, the dunes seclude areas of Sitka spruce and shore-pine, and by 3.25 miles the abutting dunes become low and rolling. Near the end of the spit, gain better views of the arch features suggesting the name "Three Arch Rocks." This vital seabird nesting site is part of the greater Oregon Coastal Wildlife Refuge system. The largest of the rocks is Shag Rock, the small westernmost one is Storm Rock, and

Walking on Netarts Spit, Cape Lookout State Park

the middle one is known either as Finley Rock or Mid Rock. Cape Meares and the mouth of Netarts Bay likewise gain presence.

At the end of the spit, lower your voices. As many as fifty wary harbor seals use the shoreline for sunning. Carry binoculars and keep a respectful distance—one that does not alarm the seals or alter behavior. Yawning, scratching, and undulating passes between sand and water are commonplace.

No matter how far you make it, return as you came with Cape Lookout your guiding landmark.

7. CAPE LOOKOUT

Features	▪ Dramatic headland, superb views, memorial plaque
Distance	▪ 4.8 miles round trip
Elevation change	▪ 400 feet
Difficulty	▪ Moderate
Season	▪ Year-round
Map	▪ Cape Lookout State Park Hiking Trails brochure
Information	▪ Oregon State Parks; day-use or campground fee

On the Cape Trail, you will traverse the steep treed flanks of Cape Lookout, wending to viewpoints with a grand signature view at the cape's tip. Where the trail traces cliff rims, find exciting windows to the south and north. The tip's outlook stretches south and west. The gathered views span some 80 miles of Oregon coast from Tillamook Head to Cape Foulweather. The forbidding weathered and surf-battered cliffs contribute drama but do pose danger; keep back. A bench and rocky seating are available at trail's end. Bring a sandwich,

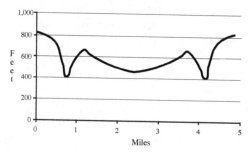

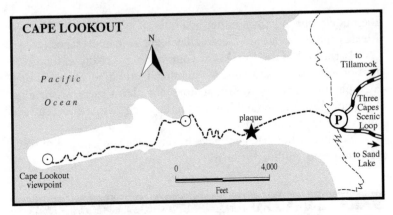

because you might want to linger. Whalewatchers give the cape tip a thumbs up.

This trail sits at the southern extent of Cape Lookout State Park off Three Capes Scenic Loop. Reach the campground and core of the park about 12 miles southwest of Tillamook (follow signed route off Third Street); the trailhead is about 2.5 miles farther south. RVers may prefer the less winding Sand Lake route to the trailhead and park. It heads west off US 101, 11 miles south of Tillamook; a sign reads: "To Sand Lake, Three Capes Scenic Loop, and Cape Lookout." Go 4.3 miles to a stop sign and proceed forward on Cape Lookout Road. Reach the trailhead in another 3.3 miles, with the campground beyond.

Start on the left path heading west, avoiding the north-south trending Oregon Coast Trail which heads right at the trailhead and left 250 feet down the Cape Trail. Sitka spruce, western hemlock, and western red cedar rise above a thick mat of fern, salal, waxmyrtle, and salmonberry. Discover a few massive Sitka spruce, as well as scenic snags, nurse logs, stumps, and extensive root balls. The environment is lush owing to its 100 inches of annual rainfall.

About 0.5 mile into the trail, search the outcrop slope to your right for the plaque paying tribute to the crash victims of the B-17 bomber that struck the cape cliffs in 1943. In the same vicinity, the trail serves up the first view south overlooking a remote beach, Sand Lake Recreation Area, Cape Kiwanda, Haystack Rock, and Cascade Head. Fog, cloud, and mist can rewrite the view; clear days present a distant Cape Foulweather.

As the trail descends, boardwalks (slippery when wet) advance the trail. Beyond the 1-mile post look for the trail to level at a saddle before slipping onto the cape's north flank. View Netarts Spit, Cape

Meares, and Three Arch Rocks. The fenced area ahead adds a stirring look at the cape's vertical plunging cliffs and the turbulent cove below. Views continue to build and perspectives flip back to the south. Forest strolls bridge cliff segments.

At 2.4 miles, claim the cape tip and viewing bench nearly 500 feet above the sea. The tip is a great place to surrender to the site's power and solace and to soak in the warm rays. Winds heighten vigor, while passing whales may draw you to your feet. Cape Lookout juts 2 miles into the blue swells of the Pacific Ocean for prime viewing. Scan for spouts, glassy footprints, and the actual leviathans. Nesting seabirds and passing sea lions may also catch your eye. Backtrack when ready.

OF SPECIAL INTEREST

Each winter, Cape Lookout is one of thirty sites along the Oregon Coast staffed by volunteers during Whale Watch Week, which occurs at the peak of the gray whale migration season. Check newspapers for dates. On average, during the height of migration, nearly thirty gray whales an hour swim past the Oregon coast. Look for spouts visible up to 5 miles out. Volunteers can guide your search and provide gray whale information.

Cape Lookout Trail, Cape Lookout State Park

8. HARTS COVE

Features ■	Headland meadow, coastal vistas, waterfall
Distance ■	5.4 miles round trip
Elevation change ■	700 feet
Difficulty ■	Moderate to difficult
Season ■	July 16 through December 31
Maps ■	Hebo District Hiking Trails brochure; USFS Siuslaw National Forest
Information ■	Hebo Ranger District; no overnight camping

In Cascade Head Scenic Research Area, this trail wraps around hillsides and cuts through steep drainages to emerge at a picturesque headland meadow that serves up spectacular ocean, cliff, and coastline views. What's even more special is the meadow's south rim, which overlooks a postcard-pretty waterfall as it dives from a coastal cliff into the sea at Harts Cove. Often atop a nearby snag, a bald eagle shares this view and in morning deer may linger in the meadow. In November and December, the headland is ideal for seeking gray whales. Seabirds can delight anytime. When bathed by the sun, the relaxing meadow invites you to kick off your boots and pull up your day pack for a pillow.

Reach this trail off US 101, 3.5 miles north of its junction with OR 18 (north of Lincoln City) or 3.3 miles south of Neskowin. There turn west onto gravel Cascade Head Road (FR 1861). Trailhead parking is at the road's end in 4 miles.

A quick switchback descent through alder stand and choked second-growth hemlock leads to the Cliff Creek bridge crossing (0.75 mile) and an old-growth gallery of fabulous stout, tall Sitka spruce with outstretched arms. The forest bursts with beauty and diversity. Snags riddle the multistoried grove and ferns abound.

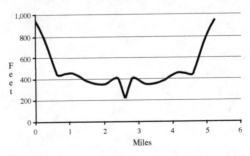

Harts Cove Trail, Neskowin Crest Research Natural Area, Siuslaw National Forest

The grade eases with the rounding of the slope. By 1.2 miles, the sound of the surf and the barking of unseen sea lions urge you on. Enter Neskowin Crest Research Natural Area. Through forest succession, western hemlocks will slowly replace this area's 250-year-old spruce trees. Soon, the Harts Cove Viewpoint bench invites you aside for a view of the cove and the grassy headland destination footed by steep, dark cliffs.

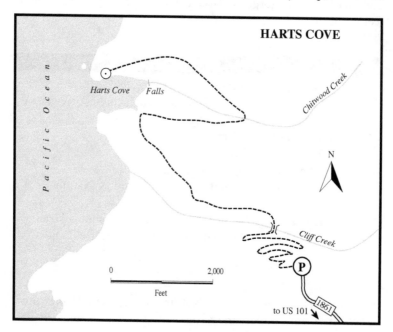

Gulls, red-tailed hawks, pigeon guillemots, and woodpeckers may be spied. The trail then drifts inland to round Harts Cove. Across Chitwood Creek, the forest briefly opens up, but big trees again enclose the trail before it bursts out onto the meadow-topped headland.

A narrow trampled path descends through the meadow. Southern views find Two Arches, an offshore rock with side-by-side ocean gateways, and Harts Cove, with its steep moss-decked cliffs, cascade to the sea, and nearby weather-shaped trees. The 60- to 80-foot falls on Chitwood Creek spills as a graceful plume. Depending on tide, either a small sandy beach or open water catches the spill.

Views north present Capes Kiwanda and Lookout along with Haystack Rock. Explorations across the grassland add a western vantage, looking out at the offshore rocks with their seabird colonies. On the odd occasion, a puffin may fill your binocular image. Return as you came.

OF SPECIAL INTEREST

Cascade Head rises 1,800 feet above the ocean. Its prairie meadows support rare plant species and provide habitat for the endangered silverspot butterfly. This headland is so named for its three creeks that carve deep-cut gorges and cascade over its flank spilling 60 to 80 feet to the ocean.

9. SALAL HILL

Features ▪	Lighthouse, whalewatching, birding
Distance ▪	0.7-mile round trip, including paved loop around lighthouse
Elevation change ▪	150 feet
Difficulty ▪	Easy
Season ▪	Year-round, dawn to dusk
Map ▪	Yaquina Head Outstanding Natural Area brochure
Information ▪	Salem District, BLM or Yaquina Head Outstanding Natural Area; fee (Golden Eagles accepted), no pets in wildlife viewing area

In Yaquina Head Outstanding Natural Area, north of Newport, several short trails explore the headland from tidepool to bluff. This

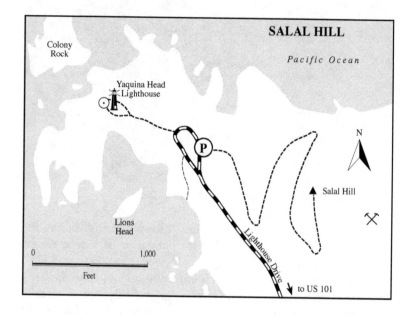

easily accomplished hike tops an aptly named frontal hill for a gratifying overlook of this rugged section of coast. It's one photographers won't want to miss. At the site, admire the classic beauty of Yaquina Head Lighthouse, Colony Rock (an important seabird nesting site), Seal Island (where harbor seals haul-out), and sweeping coastline and horizon views. From November to March, gray whale migrations add to the discovery.

From US 101 at the northern edge of Newport, take the marked turn for the outstanding natural area and head west on Lighthouse Drive to the lighthouse parking area at road's end. Pass the fee collection site and the visitor center tucked back in a quarry. The visitor center is open daily 10:00 A.M. to 4:00 P.M., with lighthouse hours varying. The lighthouse and its observation deck hold a front row seat

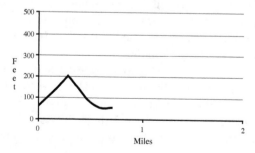

Colony Rock, Yaquina Head Outstanding Natural Area

to this coastal drama; Salal Hill offers balcony viewing. Locate the trail to Salal Hill at the east end of the lighthouse parking area near the chemical toilets.

The 0.3-mile Salal Hill Trail is uncomplicated. Ascend the stairs from the parking area to climb in switchback fashion on an earthen footpath along the salal and wildflower slope to top the hill east of Yaquina Head Lighthouse. The final distance traces the summit ridge on the back side of Salal Hill overlooking the visitor center area and the quarry cliffs. A good chunk of the Yaquina headland was privately quarried before the government retrieved this treasure, but the Bureau of Land Management (BLM) has made the most of these gaping holes, nestling the visitor center in one and building an experimental tidepool in another.

Views engage throughout, changing in scope and perspective. Salal, the signature plant, is a woody shrub with leathery evergreen leaves and waxy bell-shaped white and pink flowers. Wild rose weaves throughout the salal, while salmonberry patches the slope. Rare and common wildflowers join in the parade of bloom.

From the hilltop, admire the shining white 93-foot lighthouse tower (the tallest in Oregon) against the stunning backdrop of the sea. Its beacon's signature flash pattern is visible from 19 miles out. The glass prisms of its lens dance in the sunlight, and gulls often decorate the rooftop of the lighthouse building.

When whalewatching, look for spouts (the exhaled vapor), glassy footprints showing the site of the last dive, and breaches (where whales break the surface of the water). Whale spouts shoot up to 12 feet high and can be viewed as far as 5 miles out. Although twenty-six species of whale have been spied off the Oregon coast, 95 percent are gray whales.

Authorities estimate that as many as thirty an hour pass along the Oregon shore late December through early January. About one hundred gray whales remain nearly year-round.

Although the hilltop vantage allows visitors to view the comings and goings and noisy commotion of the sanctuary birds, the best birdwatching is from the lighthouse observation deck, back at the trail's start; no pets. April through July, common murres, Brandt's and pelagic cormorants, and pigeon guillemots stand shoulder-to-shoulder atop Colony Rock. A few tufted puffins nest deep in the rock, and gulls nest on the headland cliff. Colony Rock holds the unique distinction of being the nearest nesting colony to the United States mainland, so the views are a treat. Morning has the best lighting for both area photography and wildlife viewing.

10. HISTORIC 804 TRAIL

Features ■	Exciting assault of surf on rocky shore
Distance ■	1.5 miles round trip, can be extended on beach
Elevation change ■	Minimal
Difficulty ■	Easy/barrier free
Season ■	Year-round, except when seas or winds are especially high
Maps ■	None
Information ■	Oregon State Parks; do not approach sea lions

Part of the Oregon Coast Trail, this trail follows a remnant section of the early wagon route between Waldport and Yachats—Lincoln County 804. It tours at the edge of one of Oregon's most dramatic shorelines. Here, you can feel the rumble of the ocean at your body's

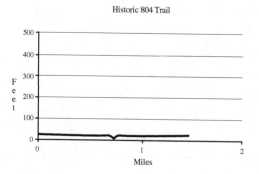

Historic 804 Trail

core, while the salt mist clings to your skin. The thundering assault of surf on land is wild and beautiful: skyward shooting spray, blow holes, churns, cascades, and foam. The white streaming water dramatically accents the low ragged basalt shore. Although some homes and hotels back the trail, eyes remain locked on the sea. North of this rugged shore, open beach carried the early-day highway and now offers an opportunity to extend the hike.

The trail begins in Smelt Sands State Recreation Area, west off US 101 at the north end of Yachats; watch for park signs. The park has picnic tables, a restroom, and beach and trail access.

Hike west from the interpretive board, turning north upon reaching the now-surfaced historic path. This route carried the Alsi Indians, stagecoach passengers, and early settlers along this section of coast. It passes between the low coastal terrace and the eroded shoreline rock ledges and tongues battered by the sea. It's a wave-watchers paradise. Stirring white water images come fast and furious. Winds can aggravate the sea and heighten the intensity of the moment.

Small pocket beaches of cobble and gravel are tucked between the fury. Agates and jasper can be found in their midst. Tidepools hold starfish, sea anemone, mussels, and crabs, but never take your

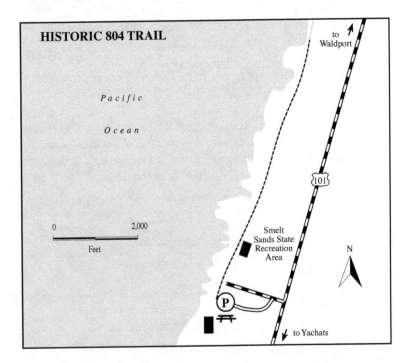

Rocky coast along Historic Trail 804, Smelt Sands State Recreation Area

eyes off the sea. Before homes and hotels, Native American summer camps (600 B.C. to 1620 A.D.) dotted the coastal terrace. Bountiful shellfish drew the Native Americans here, and the middens (heaps of disposed shell) grew as deep as 40 feet. Most of the middens have since been excavated, with the shells used to surface the early streets of Yachats.

Salal, low-growing Sitka spruce, and wildflowers edge the route. Mostly the viewing is nonstop, save where the spruce and salal are a bit taller and fuller. Viewing benches and a small picnic area at 0.5 mile suggest you linger in comfort. At 0.75 mile the route grades to the beach, which calls most hikers to continue the walk. How far you go depends on the tide and your will and ability, but know the time of the next incoming tide before getting too adventurous.

While the clash of rock and water is the recommending feature of this stroll, you may also spy oystercatchers, terns, brown pelicans, common murres, cormorants, and of course—gulls. Garter or red racer snakes may slither across the trail.

OF SPECIAL INTEREST

Smelt Sands State Recreation Area pays tribute to the annual summer smelt runs that occur along this shore. The surf smelt lay their eggs in the shoreline gravel. Historically, the native peoples dip-netted the smelts; contemporary fishermen follow in their tradition.

11. RESTLESS WATERS–COOKS CHASM

Features ■	Thrilling rocky coast, wild beach cove
Distance ■	1.8 miles round trip
Elevation change ■	100 feet
Difficulty ■	Easy (more difficult under wet conditions)
Season ■	Year-round
Maps ■	Cape Perpetua Hiking Trails brochure; USFS Siuslaw National Forest
Information ■	Waldport Ranger District or Cape Perpetua Interpretive Center; Northwest Forest Pass

You won't want to miss this hike in Cape Perpetua Special Interest Area. It travels one of Oregon's most rugged coastal stretches and holds nonstop excitement. Discover a thumping surf that vibrates in your throat, geyserlike sprays, cruel rocky shores, and a picturesque beach cove. The ever-changing images of the restless water, jet black rocks, and sheer power are spellbinding. Rising above the trail is 800-foot Cape Perpetua, named by Captain James Cook. Gray whales are sighted offshore, but are best spied from the headland summit, where the line of view is better and the competing points of interest less alluring. Oystercatchers, turnstones, and gulls pause on the drier rocks.

Start at Cape Perpetua's Devils Churn Viewpoint Parking, west

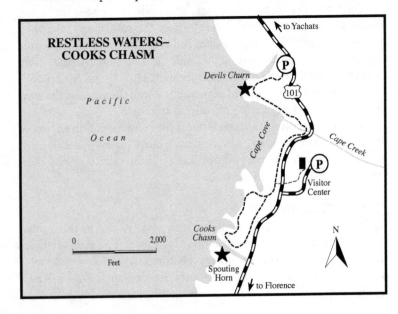

off US 101, 10.6 miles south of Waldport; 2.3 miles south of Yachats. To obtain the trails brochure, the visitor center is just a bit more south. Center hours are 9:00 A.M. to 5:00 P.M. daily in summer; 10:00 A.M. to 4:00 P.M. weekends in winter.

This hike links the Trail of Restless Waters, Cape Cove Trail, and Cooks Chasm Trail. The route passes beneath ancient and wind-distorted spruce and through salal. The collision of water and rock captivates with crash, spray, and trailing cascades. Throughout the hike, be careful on any wet stairs, path, or rock. Also, keep an eye out on the waves while enjoying the side spurs to shore.

From the seaward side of the lower parking level, descend the paved Trail of Restless Waters, switchbacking to the Devils Churn spur (0.1 mile). Stairs descend to this attraction where tides thunder in and out of a long, narrow chasm, churning foam and shooting spray.

At the north end of Cape Cove, a stairway descends to the lava shores and a tidepool menagerie. Sea urchins and anemones, starfish, limpets, mussels, and camouflaged fish attract the curious but no collecting. Ahead, keep right on the Cape Cove Trail; it cups the site's scenic sandy beach. At 0.4 mile, a spur descends to the beach.

En route to Spouting Horn, find a fairly steep, unsurfaced stretch, where the trail gets pinched up to US 101. The foot trail resumes past the small interpretive turnout. Walk past the tunnel to the visitor center at 0.6 mile, staying on the coastal trail system. In 100 feet is the loop junction for the Captain Cook Trail; bear right passing a shell midden and tidepool overlook.

At 0.9 mile arrive at the overlook landing for Cooks Chasm and Spouting Horn. Here, a sea finger penetrates the land and water mounts in a sea cave beneath the basalt ledge only to be forced up through an aperture in a billowing spout. When conditions come together just right, it's a glorious display. Return as you came or take the inland arms of the Captain Cook and Restless Waters loops, touring in coastal forest.

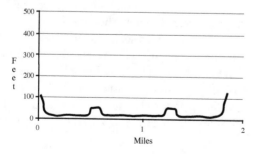

Devils Churn, Cape Perpetua Special Interest Area, Siuslaw National Forest

OF SPECIAL INTEREST

On March 7, 1778, the log of Captain James Cook records the sighting of this significant headland that he named Cape Perpetua. At the time of Cook's visit, Native Americans occupied the area, subsisting on shellfish. Shell mounds offer a clue of their early presence.

12. HECETA HEAD

Features	■	Lighthouse, coastal views, beaches
Distance	■	4 miles round trip (1 mile round trip to lighthouse)
Elevation change	■	400 feet
Difficulty	■	Moderate
Season	■	Year-round
Map	■	Carl G. Washburne State Park brochure
Information	■	Oregon State Parks; fee

This trail visits Oregon's most photographed lighthouse—Heceta Head Lighthouse, which occupies a charismatic coastal bluff at the edge of the sea. The lightkeeper's house on a lower terrace is now a U.S. Forest Service property operated as a bed & breakfast; it holds the Heceta Light Station Interpretive Center. The hike travels coastal bluff and spruce-forested slope between the cobble beach at Heceta Head Lighthouse State Scenic Viewpoint and a sculpted sandy beach to its north in Carl G. Washburne State Park. Heceta Head and Hobbit Trails combine to fashion the hike, which not only applauds the lighthouse but also the imposing nature of the coastal headland.

Start at the parking area for Heceta Head Lighthouse. It is west off US 101, 11.8 miles north of the US 101–OR 126 junction in

Florence; 33 miles south of Waldport. The gravel trail leaves the picnic area wrapping north uphill toward the attractive lightkeeper's house, gleaming white against the dark headland backdrop.

Below the lightkeeper's house, find a vista spur onto a headland appendage offering southern views of the serial headlands, Devils Elbow Cove, Cape Creek and its road bridge, and Parrot and Conical Rocks. With privately operated Sea Lion Caves just to the south, it's not uncommon to see or hear sea lions. To the north overlook Heceta Churn between the promontory you are on and the main headland.

Walk past the lightkeeper's house, traveling among storm-shaped seaward Sitka spruce, salmonberry, fern, and salal. The trail's continuation switchbacks uphill to the right, just before the lighthouse (0.5 mile); delay taking it. The charming lighthouse with its auxiliary buildings occupies a small grassy terrace 205 feet above the sea. The lighthouse is painted classic white and sports a red cap; its beacon is the brightest on the Oregon coast. A picnic table and bench invite you to linger, whether to admire the scene or to spot whales, sea lions, or the seabirds that nest on the offshore rocks.

Switchbacks and sets of stairs then carry the trail up the steep

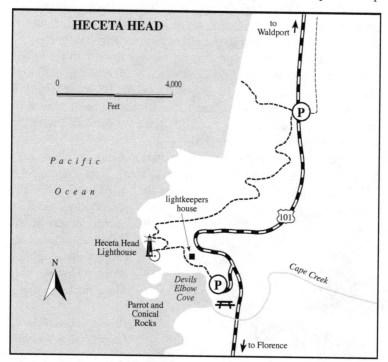

HECETA HEAD

to Waldport

0   4,000
Feet

Pacific

Ocean

lightkeepers house

101

Heceta Head Lighthouse

N

Devils Elbow Cove

P

Parrot and Conical Rocks

Cape Creek

to Florence

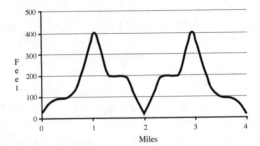

coastal headland, cloaked in Sitka spruce. The mood varies as the trail passes through ancient, candelabra-trunk, choked, and parklike stands of the scaly bark tree. At the start, spurs branch to views of the beacon and seascape, but keep back from the edge—this is an unforgiving landscape.

The primary trail turns right at 0.6 mile, heading inland to skirt a headland crease with vertical cliffs and a tormented sea (viewed from informal left spurs—use caution!). Benches dot the route, while balls of licorice fern adorn the spruce. Midway, the hike enters its descent. Be careful if the trail is wet; the earthen bed is slippery. More salmonberry and fern appear as the forest opens up. Past an abandoned link to US 101, meet the Hobbit Trail and turn left. This twisting descent through an enchanting thicket of salal, black huckleberry, rhododendron, waxmyrtle, shorepine, and spruce seems ideal for fairy-tale beings.

At 2 miles reach the thin channel passage leading to the beach, noting where you arrived. Eroded sunset-colored sandstone cliffs back the beach and contribute to its sculpted character. Because of the cliffs and the tributaries crossing the beach, how far you can roam depends on the tide. Don't risk becoming stranded. Return as you came, retracing the Hobbit and Heceta Head Trails.

Tip: To find out about the light station tours (available on a limited schedule), contact Carl G. Washburne State Park at 541-547-3416 or Jessie M. Honeyman State Park at 541-997-3851. For information about an overnight stay at the lightkeeper's house, contact the Mapleton Ranger District (See Appendix G).

Parrot and Conical Rocks, Siuslaw National Forest

13. BAKER BEACH

Features	▪	Lightly traveled, undeveloped beach
Distance	▪	Up to 6.2 miles round trip
Elevation change	▪	None
Difficulty	▪	Easy to moderate
Season	▪	Year-round
Map	▪	USFS Siuslaw National Forest
Information	▪	Mapleton Ranger District; fee/Northwest Forest Pass, leash dogs

Baker Beach has just the formula to erase the work-a-day woes. Part of the greater Coos Bay Dune Sheet, Baker Beach offers a taste of the setting found along the premier dune fields and beach strips of Oregon Dunes National Recreation Area, farther south. This hike follows the wild strand south to Sutton Creek. The deep dune field backing Baker

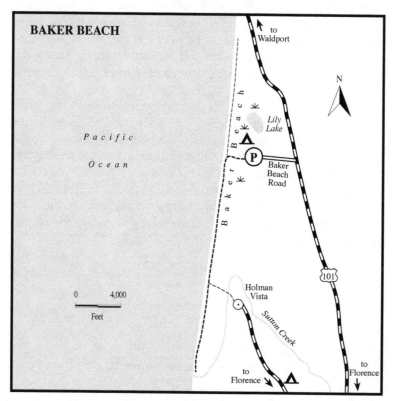

Beach invites side trips for beach and dune overlooks. Discover 10- to 20-foot-high mounds with dips, rises, and shallow depressions. But from March 15 through September 15, stay below the high-tide line, respecting the nesting habitat of the threatened western snowy plover. Views to the north include Heceta Head, its lighthouse, and the cliffs and headland at Sea Lion Caves. Views south span the coastline to North Jetty and the Siuslaw River.

From US 101, 5.6 miles north of Florence, turn west onto gravel Baker Beach Road. Travel 0.4 mile to road's end, the broad beach parking area, and a primitive campground. A 0.3-mile footpath then winds through the coastal scrub and around and over dunes to arrive at the beach. On this crossing, beware of the gorse, an invasive unyielding spiny shrub.

Upon reaching Baker Beach, discover the pole markers that will signal your return to the parking area on the way back. Turn south. Another mile of beach stretches north but requires the wading of the outlet of Lily Lake and the crossing of Berry Creek. Travel an inviting broad, flat, sandy strand mostly bordered by low dunes. Like coarse hair, golden green grasses spread between and over the smooth dune contours. Closer to the dunes, you will encounter loose sand and wind-whipped patterns. At the beach's seaward edge, travel tidal-etched and compressed sand.

At the tide line, a thin glassy sheet of water tosses back the reflections of shorebirds. Peppering the beach are the small holes left by both the dug-in crustaceans and the searching shorebirds. As horseback riders share Baker Beach, photographers can sometimes capture rider and horse splashing through the tide.

After 1.2 miles, find over-the-shoulder looks at Heceta Head Lighthouse; it was previously blocked by the angle of the cliffs. Sea lions or harbor seals may be spied; North Jetty to the south is a favorite hangout for these guys.

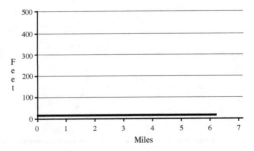

Dune grass at Baker Beach, Siuslaw National Forest

In another 0.5 mile, Sutton Creek passes parallel to the beach but is mostly hidden by the low, rolling dunes. Where cedar posts cross over the dunes, you can follow them to a Sutton Creek fording. Across the water is Sutton Creek Recreation Area and Holman Vista, an estuary overlook. You can see the deck from atop the dunes.

Remaining on the beach, the low dunes give way to a drift log–strewn flat between the ocean and the Sutton Creek estuary. At the mouth of Sutton Creek (3.1 miles), gulls congregate and bathe. This watery stop signals the turnaround; across the creek, Heceta Beach stretches south. Return as you came, trading southern views for northern ones.

OF SPECIAL INTEREST

Opposite the southern end of Baker Beach, Sutton Creek Recreation Area spreads east and encompasses twelve different habitats, including dunes, a Darlingtonia (cobra plant) bog, and coastal lakes. The diverse realm supports some 300 species of wildlife—native and migrant, and has a network of trails as well as camping.

14. SOUTH JETTY BEACH

Features	■	A prime Oregon Dunes National Recreation Area beach
Distance	■	Up to 7.4 miles round trip
Elevation change	■	None
Difficulty	■	Easy to moderate
Season	■	Year-round, but best May 1 to September 30 and all weekends and holidays, when the beach is closed to street vehicles
Map	■	USFS Oregon Dunes National Recreation Area
Information	■	Oregon Dunes National Recreation Area; fee/Northwest Forest Pass

Here, at the southernmost reach of coastal trails in this book, you just get to dip your toe into Oregon Dunes National Recreation Area. A wild beach experience awaits in summer; the rest of the year, you can see evidence of the flip-side of the area offering—beach driving. South Jetty stretches into the sea at the north end of the beach. At the south end find the marker signaling the divide between the open driving beach and this restricted-access beach. Dunes back the strand and the vast ocean draws the gaze to the horizon. Shorebirds are travel companions.

At the southern outskirts of Florence, 0.8 mile south of the Siuslaw River Bridge, turn west off US 101 for South Jetty Dune and Beach Access. Six parking areas access the beach; for this hike start at Beach Access 6, in 5.7 miles. An alternative start would be from the jetty, 0.2 mile farther on rutted unpaved road. Park law enforcement vehicles patrol the beach.

Cross through the rumpled dunes with shorepine depressions,

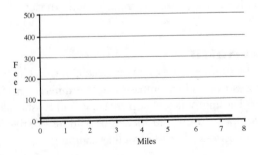

South Jetty Beach, Oregon Dunes National Recreation Area

reach South Jetty Beach in 0.1 mile, and turn south. But before strolling away, study where you came out of the dunes and take a moment to view the jetty, 0.2 mile north; it will help signal your point of return. In summer, footprints or the presence of other people will likely show where to turn in. In winter, though, you may have the beach all to yourself, despite its being open to driving, making the return harder to find.

The dunes are flattish at the start, but build in stature and show subtle changes in character. The sandy strand is broad and offers easy walking. There are no cobbles or pebbles, just clean fine sand. Embedded in the sand, picturesque red drift stumps punctuate the beach, marking off distance. Washed-in kelp streamers, broken clam shells, and the occasional broken sand dollar are among the discoveries. The waves arrive one after the other in a long, unbroken series. Morning hikers can find a canvas of unmarked sand to sink their feet into—unless the shorebirds got there first.

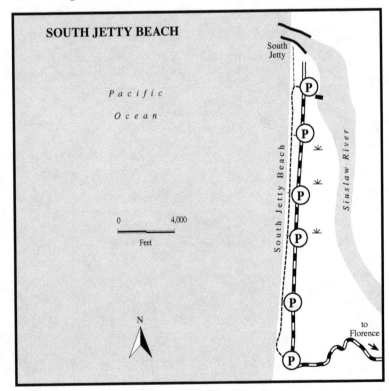

Between accesses you are often alone with your thoughts. Admire the big arc of sky, which can be a brilliant blue with puffy clouds or show the inward march of the ocean fog. As the seaward dune builds, the parking-bench access spurs require a steep climb up and over, but again, they are not that easy to detect. The voice of the ocean can change from a rumble to a crash and rush.

How far you wander will depend on you, but likely you will want to turn back before reaching the section of beach open to driving (3.7 miles). The sign is your clue.

Tip: Along this section of coast, onshore winds clock their greatest average velocity in summer—this is, after all, dune habitat. In winter, the wind is less frequent, but that's when storms bring the strongest blasts.

COAST RANGE

Stretched between the Willamette Valley and Oregon coast rests Oregon's forgotten mountain range—the Coast Range. Cloaked in rainforest Douglas fir, Sitka spruce, and western hemlock, the range was virtually left to loggers, but it's been rediscovered in recent years for its recreational potential. No longer is it just a passing image in the windshield but a destination, and a fine one at that.

The Coast Range houses vital wildlife habitat for species as diverse as the Roosevelt elk, the northern spotted owl, and the rare silverspot butterfly. Laced by churning rivers and quiet waters, the range still secludes pockets of old-growth Douglas fir and Sitka spruce; towering waterfalls; record-size trees; summit meadows; and coastal, mountain, and valley vistas. The peaks themselves are steep and rugged. The western reaches closely pair with the coast.

The Corps of Discovery wintered in the shelter of the Coast Range. The range was only descriptively mentioned in the journal of Meriwether Lewis as being separate from the Cascade Range isolated by a large river valley. In Native American legend, prominent Coast Range features embody events and figures from the spiritual world. The mountains themselves unfold stories of homestead efforts and of early-day logging done with springboards and sleds.

But the temperate rainforest which signaled the near loss of this recreation land also signaled its resurrection. Beneath the towering trees, fine trails journey through a lush undergrowth of salal, sword fern, huckleberry, oxalis, and Oregon grape. Moss-draped alders and maples claim the lower foothills and the riparian settings along the prized waterways. When water droplets bejewel the setting or fog drags its misty fingers through the branchwork, the forest takes on a magical quality.

The Coast Range is accessible year-round, with a moderate climate. The frequent heavy rains of winter and early spring reveal the ancient forests and waterfalls in their true element and full glory. During the rest of the year, the range has its share of fair days for unencumbered

Saddle Mountain summit view at dusk, Saddle Mountain State Park

touring and exceptional viewing. Snow occasionally caps the highest peaks and brushes the passes, but its presence is mostly fleeting.

What you should know, if you go: Fall through spring, the Coast Range does receive ample rainfall, after all, these are rainforests you are walking in. Wear (or carry) a good suit of rainwear and pre-treat boots with a liquid seal. Rain pants are a good investment because even when the rain showers stop, the wet vegetation can quickly soak legs. When traveling in the Coast Range in winter and spring, it is particularly advisable to phone ahead to learn of road and trail conditions. Slides and washouts are common in this steep rain-soaked mountain range. But on the plus side, despite all the water, the Coast Range has notably few mosquitoes.

15. SADDLE MOUNTAIN

Features ▪	Summit view, more than 300 species of wildflowers
Distance ▪	5.9 miles round trip (5.4 miles omitting spur)
Elevation change ▪	1,600 feet
Difficulty ▪	Difficult
Season ▪	Spring through fall
Map ▪	Saddle Mountain State Park brochure
Information ▪	Oregon State Parks

For the investment of a bit of sweat and a satisfying workout, you can raise your figurative flag atop Saddle Mountain's bald top (elevation 3,283 feet) for one of the best vistas in Oregon's North Coast Range. Views span two states—Oregon and Washington. To the east-northeast, Mounts Rainier, St. Helens, Adams, and Hood represent the Cascade volcano chain in dazzling snowy-crown elegance. To the west, clear-day

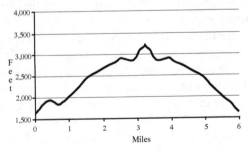

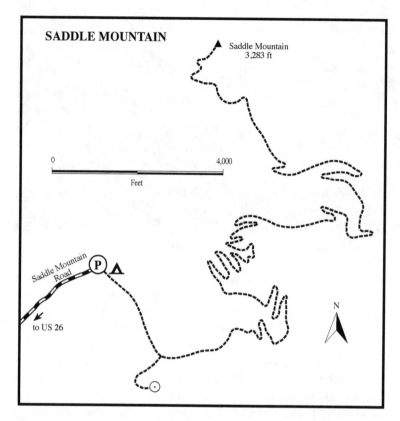

views stretch to the western horizon, overlooking the Pacific Ocean, Astoria, and the Columbia River mouth. Hikers of all ages challenge this summit, so lace on your boots, set a pace that's right for you, and come along. There are rewarding discoveries even if your feet never touch the top.

From the US 101–US 26 junction, south of Seaside, drive about 10 miles east on US 26. Turn north at the sign for Saddle Mountain State Park and proceed 6.9 miles on winding, paved road to the park at road's end (State Park fee required). On summer weekends, spillover parking can line the road leading into the park—a testament to the trail's popularity. Midweek and off-season visits promise a more peaceful mountain encounter. Be sure to carry enough water for the climb.

At the east side of the parking area, follow the wide, paved swath, which soon becomes foot trail. In 0.2 mile, a 0.25-mile spur branches right topping an outcrop for the first vista. Admire treed and rocky Saddle Mountain, its pronounced volcanic dikes (raised rock veins),

Saddle Mountain, Saddle Mountain State Park

and the surrounding Coast Range. Native Americans believed a revered murdered chief ascended as an eagle from the Saddle Mountain summit to become the creator of thunder and lightning. Past the 0.2-mile junction, the primary trail remains mostly shaded, passing through second-growth fir and alder. The understory is varied and textured.

Where the trail pulls into the open in about a mile, shade becomes prized and the path is gravelly. Avoid taking shortcuts, which cause erosion and kill vegetation. In another mile claim the ridge top, earning views north. The open, thin-soiled meadow parades a springtime bounty of prairie smoke, Siskiyou fritillary, Indian paintbrush, Oregon iris, and monkeyflowers. The steep south-facing slope houses a rock-garden community, where the amateur botanist might detect such rare species as the crucifer, Saddle Mountain saxifrage, and Saddle Mountain bittercress. More common species are nodding onion and yellow fawn lily. Again, keep on the trail and rein in little ones and pets to protect this botanic treasury.

Loose crumbly rocks slow and complicate the final hard charge to the summit. That's why ground-gripping shoes that provide ankle support are important. Use the provided cable for steadying yourself. The summit view makes up for the trouble of the climb. Glass fragments hint at a one-time lookout site; from here, the Tillamook fire of 1933 was first reported. The parkland spreading from the summit features mostly second-growth forest.

When ready to surrender the view, return down the primary trail, allowing adequate time for the first precarious leg of the descent.

16. NIAGARA FALLS

Features ▪	Two 100-foot waterfalls, each of different character
Distance ▪	2 miles round trip
Elevation change ▪	350 feet
Difficulty ▪	Moderate
Season ▪	Year-round
Map ▪	USFS Siuslaw National Forest
Information ▪	Hebo Ranger District; no overnight camping

Perfect for the family outing, this short Coast Range trail descends in second-growth forest to a magical box canyon graced by the silvery plummets of two 100-foot waterfalls. Niagara Falls, which lends its name to the trail, spills as a free-fall horsetail, while Pheasant Creek Falls skips down its cliff in lacy streamers and showery cascades. When swollen by winter rains, the falls are in full, wild glory—worth every blink of the raindrop-laden eyelashes. Summer visitors find the cliffs traced by graceful droplet threads. Plant enthusiasts particularly enjoy the trail in March and April, when the wand of spring brings out color and variety.

From US 101 at Beaver (4 miles north of Hebo; 17 miles south of Tillamook), go east on County Road 858, Nestucca River Road, for about 12 miles. Turn right (south) on FR 8533, continue another 4.2 miles, and turn right on FR 8533.131. Go 0.7 mile more to locate the trailhead and parking on the left. Find adequate parking for half a dozen vehicles.

Housed in a classic setting of second-growth Douglas fir, this pleasant trail descends and contours a hillside passing through a Coast Range canyon to the waterfall spectacle. Vine maple and salmonberry create

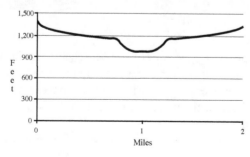

Niagara Falls, Siuslaw National Forest

a midstory, while the jagged tops of fire-scorched snags bring visual interest to the same-age forest. A few heavily branched, old-growth "hooter" trees draw eyes skyward. Elk tracks, the harvest mound of an industrious squirrel, or the noisy chastise of a Steller's jay can further add to discovery.

The descent begins meandering and slow. Later, a few slightly

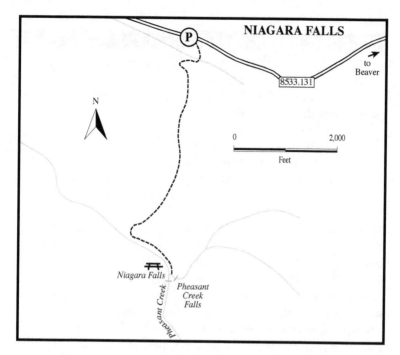

steeper segments punctuate the otherwise comfortable descent. Bridges span alder-lined tributaries and a couple of wooden benches invite pause. Switchbacks come faster. Where the trail breaks into the natural opening, enter the waterfall box canyon. The two falls adorn a side stem and the main stem of Pheasant Creek, with Niagara Falls on the main stem.

Viewing is from a dual-purpose bridge and observation deck at the base of Pheasant Creek Falls (0.9 mile) and a picnic table at trail's end. From the deck, admire both of the falls in their basalt amphitheater bowl. The picnic table presents Niagara Falls. Moisture from the falls nurtures moss and fern. Bigleaf maples and alders join the evergreens in the canyon bottom. The return is as you came.

OF SPECIAL INTEREST

The Nestucca River, a state scenic waterway en route to the trailhead, is paired with a companion byway (Nestucca River Road) for convenient viewing and access. The byway runs between the Willamette Valley at Carlton and US 101 at Beaver and offers an alternative, slow scenic route to or from the coast. BLM recreation sites along the corridor offer camping and picnicking.

17. DRIFT CREEK FALLS

Features	■	Suspension bridge, canyon waterfall, big trees
Distance	■	3 miles round trip
Elevation change	■	400 feet
Difficulty	■	Moderate
Season	■	Year-round
Map	■	Trail brochure
Information	■	Hebo Ranger District; Northwest Forest Pass, no overnight camping

Not to be confused with Drift Creek Wilderness in the Waldport Ranger District, this Drift Creek has its own surprises, including an impressive 240-foot suspension bridge hanging 100 feet above the Drift Creek chasm. What's even more unusual is that the bridge is a destination, not merely a means of advancing the trail. Despite minimal sway—not more than a couple of inches—the suspension bridge puts a bounce in your step. Below the bridge sits the 75-foot waterfall that spills into Drift Creek. Giant western hemlocks grace the bridge site, and a picnic table welcomes extended viewing of the dramatic canyon and its special piece of architecture/engineering.

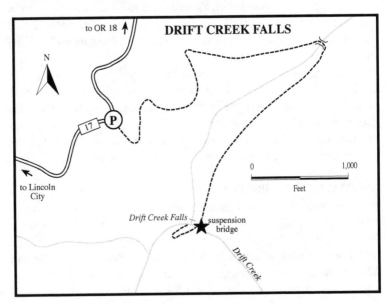

You can reach this family-friendly trail from the tiny community of Rose Lodge (east of Lincoln City). Turn south off OR 18 near milepost 5 on Bear Creek Road; the turn is signed. Initially paved, Bear Creek Road changes to gravel and narrows. Follow it 3.1 miles to paved, single-lane FR 17, which continues the tour. Keep right to remain on FR 17, following it for 5.7 miles to the trailhead parking lot on the left. On twisting single-lane FR 17, drive cautiously and expect other vehicles. In the off-season, phone ahead to confirm that the roads and trail are passable. At the trailhead, a vault toilet serves hikers.

For an optional route, from US 101 about 4 miles south of Lincoln City (24 miles north of Newport), turn east on County Road 109 (Drift Creek Road) and continue right (south) on South Drift Creek Road, reaching FR 17 in 1.9 miles. Turn left and follow FR 17 for 10.3 miles to reach the trailhead on the right. An occasional sign helps point the way.

This uncomplicated hike strings through changing forest settings. Descend through an even-age Douglas fir forest, openings of sword fern and salmonberry, a stand of young mixed evergreens with interlacing red alder, and the mossy drainage forests. Big trees are found deep in the canyon heart. Despite the steepness of the canyon slope, switchbacks and contours ease descent. The sound of rushing water accompanies travel almost from the start.

Where the trail enters a side canyon, cross a footbridge. When conditions are wet or frosty, bridges can be slippery. The drainage now directs you downhill at a quick pace. At a snaking bend at 1 mile, cross a footbridge over the side fork of Drift Creek. Below the trail, notice the gorge on this fork, which feeds to the 75-foot waterfall. In another 0.25 mile cross Drift Creek canyon on the suspension bridge and from it, overlook the waterfall's plunge into Drift Creek. Because the waterfall fork and Drift Creek are of comparable size, they unite in theatrical style.

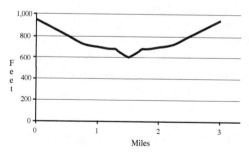

Drift Creek, Siuslaw National Forest

As you cross the bridge, gain an eagle's point of view, staring down on treetops. Attractive, 125-year-old hemlocks rise at the bridge's end. By keeping to the foot trail, hikers pursue the merged waters downstream through a beautiful forest gallery of big fir and hemlock to arrive at creek level for a side-angle look at the falls and its cliff jut. When fed by winter rains, admire a white chute smacking the green pool of Drift Creek. Cascades race away from the plunge pool. Upstream, the bridge draws a bold line across the canyon. Backtrack when ready.

18. MEADOW EDGE–MARYS PEAK SUMMIT

Features	360-degree panoramic view, noble fir forest, high meadows
Distance	3 miles round trip
Elevation change	600 feet
Difficulty	Moderate
Season	Spring through fall
Maps	Marys Peak Recreation Area brochure; USFS Siuslaw National Forest
Information	Waldport Ranger District; Northwest Forest Pass

This hike has two components: the dense noble fir forest and open tall-grass meadows of the Meadow Edge Trail coupled with the panoramic

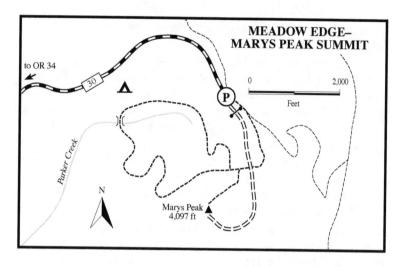

views from atop Marys Peak reached via the summit spur. Marys Peak (elevation 4,097 feet) is the highest peak in the Coast Range and extends a piecemeal 360-degree panorama sure to make your head spin. Views stretch from Washington to southern Oregon, spotlighting the Cascade volcanoes, Willamette Valley, and Coast Range—maybe even the glint of the Pacific Ocean. When fog fills the valley, Marys Peak rises like an island above the foamy sea. In addition to the noble fir, Marys Peak Scenic Botanical Area (a protective U.S. Forest Service designation) is noted for its wildflower calico. Despite the peak's popularity, the terrain is wild enough for bobcat.

To drink in this Coast Range high from OR 34, 10 miles west of Philomath, 8.5 miles east of Alsea, turn north onto Marys Peak Road (FR 30). Trailhead parking is in 9.6 miles at the observation point parking lot (generally open April 1 through November 30).

From the southeast corner of the observation point parking, head south along the meadow-forest transition zone at the eastern edge of

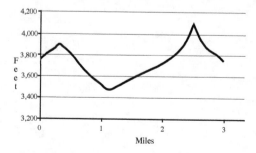

the crest to cross the service road at 0.25 mile. There find the Meadow Edge Trail and be on the watch for deer.

The 2-mile Meadow Edge Trail (a loop) is well marked with legends and map boards and quickly disappears into the noble fir forest. In a matter of strides, bypass the unmarked summit spur, which veers left; save it for the finale. Just beyond it, the Meadow Edge Trail forks for the loop; go clockwise. Noble firs prefer this lofty elevation of Marys Peak and are recognized by their classic shape and blue-green needles, rigid branches, and upright cones in late summer and early fall. Where the trail snakes through a meadow of waist-high grasses, bracken fern, and lupine, views stretch west.

The trail continues alternating between forest and meadow, with a brief riparian stretch along Parker Creek, where nettles, monkeyflowers, ferns, salmonberry, and a profusion of water-loving plants grow. Fireweed, thistle, columbine, and daisy color the former roadbed traced by the trail. Avoid the spurs branching to either the creek or the campground. Meadow-edge travel concludes the loop at 2.2 miles.

Upon completion of the loop, take a few steps forward and hook

Buttercups on Marys Peak, Siuslaw National Forest

right to add the summit spur. Its path ascends from forest to switchback up through the steep high meadow to arrive near the communication towers (2.5 miles). Wildflowers dot the summit grasses and rocky niches. Every direction competes for attention. Mounts Hood, Jefferson, and Washington; Three Fingered Jack; the Three Sisters; and Bachelor Butte highlight eastern views. The western horizon holds the rolling outline of the Coast Range and the Alsea River Valley. Clear days add Washington State's Mounts Adams, St. Helens, and Rainier. When ready, backtrack to the Meadow Edge Trail, cross back over the service road, and return to parking.

OF SPECIAL INTEREST

Marys Peak is the most prominent feature in the Coast Range. The Coast Range formed some 40 million years ago in a massive collision between the sea floor and the North American continental shelf. Molten lava then belched up through the uplifted mountain terrain adding erosion-resistant layers, called sills. Marys Peak was once taller, but the looser sediments eroded away. Today, the topmost 1,000 feet is all hard sill. An auto tour route and longer trails tracing the north and east flanks offer other ways to see the mountain.

19. PAWN OLD GROWTH

Features ▪	Outstanding old-growth grove, 500-year-old trees
Distance ▪	0.9 mile round trip
Elevation change ▪	100 feet
Difficulty ▪	Easy
Season ▪	Year-round
Map ▪	USFS Siuslaw National Forest
Information ▪	Mapleton Ranger District

Old growth has a magical quality, awakening the senses as you wander among the big trees. This 10-acre old-growth grove along Taylor Creek and the upper North Fork Siuslaw River is dark, deep, and mysterious. Many of the trees tower more than 200 feet tall and approach 500 years in age. Because historically, lightning-caused fires swept the Coast Range every 125 to 175 years, any untouched old growth remains primarily in pocket stands like this one. Hummingbirds, wrens, snails, and even elk may be spied here.

Hiker bridge on Pawn Old Growth Trail, Siuslaw National Forest

A pleasant drive along the North Fork Siuslaw River leads to this trail. From US 101 in Florence, drive 1 mile east on OR 126 and turn north onto North Fork Siuslaw River Road. Follow it for 17.3 miles, coming to a fork. Bear right and cross the North Fork bridge to arrive at the trail parking on the right-hand side of FR 2553. A brochure is available. Pets must be leashed.

Lovely but short, this self-guided lasso-shaped trail begins with the footbridge crossing of alder- and salmonberry-lined Taylor Creek before easing uphill in gentle switchbacks. The trail blends into its mossy, lush old-growth setting, passing through and over logs and dipping beneath low-swung branches. The big western hemlock and Douglas fir trees draw eyes skyward, but the tops remain elusive. Be careful where the trail crosses logs and roots; they are slippery when wet.

The Douglas fir trees show tremendous size and deeply corrugated

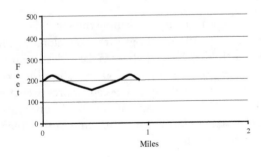

bark, while vine maples weave a midstory of delicate contrast. Bases of some trees wear the scorching from past fires. Western hemlock, a climax species, will one day take the place of the ancient Douglas firs. Snags, nurse logs, and an enormous red alder—38 inches in diameter, add visual variety.

Where the trail forks; bear left for a clockwise loop. The cut passages through logs reveal the diameters and age rings of the former colossi. Besides showing off the big trees, the loop presents a dark hemlock stand; a hardwood grove of alder, cascara, bigleaf maple, and vine maple; and a stretch near the North Fork Siuslaw River—each with signature discovery. The North Fork supports steelhead as well as silver and Chinook salmon. Close the loop and backtrack to the trailhead.

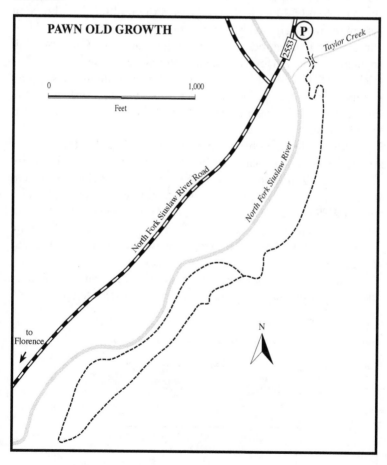

20. SWEET CREEK

Features ■	Scenic waterfalls and cascades
Distance ■	5.2 miles total round trip (can be shortened)
Elevation change ■	400 feet
Difficulty ■	Easy to moderate
Season ■	Year-round
Maps ■	Sweet Creek Trail map; USFS Siuslaw National Forest
Information ■	Mapleton Ranger District

If you want to immerse yourself in a lush green setting along a beautiful waterway graced by nearly a dozen cascades and waterfalls that measure between 4 and 75 feet high, then this is the trail for you. The trail system segmented by creek flows has four sections. This hike combines three of the four segments for a 5.2-mile round trip. One brief trail segment is improved for wheelchair access, and catwalks span the hike's trickier cliff reaches. The bulk of the journey is along the skipping waters of Sweet Creek. Its confluence water, Beaver Creek, holds the concluding falls. In presenting Sweet Creek Falls, the largest plummet, the hike visits both banks.

To take this delightful yet little-known hike, in the town of Mapleton, go 0.2 mile east on OR 126 from its junction with OR 36. Upon crossing the river bridge, turn south on Sweet Creek Road. Go 4.5 miles and bear left to remain on Sweet Creek Road, which later becomes FR 48. Proceed 5.8 miles to the Homestead trailhead, where the 0.1-mile all-ability trail starts. (There's a vault toilet.) A half mile farther find Sweet Creek Falls trailhead, with Wagon Road trailhead 0.7 mile past that.

Starting from Homestead trailhead, the upstream tour follows the 4-foot-wide, all-ability trail in a setting of tall Douglas fir, red

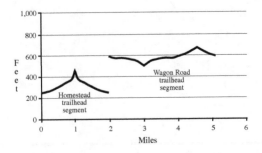

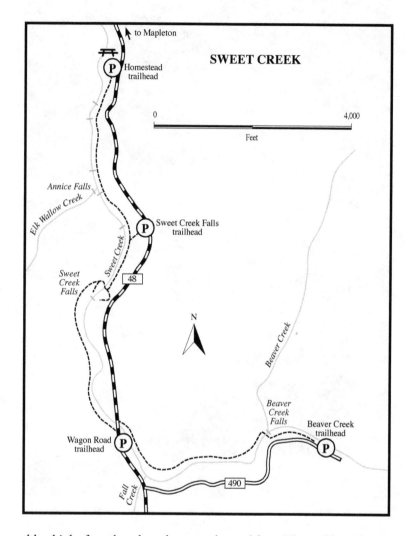

SWEET CREEK

to Mapleton

P Homestead trailhead

0   Feet   4,000

Annice Falls

Elk Wallow Creek

P Sweet Creek Falls trailhead

Sweet Creek

48

Sweet Creek Falls

N

Beaver Creek

Beaver Creek Falls

Beaver Creek trailhead P

Wagon Road trailhead P

Fall Creek

490

alder, bigleaf maple, salmonberry, and sword fern. The trail hugs bending Sweet Creek, revealing its bubbling cascades, outcrop ledges, bowls, and gorges. At 0.1 mile, the all-ability trail is replaced by foot trail and elevated grate (the catwalk), tracing a moss- and plant-adorned cliff.

Cascades and falls span the 20-foot width of the creek; the drop count will vary depending on the amount of water and your perception. Water slides, boulder-divided waters, plunge pools, and side creeks add to the hike's appeal, as do benches and interpretive signs. Winter hikers may spy fish jumping the watery tumbles to upstream spawning beds.

Sweet Creek on Sweet Creek Falls Trail, Siuslaw National Forest

At the Gorge Area, the flow is contained by steep, vegetated walls; find a catwalk here. Then, at 0.75 mile, avoid the left spur to Sweet Creek Falls trailhead and proceed upstream for Sweet Creek Falls. The upper 75-foot double falls feeds a central steep cascade before coming to the pinched lower 50-foot drop.

Where the trail halts at the head of the lower falls, backtrack to Homestead trailhead (2 miles). A short drive to Wagon Road trailhead then provides access to the next two trail segments. By taking the west bank trail downstream from the Sweet Creek road bridge, rediscover

Sweet Creek Falls from a new vantage. This 1-mile segment follows the trace of the Sunset Wagon Road through second-growth forest, coming to a pair of viewpoint spurs at 0.9 mile: straight ahead is the upper viewpoint; to the left, the lower one.

Backtrack to the Wagon Road trailhead and continue upstream along Sweet Creek to view the Beaver Creek confluence and its waterfall contribution. This 0.6-mile segment follows the east bank of Sweet Creek upstream from the road bridge, touring a verdant forest–riparian setting with some big Douglas firs. Terraced, multidirectional Beaver Creek Falls is about 25 feet high and equally as wide in an enchantment of greenery. Beyond the falls stretches the final 0.1-mile trail segment to Beaver Creek trailhead, but it requires wading or another drive to reach it. End back at Wagon Road trailhead.

OF SPECIAL INTEREST

Sweet Creek is named after an 1843–Oregon Trail pioneer, Zara Sweet. He and wife, Maria, eventually settled in this area in 1876. Maria kept a diary of their time on Sweet Creek; entries mention flood, hardship, daily routine, and the passing of an 1881 comet. Excerpts are in the trail-map flier.

WILLAMETTE VALLEY

The Willamette Valley is the dramatic geographic feature separating Oregon's Coast Range and Cascades. Despite holding the state's metropolitan areas, much of the valley remains rural with productive farms, orchards, berry fields, and vineyards. Sheep graze the green pastoral hills and dales. Peculiar newcomers: emu, ostrich, bison—and even camel—may cause heads to spin in a doubletake.

This fertile bottomland extended an invitation rivaling gold, beckoning pioneer homesteaders west. The yellow-brick road was the grueling 2,000-mile Oregon Trail. Oregon City, along the I-5 corridor, is one of two Oregon cities claiming the title "End of the Oregon Trail." The other is The Dalles, in the Columbia River Gorge.

Since the days of the pioneers, the broad untamed drainage of the Willamette River has been contained, its prized lands claimed and cultivated, and its cities born. Despite the large private ownership of this region, the Willamette Valley still boasts cherished reaches, where visitors can pace off its wonder. National and state wildlife lands, state parks, and a prized forest park in the heart of Portland are just some of the valley sites where hikers can admire the habitats, wildlife, mood, and overall beauty of the valley.

A Sauvie Island walk with bald eagles, a Willamette River stroll where the earliest missionaries established a base, and hikes in a sterling waterfall realm, all await, as do bald hilltops for panoramic viewing. When not exploring the hiking trails, you might want to check out the liquid trail of the broad, quiet-flowing Willamette River.

In the Pacific Flyway, the Willamette Valley is a traditional wintering ground for the Canada goose. In the face of mass cultivation and shrinking goose habitat in the 1960s, the government stepped in to preserve the remaining habitat. Additional wetlands are protected by city and county parks along the I-5 corridor. Common valley wildlife sightings include ospreys, geese, herons, hawks, kingfishers, deer, beavers (the state mammal), river otters, and muskrats.

The Narrows, Sauvie Island Wildlife Area

Blackberry brambles are a valley standard and wild rose is common.

In this region, you will find a mild climate for year-round activity, but keep your rainsuit and umbrella handy. Snow can dip to the foothills, with the valley floor having a couple of fleeting snowy episodes each winter. Morning fog can lie in the valley almost any time of year, burning off by afternoon. Hot summer days make a riverside walk appealing.

What you should know, if you go: While walking the trails, and particularly if you should leave the trail, watch out for poison oak—it finds favor on the oak hillsides and on the valley floor. Because the valley is a leading grass seed producer, it holds the dubious distinction of "hay fever capital of the world," so come prepared with allergy tablets and tissue. Binoculars are usually worth carrying, especially in the more open valley terrain. Birds, animals, and landmarks all suggest study.

21. OAK ISLAND

Features ■	Bald eagles and waterfowl, oak woodlands, wetlands
Distance ■	2.6 miles round trip (3.4 miles with spurs)
Elevation change ■	None
Difficulty ■	Easy
Season ■	April 16 through September 30 (winter closure protects birds), daylight hours
Maps ■	Sauvie Island Wildlife Area maps and brochures
Information ■	Sauvie Island Wildlife Area; parking permit, dogs on leash

If birding is a passion for you, Sauvie Island, in the floodplain of the Columbia and Willamette Rivers, is one of the best locations in the state to take your binoculars for a walk. The selected Oak Island Trail

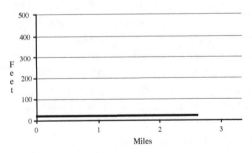

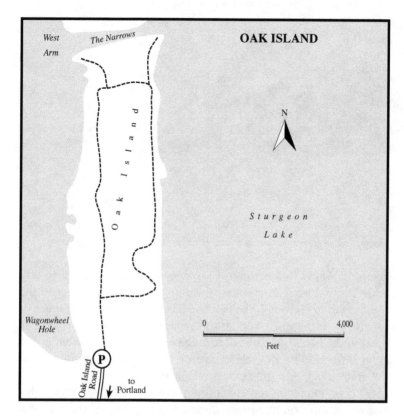

is a superb introduction to the Sauvie Island oak lowland, open water, and wetland and field habitats. More than 250 bird species are recorded here annually. Fall migration brings 300,000 ducks and geese, and the bald eagles that feed on the weakened birds.

To reach the trail, from US 30 northwest of Portland, take the marked exit for Sauvie Island Bridge. Cross over Multnomah Channel and follow Northwest Sauvie Island Road to a Y-junction (2.6 miles from US 30). To obtain brochures and information, head left to the headquarters, which is on the right in 0.2 mile. For the trail alone, head right on Reeder Road for 1.2 miles and turn left on Oak Island Road, following it to its end and the trailhead in about 3 miles. Purchase Sauvie Island Wildlife Area parking permits at outlets where Oregon Department of Fish and Wildlife fishing licenses are sold or on Sauvie Island at the market on the left as you follow Northwest Sauvie Island Road away from the bridge.

The Oak Island hike begins on the cabled-off 2-track heading

Turtles at The Narrows, Sauvie Island Wildlife Area

north. Travel is in a setting of Oregon white oak above a scruffy understory. When the leaves are missing, the big oaks may reveal the bandit-eyes of raccoons. Skeins of honking geese, the lilting notes of songbirds, or the rustle of pheasant can vie for attention. Bald eagles roost in the bare oaks, late fall through early spring. But what's truly great is the wildlife viewing starts even before you reach the loop at the grate at 0.3 mile; grassy tracks shape the loop.

This 2-mile loop presents open grassy expanses, oak savannahs, and the island's rimming lake waters. If you proceed straight for a clockwise tour, you will circle the island interior with the open water of Wagonwheel Hole and West Arm seen beyond the fields to the west. Marsh hawks patrol the open fields, and where the fields are more overgrown, find blackberry brambles. A wonderfully noisy backdrop of squawks, honks, whistles, whoops, calls, and melodic arias engages even when the sources go unidentified.

At 1.2 miles, find the first of a pair of spurs heading left (north) to The Narrows, which links Sturgeon Lake and West Arm. Each spur measures 0.2 mile, with the chance for more eagle sightings. The loop's return traces the Sturgeon Lake shore, which can be grassy, weedy, shrubby, or dotted by small alders and cottonwoods. Find open views of the water, plopping fish, and herons, ducks, and other waterfowl. To the right stretches an oak-cottonwood savannah. At 2 miles, be alert for where the trail turns right, passing a bench and memorial to close the loop (2.3 miles); avoid the trail continuing along the lake. End at the trailhead at 2.6 miles (3.4 miles if you took the spurs).

OF SPECIAL INTEREST

The Multnomah Indians harvested the Sauvie Island bounty in summer and fall. Lewis and Clark dubbed this island "Wap-pa-to," the Native American name for the abundant, arrow-leafed wild potato growing here. Although water changes have made this plant a rare find, it can still be seen on the island. Later, the island was the site of the Hudson's Bay Company dairy that supplied Fort Vancouver in Washington.

29. WILDWOOD, GERMANTOWN ROAD

Features ▪	National recreation trail through urban forest
Distance ▪	Up to 10 miles or more round trip
Elevation change ▪	100 feet (hiking south); 300 feet (hiking north)
Difficulty ▪	Easy to difficult
Season ▪	Year-round; open between 5:00 A.M. and 10:00 P.M.
Map ▪	Portland Parks Bureau trail map
Information ▪	Portland Parks and Recreation Department, Hoyt Arboretum

In Portland, when the wilderness stirring overtakes you and you can't break the bonds of the city, this premier 30-mile-long national recreation trail (NRT) that strings through the city's metropolitan wilderness park, Forest Park, soothes the restlessness within you. Forward-thinking city planners set aside this 5,000-acre open space of natural habitat for a city retreat and wilderness touchstone. The Wildwood Trail is a family trail, one for all ages. Travel is primarily through mixed Douglas fir–bigleaf maple forest. The southern end of the trail is more civilized, touring the prized parks of Portland's northwest hills. North of Cornell Road nomads enter the forest core. Multiple access points allow hikers to vary starting points and customize their walk's length. The hikes from Germantown Road are representative of the offering.

To reach the Germantown Road offering, start from St. Helens Road (US 30) in northwest Portland. Just north of the St. Johns Bridge, take the indicated northwest turn for Germantown Road. Germantown Road holds three trailheads; the selected one is on the left side of the road in 1.7 miles and has parking for up to six vehicles. Trailheads near the World Forestry Center in Washington Park and off Skyline

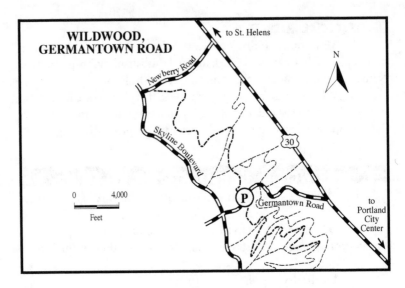

Boulevard, a major route through the Portland hills, offer other potential starts.

Throughout its 30 miles, the Wildwood Trail rolls out a 3-foot-wide, leveled bed and a comfortable grade for its slope-contouring journey. During heavy rains, expect some muddy spots. A number of side trails and fire roads connect to and explore outward from this primary artery. The Wildwood is a hiker-only trail, but mountain bikes can be encountered at crossroads. Junctions, for the most part, are well marked and allow hikers to navigate loops and fashion side tours with the use of the park map. Diamond markers counting off 0.25-mile increments along the Wildwood can further help hikers stay on track.

From Germantown Road, the Wildwood Trail heads out in both directions. To the north it continues about 5 miles to the park's northern boundary. Be careful crossing Germantown Road to begin this hike.

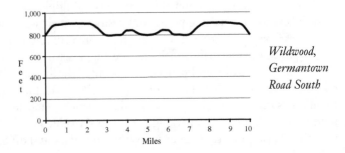

Wildwood,
Germantown
Road South

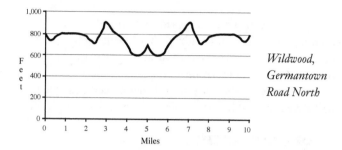

Wildwood, Germantown Road North

Hiking south you can determine your own turnaround; cross-trails, crossroads, or the gas line road/trail at about 5 miles, signal likely spots.

In either direction, the trail passes through deep second-growth woodland with Douglas fir, western hemlock, bigleaf maple, and alder, quickly erasing the reminders of the city. Sword fern, salal, and red huckleberry contribute to the understory, while vine maple, hazel, and cascara shape the midstory. Salmonberry favors the trickling drainages and small streams. In places, a nonnative ivy invades, twisting up the tree trunks. Seasonal changes alter the discovery. The forest floor shows a variety of blooms in spring, with trillium being particularly well represented. In autumn, the deciduous trees and shrubs add bursts of yellow and orange.

Wildwood National Recreation Trail, Forest Park

Some fifty mammal species make Forest Park their home, and more than one hundred kinds of birds have been sighted in its realm. The multistory forest with its shadow and light play, wind rustling in the treetops, and overall relaxation succeeds in offering solace and renewal, so key for city dweller or visitor. It has served this role for more than half a century and becomes increasingly more significant every year.

OF SPECIAL INTEREST

In its more "civilized" southern extent, the Wildwood Trail enters Hoyt Arboretum, a planned forest that unites native Northwest trees, shrubs, ferns, and wildflowers with more than nine hundred types of trees and woody shrubs from around the world. It also visits the grounds of Pittock Mansion, the home of newspaper magnate Henry Pittock, which sits atop a hill offering the trail's best views.

23. POWELL BUTTE

Features	▪	Volcano vista, birding, wildflowers
Distance	▪	2 miles round trip (options to vary or extend)
Elevation change	▪	200 feet
Difficulty	▪	Easy
Season	▪	Year-round; gated at sunset
Map	▪	Nature park map
Information	▪	Powell Butte Nature Park; dogs must be leashed, stay on designated trails

In east Portland, Powell Butte (elevation 630 feet) lifts visitors above the city to an open panoramic view that sweeps 360 degrees and includes the volcano lineup from Mounts St. Helens and Adams in Washington State to Mount Jefferson in Oregon. Local landmarks,

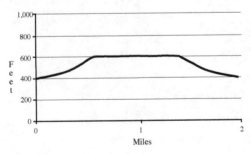

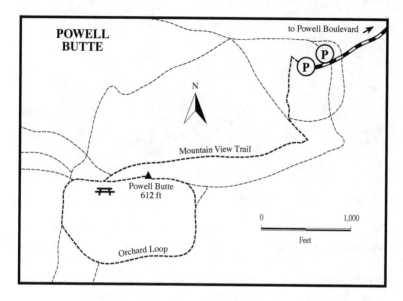

POWELL
BUTTE

to Powell Boulevard

N

Mountain View Trail

Powell Butte
612 ft

0   1,000

Feet

Orchard Loop

too, are pinpointed. Formed on a cinder cone of an extinct volcano, broad, flattish Powell Butte and its surrounding area shape an inviting 640-acre open space. The western extent of Powell Butte is largely Douglas fir–forested; the eastern face is meadowy, recording where the butte was once farmed and used as pasture. Nine miles of trail web the park. The selected hike explores the meadow reaches of Powell Butte, traveling the wheelchair-accessible Mountain View Trail to the multiple-use Orchard Loop, which rings the summit. Wildflowers, birds, and mammal sightings can pepper the discovery.

From Powell Boulevard in east Portland about 3 miles east of I-205, turn south on Southeast 162nd Avenue, entering the park. Trail parking, a trail information board (where brochures are typically stocked), restrooms, a drinking fountain, and picnic tables are reached in 0.5 mile. By bus, take Portland's Tri-Met bus #9 (Powell Boulevard) to Southeast 162nd Avenue and walk the 0.5-mile entrance road to the trailhead. The park is closed to horses and bicycles December through February.

From the map board, follow the gently ascending paved path of the Mountain View Trail. A pleasing look at Mounts Hood and St. Helens, with Mount Adams peering above the Cascades to the north-east launches the journey. The trail traverses a grass-wildflower meadow dotted by pockets of shrubs, a remnant walnut orchard, red alders, and brambles. The park nearly breaks the shackles of the city,

Meadow with trees and Mount Hood, Powell Butte Nature Park

but the roadway drone still competes with the birdsongs at the lower reaches. Benches and changing views welcome travelers. Primary junctions are generally well-marked for plotting alternative travel or returns (carry the park map). Avoid all secondary routes; these are being closed and brushed out to restore natural habitat.

In spring and summer find an array of wildflowers; chicory and yarrow are the players of late summer. In fall the red berries of elderberry delight the eye. Throughout the park, the English hawthorn and other nonnative vegetation have been targeted for removal. Bird sighting can include Steller's jays, red-shafted flickers, various hawks (particularly at the summit), grosbeaks, savannah sparrows, dusky flycatchers, and if you are super fortunate—a great-horned owl. Fox, deer, coyote, and even a mountain lion have been spied, but because this park is popular with dog-owners such sightings are unusual.

The climb increases passing through a hedgerow of wild hawthorn and young trees. At the summit orchard, meet the Orchard Loop at a T-junction (0.6 mile) and go left to reach the viewpoint and vista finder a few strides farther. Picnic tables disperse the summit's old orchard of cherry and apple trees.

The mountain view finder is essentially a gravel compass with beams radiating to major landmarks. Faint inscriptions name the features, their elevation, and their distance from you. The packed-dirt track of the Orchard Loop is fairly easy to follow, except at the mountain view finder. The cleanest route from here is to go right at the trail fork, crossing over the broad summit and then continue right (west) along the southern rim. Hawthorn abounds. By keeping right, you will return to the Mountain View Trail at 1.4 miles and can return as you came.

24. WILLAMETTE MISSION STATE PARK

Features	▪	Willamette River views and access, historic mission site
Distance	▪	3.7 miles round trip (4.2 miles round trip with spur to Jason Lee Monument)
Elevation change	▪	Minimal
Difficulty	▪	Easy to moderate
Season	▪	Year-round, but winter flooding on Willamette River can close trail
Map	▪	State park map
Information	▪	Oregon State Parks; day-use fee

Ideal for a picnic basket, this engaging lasso-shaped hike travels along the Willamette River, passing through lush cottonwood-riparian habitats, grassy clearings, and abandoned filbert groves. In October when the nuts drop, hikers, like the squirrels, fill their cheeks. At the trail's start or end, you may add a side trip to the Jason Lee Monument. In 1834, the Reverend Jason Lee and four assistants established a mission on the Willamette River floodplain and set about teaching and converting the native peoples of Oregon Country. The great flood of 1861, which shifted the river channel from its mission-days location (at what is now Mission Lake) to its present location, erased all trace of the mission. Park plans, though, call for construction of a replica mission building in 2002–2003.

From I-5 exit 263, the Brooks exit, go west on Brooklake Road, following signs to the state park. At the junction with Wheatland Road at 1.9 miles, turn right. Continue past the main entrance on the left in 2.4 miles, reaching the junction with Matheny Road in another 0.8 mile. Turn left and go 0.5 mile more to find riverside parking on your left at the Wheatland Ferry site. The park is open for day use only.

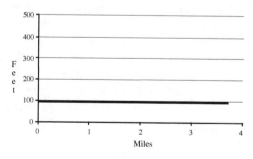

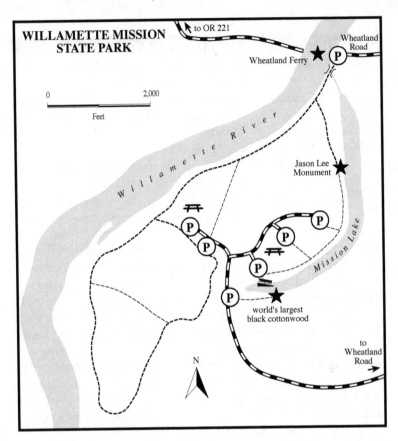

By starting at the river trailhead, hikers gain access partway to the picnicking, restrooms, and drinking fountain at the Filbert Grove Picnic Area of the main park. The primary tour is paved; only the spur is on grassy track. The hike follows the east shore of the Willamette River upstream, offering limited views. Beautiful cottonwoods 6 feet in diameter, dogwood, ash, blackberry bramble, sword fern, wild grape, filberts, and poison oak edge the trail. Heron rookeries, nesting ospreys, bald eagles, Canada geese, kingfishers, cedar waxwings, chickadees, and a complaining raven or two are just some of the feathered discoveries.

Bypass the spur to Jason Lee Monument at 0.1 mile. Short somewhat steep-pitched spurs branch to river accesses and bench seating at 0.75 mile and 0.9 mile, with the loop junction found in between at 0.8 mile. For this hike, keep toward the river; trails heading left lead into the main park. Locator maps at primary junctions will help you track progress.

Wheatland Ferry, Willamette Mission State Park

The Willamette River flows broad, smooth, and sleepy, drawing canoeists as well as mallards and mergansers. Cross river views find similar rich woods or an eroded bluff, with the ferry creeping back and forth across the river downstream. By summer, broad gravel bars address the river and call agate hunters to their knees. Killdeer guard nests in the gravel.

After the trail passes through a snag-dotted grassy meadow, cross the horse trail and continue forward at the paved triangle junction, for the full loop. Showcase bigleaf maple–riparian tanglewoods bridge the meadow stretches; in fall, enjoy a leaf shuffle. At 1.75 miles, the loop curves left; avoid the dirt path to right. Ahead, keep right past the cutoff trails and skirt the horse staging area to enter Filbert Grove Picnic Area (2.7 miles).

When ready to move on, follow the paved path heading west behind the restroom to close the loop at the 0.8-mile junction (2.9 miles). Backtrack right along the river trail to return to the trailhead at 3.7 miles (4.2 miles with Jason Lee spur). The monument explains the mission history, overlooks Mission Lake, and reveals the historical Mission rose.

Tip: While at the park you might want to visit the world's largest black cottonwood tree, which overlooks the southeast corner of Mission Lake. More than 250 years old, the tree exceeds 26 feet in diameter and stands 155 feet tall.

25. SILVER CREEK CANYON, SOUTH LOOP

Features ■	177-foot South Falls, 93-foot Lower South Falls
Distance ■	2.1 miles round trip
Elevation change ■	400 feet
Difficulty ■	Moderate
Season ■	Year-round
Maps ■	Silver Falls State Park map and trail guide
Information ■	Oregon State Parks; day-use or camping fee required, no pets

Tucked in the rural and fir-forested foothills east of Salem, Silver Falls State Park houses ten major waterfalls that range between 27 and 178 feet high, with five falls plunging more than 100 feet. This hike takes you to the starring feature of this secluded canyon—the 177-foot South Falls—one of the most photographed falls in the state. The hike shapes a loop around the premier falls, adding a spur to its lower counterpart, the 93-foot showery drop of Lower South Falls. These falls can be admired from a variety of perspectives, as well as from beneath the showery plummets. Fascinating basalt cliffs and cavernous hollows, tree casts (impressions of the living trees at the time of a volcanic eruption), a sparkling creek, and the charming tight canyon further engage hikers.

To reach this waterfall realm from OR 22 east of Salem, take exit 7 for Silver Falls State Park and OR 214. Follow twisting OR 214 northeast to the park in 15.5 miles; signs mark the junctions. For this hike start at the South Falls Day-Use Area at the lodge. Map boards at the trailheads and at junctions along the trail aid in navigation.

As you take the paved forest path to the rim and descend toward South Falls, expect company—this is the most visited falls in the park.

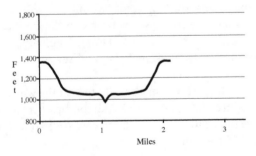

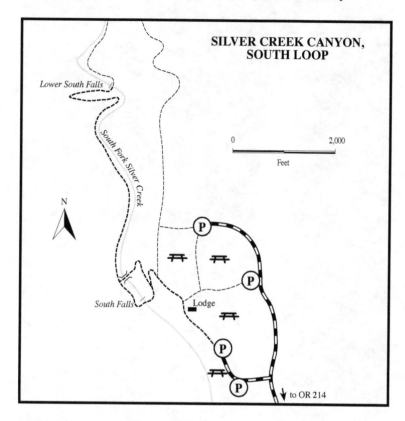

SILVER CREEK CANYON, SOUTH LOOP

Lower South Falls

South Fork Silver Creek

N

0   2,000

Feet

P

South Falls   Lodge

P

P

P

↓ to OR 214

Bigleaf maples, rich mosses, and ferns decorate the canyon, with a few big Douglas firs near the rim. Soon, a right spur offers a detour to the silver threads of seasonal Frenchie Falls. At the next junction, keep left for clockwise travel to South Falls; a right leads to the footbridge below South Falls.

South Falls is a dazzler, its image varying with each season. It is most frequently viewed in summer, but springtime charges the waterfall with bombastic energy and electrifies the surrounding greenery. Autumn paints the canyon in hues of yellow, while winter creates a fantasy-scape of rushing water, blue ice, and icicles.

From beneath the falls, you can peer out through the thick spraying chute at the canyon and plunge pool. Silver Creek's headward erosion carved out this canyon showcase of waterfalls and scenic amphitheater bowls. While in the cliff hollow of South Falls, pause a moment to search the ceiling for tree casts. But be careful while you're looking up, mist can make parts of the trail slippery.

South Falls, Silver Falls State Park

Continue down along the opposite wall, hiking past the footbridge to descend to Lower South Falls. The bridge holds the hike's return to the rim. For the loop alone, the total distance is 0.7 mile. Following the South Fork of Silver Creek downstream, enjoy the rich cedar-fir-maple canyon with cascading greenery before stairs facilitate the steep descent to the broad shower of Lower South Falls. It has a dimensional character consisting of a see-through outer veil and inner cascading streamlets.

Although the trail continues for a 7.5-mile loop visiting each of the ten falls, this hike turns back at Lower South Falls. Be careful in the recess of Lower South, the trail's scenic rock wall can collect puddles. Backtrack to the bridge at South Falls and cross it, snaring one last camera angle on the sterling beauty. Then return uphill closing the loop and backtrack to the lodge (2.1 miles).

OF SPECIAL INTEREST

Silver Creek Canyon's geologic history traces back 26 million years to when the ocean covered much of Oregon. After the ocean receded, lava from the Columbia River Flow buried the lower sandstone strata. The unequal hardness of the lower and upper rock layers explains the unique erosion pattern seen at the waterfall headwalls.

26. SILVER CREEK CANYON, NORTH LOOP

Features ■	Four major waterfalls, picturesque creek canyon
Distance ■	3 miles round trip
Elevation change ■	400 feet
Difficulty ■	Moderate to difficult
Season ■	Year-round, with temporary seasonal closures
Maps ■	Silver Falls State Park map and trail guide
Information ■	Oregon State Parks; day-use or camping fee required, no pets

You won't want to miss this sampling of the quieter north end of Silver Creek Canyon at Silver Falls State Park, the largest state park in the state at 8,700 acres with ten major waterfalls. The selected north canyon loop visits four named falls, including the 136-foot North Falls and the 106-foot Middle North Falls. The loop travels canyon and

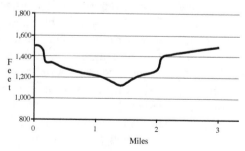

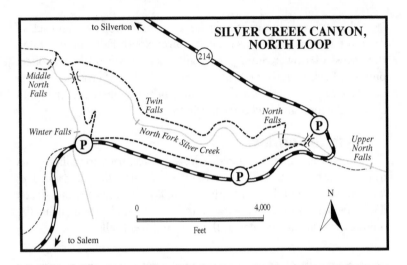

rim for a rich sensory experience. Silver Creek is a beauty, black and glassy. Picturesque bigleaf maples and draping cedars complement the creek, mosses and ferns adorn the cliffs, and Douglas firs stand watch at the rim. Spurs can expand the hike, rounding up four additional waterfalls for only 1.4 miles of additional walking.

From OR 22 east of Salem, take exit 7 for Silver Falls State Park and OR 214. Follow the park signs northeast along twisting OR 214 to the main park entrance in 15.5 miles. Now, continue past the entrance, following OR 214 to the North Falls Day-Use Area parking (about 3 miles farther). A chemical toilet is the lone amenity here. Map boards at the trailheads and at junctions along the trail aid in navigation. Be careful where the trail is wet.

The first opportunity to add a side spur comes at the start of the hike as you cross the North Fork Silver Creek bridge. The chosen hike heads right, while a 0.2-mile spur leads left to 65-foot Upper North Falls on the other side of OR 214.

For the loop, pass downstream along the dark pools and swirling cascades of the North Fork, descending to North Falls. The trail rounds up multiple perspectives on the noisy beauty. As you pass through the deep hollow behind the falls, tree casts (chimney-like impressions of the living trees at the time of eruption) can be discovered. Purportedly, in the past, the cavernous opening was used by Native Americans on vision quests.

Departing the headwall, the trail descends along the base of the north canyon wall providing creek views, showing off the lush canyon setting, and presenting 31-foot Twin Falls before arriving at the bridge at 1.2 miles. Postpone crossing and detour downstream 0.2 mile to view Middle North Falls (106 feet), arguably the prettiest waterfall in the gallery. The union of curving canyon, dimensional falls, and plunge pool is extraordinary. A dead-end spur leads behind this wall of water. Extending the detour 0.5-mile farther downstream to Lower North Falls adds the images of Drake and Double Falls as well. Seasonal Double Falls is the tallest waterfall in the park at 178 feet, but its cliff setting is the real show-stopper.

For the selected 3-mile round trip, though, turn back at Middle North Falls, returning to the 1.2-mile bridge to complete the loop. Cross the bridge following a side tributary upstream to Winter Falls, a 134-foot falls consisting of shimmery streamers tracing a nearly vertical moss-mantled cliff. Switchbacks then carry the hiker up to the Winter Falls parking turnout and the Rim Trail, which continues the loop left. On the hike back upstream, find fast travel with minimal gradient in the presence of Douglas fir and cedar. Upper North Falls makes a second bid for a visit as you cross back over the North Fork bridge to end at the parking area at 3 miles.

Upper North Falls, Silver Falls State Park

27. McDOWELL CREEK FALLS

Features	■	Picturesque creek canyon, three falls
Distance	■	2.2 miles round trip
Elevation change	■	200 feet
Difficulty	■	Easy to moderate
Season	■	Year-round (Be careful on frosty or wet stairs, decks, and bridges.)
Maps	■	None
Information	■	Linn County Parks and Recreation Department

Unless you are a native of Sweet Home or Lebanon, you've probably overlooked this quiet little treasure in the Linn County Park system. It sits in the Cascade foothills and presents three waterfalls. On Fall Creek above the McDowell Creek confluence, the park's Royal Terrace Falls tosses its 119-foot veil over the rounded ledges of a three-tiered basalt slope. The other two falls spice up McDowell Creek. When rain-swollen, Majestic Falls announces itself with booming voice and swirling mist, powerfully plunging 39 feet into a fern-dressed bowl. Downstream from it, a satiny, white 15- to 20-foot cascade spills into emerald Crystal Pool—a union of tranquil beauty.

To reach this prize, from the intersection of US 20 and Market at the eastern outskirts of Lebanon, go east on US 20 for 4.5 miles and turn north onto Fairview Road at the sign for the park. In about a mile, bear left on McDowell Creek Road and stay on it to reach the park in 7.4 miles. The park has three parking turnouts with picnic tables and trail access; the park sign is located near the uppermost (easternmost) entry, 0.5 mile farther. Bring drinking water.

A 1.1-mile trail travels McDowell Creek Canyon—it's the hikers

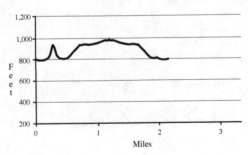

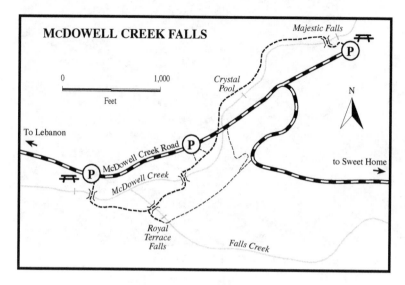

choice whether to begin at the top or bottom trailhead and whether to shuttle the hike. Mostly the trail is straightforward pursuing the creek, with side trails branching to picnic areas or shore. The mossy signs for attractions and trailheads are typically marked, but look up to find them. The trail crisscrosses the creek and crosses over McDowell Creek Road near the road bridge on the upper leg of the journey. Watch youngsters at the road crossing.

A classic low-elevation forest of Douglas fir, western hemlock, cedar, bigleaf maple, red alder, and vine maple enfolds the watery attractions. A lush and varied understory complements the shady bower. Seasonal changes alter both the character of the falls and the forest cloak. Away from the falls, cascades and low waterfalls mark McDowell Creek. Pockets of salmonberry, though, can keep you at a distance.

For viewing the tiered streaking waters of Royal Terrace Falls, a footbridge spans the stream at the waterfall's base, recessed stairs in the slope access a small, rustic top-of-the-falls viewing platform, and midway, a 10-foot spur reaches the pool and five-finger fern grotto capturing the upper-tier waters. Many photographers favor this additional camera angle. When next to Royal Terrace Falls, beware of the slope's steepness, slippery leaf mat, rickety railings, and any ongoing repairs. When hiking upstream from Royal Terrace Falls, take the lower route from the bridge at the falls base to avoid a 0.3-mile walk later on road.

Royal Terrace Falls, McDowell Creek Falls County Park

Upper and lower viewing decks present Majestic Falls. A stairway links the two decks. At Crystal Pool the trail alone affords overlooks, but the more determined onlooker can follow a descending sharp-angled secondary trail to gain closer viewing.

Who knows, once you have discovered this canyon's charms, you just might make this Linn County park a regular US 20 detour.

28. WOODPECKER LOOP

Features	■ Wildlife refuge, valley habitats, birding
Distance	■ 1.2 miles round trip
Elevation change	■ 100 feet
Difficulty	■ Easy
Season	■ Year-round; daylight hours
Map	■ Willamette Valley National Wildlife Refuge Complex brochure
Information	■ William L. Finley National Wildlife Refuge; no pets, no bikes

In William L. Finley National Wildlife Refuge, this short, easy trail surprises with relaxing discovery: the overhead passage of skeins of geese, the persistent tapping of a woodpecker, the curious stare of a deer, the slimy wake of a slug, a delicate bloom, and more. Hills, streams, marshes, and farmlands make up the 5,325-acre refuge. Along with

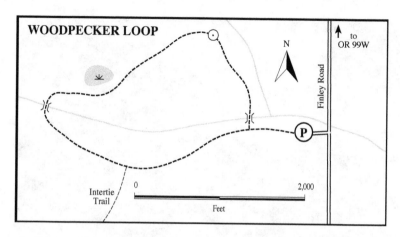

the Baskett Slough and Ankeny Refuges, Finley protects the wintering habitat of the dusky Canada goose. Woodpecker Loop demonstrates the diversity of plant and animal life found in the transition zone between the Coast Range and the Willamette Valley. The trail is aptly named with five different species of woodpecker found here, but because the trail's original name—Poison Oak Loop—has equal appropriateness, avoid straying off path. Some 212 bird species have been observed at the refuge. Binoculars and bird identification guides will enhance a stay.

Reach the turnoff for William L. Finley National Wildlife Refuge, 10 miles south of Corvallis. Turn west off OR 99W onto Finley Road at the sign and in 1.3 miles turn south. Find the comfort station along with a kiosk with a map display and refuge pamphlets in 0.8 mile; the turnoff for the trailhead is in another 1.5 miles.

Microenvironments of oak savannah, ash swale, mixed deciduous forest, and marsh contribute beauty to this wide trail designed for leisurely strolling, discovery, and study. Where the trail branches at 0.1 mile, tour the loop in either direction. Bridges and boardwalks aid in the creek and marsh crossings.

The loop's pond is a popular gathering area. Visitors pause to search the waters for life, while enjoying the tranquility of the setting. In springtime, a population of breeding rough-skinned newts occupies the pond. But by late summer, most of the water has evaporated, leaving a telltale mud hole with bird and animal tracks. Moss, lichen, and mistletoe adorn the crooked branches of nearby oaks.

Shaded by a large oak, the observation deck offers educational signboards and overlooks of the rolling, multi-textured refuge terrain.

Observation deck view, Woodpecker Loop, William L. Finley National Wildlife Refuge

To the distant east, view the purple profile of the Cascades. In late spring, deck visitors can enjoy the sights and sounds of the geese as they gather in preparation for the migration north.

Hikers do have the opportunity to extend this walk, by taking 0.5-mile Intertie Trail, which departs south, midway into the loop; look for it near the sign for Douglas fir forest. This trail links Woodpecker Loop and the refuge's Mill Hill Trail. The Intertie meanders through serene forest on a wide, cinder-surfaced bed. A boardwalk bridge spans the usually trickling drainage and an animated lighting enhances travel. Flowering shrubs add a midstory. Turn back where the Intertie meets the auto tour road.

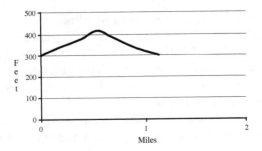

OF SPECIAL INTEREST

The refuge is named for William L. Finley, the early-day natural-ist who encouraged President Theodore Roosevelt to set aside such lands for wildlife protection. En route to Woodpecker Loop's trailhead, find the refuge's Prairie Overlook. Here, visitors are treated to the image of a native wet prairie habitat, once common to the Willamette Valley but now nearly vanquished. Historically, the Calapooya Indi-ans used fire to halt plant succession, protecting the integrity and health of the prairie. Refuge managers today follow that same practice. The National Park Service has recognized this native prairie as a National Natural Landmark.

29. MOUNT PISGAH

Features ■	Panoramic view; white oak–prairie meadow hillside, wildflowers
Distance ■	3.2 miles round trip
Elevation change ■	1,000 feet
Difficulty ■	Moderate
Season ■	Year-round, except during extreme fire danger
Map ■	Trails of the Howard Buford Recreation Area brochure
Information ■	Lane County Parks Division

This hike in Howard Buford Recreation Area, outside of Eugene, enters a classic Willamette Valley setting typically held in private ownership and reserved for windshield viewing. Here, you'll ascend a picturesque hillside of prairie grasses and Oregon white oaks, topping Mount Pisgah (elevation 1,531 feet). Its broad summit over-looks the valley mosaic, the Coast and Middle Forks of the Willamette

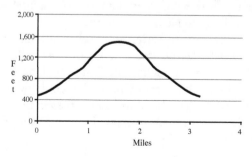

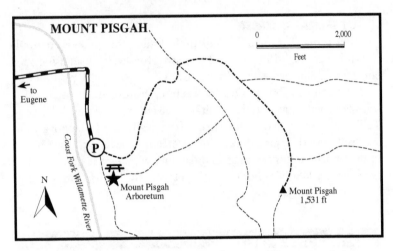

River, the Springfield–Eugene area, the Coast Range, and the near and distant Cascade peaks. Yellow monkeyflower, fawn lily, spring queen, woolly sunflower, daisy, field mustard, and Oregon iris dot the grassland with seasonal color. Wildlife sightings may include deer, rabbits, hawks, vultures, and western tanagers. For the Calapooya Indians, this mountain was a traditional hunting–harvesting ground.

From OR 58, 0.25 mile east of I-5, head north on Seavey Loop Road at the sign for Mount Pisgah. At the T-junction in 1.8 miles, turn right on Seavey Way and follow the brown road signs to Buford Park and Mount Pisgah Arboretum. The park is less than 0.5 mile ahead; the trailhead is found at the Arboretum parking area at the end of the park road.

From the hiker gate above the parking area, follow the popular West Summit Trail (hiker only) as it passes beneath powerlines to wrap and climb a natural oak–grassland slope dotted with a few Douglas fir. It traces a former road with time-softened edges and a steady grade; carry plenty of water. Early views are of the Arboretum and the round-topped mountain. Ferns, wildflowers, and poison oak interweave the grasses, while mistletoe and lichen accent the oaks.

Side trails branch from this artery of travel. At 0.5 mile, a secondary trail breaks away left, crossing over a nearby low saddle. A detour onto this saddle adds an overlook of the farmland along the Middle Fork Willamette River and Potato Hill. Hawks circle overhead. On the primary road-trail, views build to include the confluence of the Coast and Middle Forks of the Willamette River, the valley fields and cities, the Coast Range, and Spencer Butte.

At 0.8 mile, where the route turns to traverse the west face of Mount Pisgah, views span 180 degrees west. Atop the summit ridge, the trail enters an oak grove and horses may share the passage. Boulders just off the trail invite hikers to pause and enjoy the western panorama. Look for the spring queen blooms in late winter–early spring.

Follow the braided tracked-path to the summit, keeping right; other named trails arrive on your left. The summit opens a window to the east featuring the distant snowcapped Three Sisters. Atop Mount Pisgah, a bronze monument shows the topography of the immediate area. Its carved base explains the mountain's geologic evolution. Trails crisscross the broad summit revealing a 360-degree view; be sure to return via the same path you arrived on.

Tip: For additional wandering, look no farther than the base of Mount Pisgah. Here sits 210-acre Mount Pisgah Arboretum with its riparian, marsh, forest, and grassland habitats toured by interconnected short trails. Some of its oaks and maples are more than 200 years old. Trail and natural history brochures are available at the Arboretum. It is also where amenities can be found.

View from Mount Pisgah, Buford Park

COLUMBIA RIVER GORGE

Here, the mighty Columbia River slices through the Cascade Range, separating Oregon from Washington. The Gorge's nearly perpendicular 3,000-foot basalt cliffs were sculpted by the water and rock of the Missoula Floods and the ancient roiling Columbia River. Embellishing these cliffs are the silver threads of more than a dozen named waterfalls, including Multnomah Falls, the fourth tallest in the country, at 620 feet. Many unnamed plunging wisps add to the elegance.

The west end of the Gorge (featured in this book) has a sylvan temperate forest, farther east stretch picturesque grassland steppes. Douglas fir, cedar, bigleaf maple, red alder, vine maple, salmonberry, ferns, and mosses shape the western Gorge's forest–riparian habitats. Grassy wildflower meadows and sites of scree, talus, outcrops, and open cliff weave a mosaic. The skyline holds the volcanic trio of Mounts Hood, Adams, and St. Helens.

The Columbia River was key to Native American existence, with its bountiful fish runs and relatively mild climate. Tribes of the region would gather here to trade. The area entered modern history with the arrival of the Lewis and Clark expedition, in 1805. In the mid-1800s, the Gorge was both a destination and a critical decision point for the Oregon Trail pioneers. Reaching the promise of the fertile Willamette Valley required braving either the turbulent unfettered Columbia River or an arduous overland trek around Mount Hood.

When botanist David Douglas and ornithologist John Townsend inventoried the western Gorge geology, plants, and animals, they wrote the birds were so numerous that they had difficulty sleeping. In 1986, the natural and cultural wealth of the Columbia River Gorge prompted national scenic area (NSA) distinction.

Spring and summer mark favorite times to tour the Gorge with warm weather, long days, and the sprinkling of wildflowers—many rare and endangered. Autumn paints the canyons in yellow and russet and brings fish runs to the river and its tributaries. At Multnomah and Eagle

Horsetail Falls, Mount Hood National Forest, Columbia River Gorge National Scenic Area

Creeks, visitors can watch the red-sided salmon struggle upstream and rearrange the gravel for spawning. In winter, waterfalls spill at full glory and the occasional icy blast can turn them to sculpture. Wind is a signature of the Gorge, so expect it and come prepared.

Oregon's I-84 and US 30 (the Historic Columbia River Highway) conduct travel. The moss-decorated Italian stonework of the historic highway is particularly pleasing. For hiking, the area boasts a well-maintained, intricate network of trails visiting creek canyons, falls, and celebrated vistas.

What you should know, if you go: The Gorge winds delight sailboard enthusiasts but can quickly chill hikers, so carry either a windbreaker or something for warmth—even in summer, and especially if your boots are pointed skyward. During rainy, snowy, or frosty conditions, be especially cautious on trails. Wet leaves and roots can steal footing, and erosion and falling rock are possible along cliffs. If you are unfamiliar with winter travel in the Gorge, ice storms lead to treacherous road and trail conditions, check weather and road reports before heading out. If you do brave the journey, never venture below icy waterfalls—the icicles can be lethal.

30. LATOURELL FALLS

Features ▪	250-foot waterfall, 100-foot upper falls
Distance ▪	2.5-mile loop
Elevation change ▪	500 feet
Difficulty ▪	Moderate
Season ▪	Year-round (trail can be slippery in winter)
Maps ▪	None
Information ▪	Oregon State Parks

Slipping past the notice of the madding crowds, this waterfall trail in Guy W. Talbot State Park rolls out various perspectives on a picturesque

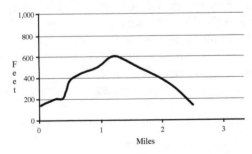

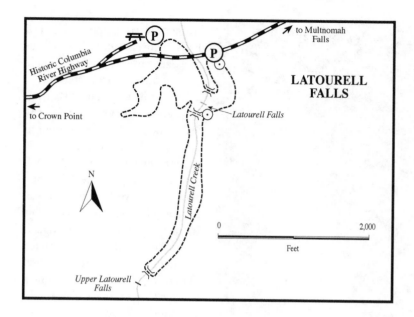

plummet and visits its upper counterpart. The primary falls belongs to the plunge (vertical-dropping) class of waterfall; the upper falls is a twisting horsetail type. This trail requires some climbing and descending between the lower and upper reaches, but the attractive woodsy side canyon and pretty spilling water coax you along.

This falls, the westernmost of the Columbia River Gorge signature waterfalls, sits alongside the Historic Columbia River Highway, about 7 miles west of Multnomah Falls (3 miles west of Bridal Veil Junction) or about 4 miles east of Crown Point State Scenic Corridor. Find the waterfall on the south side of the highway; the picnic area on the north side. A trail passing beneath the historic highway bridge links the two sites. Seasonally, restrooms are available.

When starting from the picnic area, follow the paved path upstream beneath the attractive road bridge along pretty Latourell Creek to the base of the falls for a neck-craning full-length view of the 250-foot drop. In the mist of the falls, admire the stately droplet veil as it spills over the impressive black cliff with its sections of columnar basalt and a patch of showy yellow lichen. The columns were formed by the rapid cooling of the basalt, which created tensions relieved by the hexagonal fracturing.

Cross the footbridge, and ascend the trail to the falls parking area on the south side of the highway. From there, continue steeply uphill 0.1 mile to an upper vantage before strolling higher up the canyon

Upper Latourell Falls, Talbot State Park, Columbia River Gorge National Scenic Area

slope toward Upper Latourell Falls. A foreground of deciduous trees accentuates this side-angle view of the primary waterfall.

A wide earthen path then replaces the paved one for the leafy woodland ascent. Latourell Falls remains in peripheral view until the first switchback. A bench seat at the top of the falls then provides an overlook of the creek canyon. Here, too, bypass the spur to the site of the central bridge; it was washed out, but plans call for construction of a new bridge. When in place, it would allow a shorter loop (about 1 mile total). Continue upcanyon.

Conifers, including picturesque cedars, intermingle with the leafy branches. Large spiny devil's club, trillium, false lily of the valley, bleeding heart, and red huckleberry lend texture and color. Cascading Latourell Creek, which originates on Pepper Mountain, and side tributaries vary the views.

Where the trail approaches and crosses the creek at the uppermost bridge view Upper Latourell Falls, a split-character twisting waterfall. It begins as a broad drop, bending at a midway cliff channel to emerge as a surging plume slapping the face of its plunge pool. The racing creek then departs the pool, spilling around and over rocks as it hurries toward the Columbia River.

The return leg wanders and descends the western slope, passing the spur to the middle bridge site at 2 miles. Mostly it's a woods walk back to the picnic area, reached across the Historic Highway. Be careful when crossing. Travel and photography along this trail are especially pretty under the complement of the new leaves of spring or the yellows of autumn.

31. BRIDAL VEIL FALLS AND OVERLOOK

Features	▪	A 120-foot waterfall, camas plateau, Gorge vistas
Distance	▪	1.2 miles total round trip
Elevation change	▪	100 feet (falls segment), Overlook Loop is flat
Difficulty	▪	Easy (Overlook Loop, barrier-free)
Season	▪	Year-round
Maps	▪	None (map board at trailhead parking)
Information	▪	Oregon State Parks

Sometimes you do not need to cover a lot of ground to find spectacular reward. At Bridal Veil Falls State Scenic Viewpoint, two short trails: the Falls Trail and Overlook Loop, combine for a 1.2-mile walk that takes you to both a graceful, twice-dropping terraced falls and along a wildflower–grassland plateau, rounding up prized Gorge views. Spurs along Overlook Loop lead to the fenced brink, which accentuates the perpendicular nature of the front wall cliffs. Viewpoints present the Columbia River, the Washington shore, and the famous Pillars of Hercules, a striking 120-foot basalt tower. Interpretive boards on Overlook Loop identify native plants: camas, lupine, trillium, bleeding-heart, and bride's bonnet.

Bridal Veil Falls State Scenic Viewpoint is on Historic Columbia River Highway, 3.9 miles west of Multnomah Falls (0.8 mile west of Bridal Veil Junction). Besides the two trails, the park has a picnic area, ample parking, and restrooms (open seasonally).

Look for the trails to start at the east end of the parking area near the restrooms. A map board is at the start. The Falls Trail (a hiking trail) descends east into the Bridal Veil Creek canyon. Overlook Loop journeys north toward the Gorge rim.

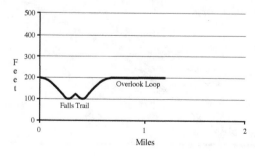

The 0.35-mile Falls Trail begins paved but changes to dirt before entering a switchback descent that is rather steep but short. Beware, loose grit can steal footing. Wear suitable shoes and plant the toes of your boots for surer steps. The trail passes through a classic western gorge habitat of Douglas fir, bigleaf maple, red alder, and low-elevation woods flora. Find the falls viewing platform upstream from the bridge.

As Bridal Veil Creek races off Larch Mountain to the awaiting Columbia River, it spills as an impressive falls through this snug corner canyon. The attractive white-lace waterfall drops in two stages, halved by a terrace pool. A grotto collects the lower pool before the creek cascades away. When ready, backtrack to the loop offering.

The paved 0.5-mile interpretive loop travels counterclockwise and is at its finest during the spring bloom, but the views are welcome anytime. The trail visits the largest concentration of camas on the western plateau of the Gorge. Oregon iris, Indian paintbrush, buttercup, and checker lily contribute additional color. Spurs lead to the Gorge vantages, which extend fine looks west toward Crown Point and Vista House, as well as the cross-Gorge looks at the Washington shore. Below view the famous river and its parallel transportation routes that send noise up the cliffs along with the wind. The loop ends back at parking.

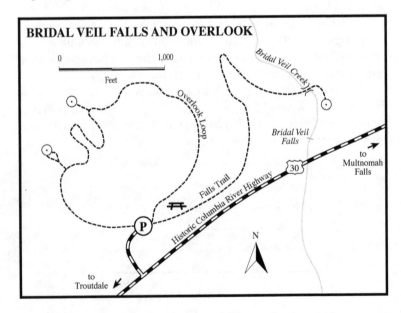

BRIDAL VEIL FALLS AND OVERLOOK

Camas, Bridal Veil Falls State Scenic Viewpoint

OF SPECIAL INTEREST

The camas, a member of the lily family, has purple, blue, or white flowers adorning its fragile stalk. The sweet bulb of this plant was a vital foodstuff for Native Americans. The name comes from the Nootka Indian term *chamass*, which translates as fruit or sweet. This flower is also quite common in the Willamette Valley; the Camassia Nature Conservancy Preserve is in West Linn.

32. ANGELS REST

Features	▪	Lofty vantage, picturesque lichen-etched rimrock, Coopey Falls
Distance	▪	4.5 miles round trip
Elevation change	▪	1,400 feet
Difficulty	▪	Difficult
Season	▪	Year-round
Maps	▪	Green Trails: Bridal Veil 15' series; USFS Columbia River Gorge National Scenic Area
Information	▪	Columbia River Gorge National Scenic Area; Northwest Forest Pass

Judging by the vertical nature of the Gorge walls, you've probably already guessed that attaining this hike's lofty vantage requires sweat

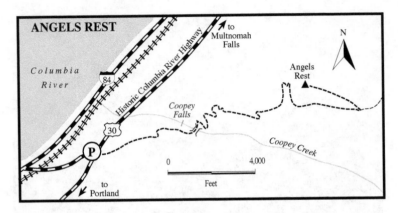

and a bit of huffing, but the thrill is worth it. The wind-charged setting, the grandeur of the Columbia River Gorge, and the richly forested Coopey Creek drainage captivate onlookers. En route, scree patch, forest opening, fire zone, and rock promontory provide fine views for less effort. On the second half of the trail, Angels Rest becomes the center of attention. The hike follows part of the greater Gorge Trail.

You'll find the Angels Rest trailhead and parking area at Bridal Veil Junction on the Historic Columbia River Highway, 3.2 miles west of Multnomah Falls. An overflow lot sits west of the trailhead; its connector trail joins the hike in the first 100 feet.

From the highway, the rocky trail heads upslope, entering a classic low-elevation forest with a few big Douglas fir and scenic bigleaf maple. The first view comes at the scree slope at 0.2 mile. View the river, the Washington shore, and Phoca Rock. Where the trail attains a terrace above Coopey Falls, keep back from the edge. The trail now pursues the Coopey Creek drainage upstream, spurs heading left lead to the creek and upper cascades. Past the bridge, find the first switchback.

The trail alternates between the forested Coopey Creek drainage and the Gorge front wall, where the drone of the highway is noticeable

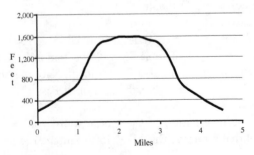

but views engage. Admire the Columbia River and its associated parks. The boughs of the firs flap in the wind as if to take flight. In the fire zone at 1.1 miles, look east to view the destination peak, as well as the river upstream. Watch out for poison oak on the second half of the journey.

At 1.6 miles a rock promontory offers views; again, stay back from the edge. When the trail again leaves the front wall, it traverses a slope of loose rock plates and slabs. Although the rock is flat to walk on, be careful: the plates can shift. This section of trail also serves up a splendid image of the head of Coopey Creek drainage. Shielded from the wind, many hikers prefer to linger at this viewpoint rather than at the summit view, which overlooks the front-wall cliffs where the wind tends to be brutal.

At the fork at 2 miles, the Gorge Trail continues right. Turn left for Angels Rest, passing the picturesque outcrops of the crest, which also extend views. Arrive at Angels Rest (2.25 miles) for a 270-degree panoramic sweep, expanding previous views with an upriver view restricted by the next ridge. When chased off by the wind, backtrack to the trailhead.

Columbia River view from Angels Rest, Mount Hood National Forest, Columbia River Gorge National Scenic Area

OF SPECIAL INTEREST

The round pebbles noticed on the surface of the trail were washed here in the great Missoula Floods. These momentous floods occurred near the end of the last ice age, around 15,000 years ago. The event started with the melting of a glacial tongue of ice that had dammed the Clark Fork River (in what is now Montana). The weakened dam then released a roiling flood carrying rock, soil, and debris. When the ice dam rebuilt, the process repeated, perhaps up to thirty times.

33. MULTNOMAH FALLS

Features ■	Nation's fourth tallest waterfall
Distance ■	2.4 miles round trip
Elevation change ■	700 feet
Difficulty ■	Moderate
Season ■	Year-round, except during winter ice storms or other hazardous conditions
Maps ■	Green Trails: Bridal Veil 15' series; USFS Columbia River Gorge National Scenic Area
Information ■	Columbia River Gorge National Scenic Area

Multnomah Falls is the most visited natural attraction in Oregon and the hub to most Columbia River Gorge visits. This high-volume (both in water and sound), twice-dropping waterfall has an upper 542-foot drop, followed by a lower 69-foot drop. Wind-whipped veils of mist peel off the vertical plummet as it spills over the ledge of a dominating 700-foot basalt cliff. The emerging creek is wild enough to be visited by spawning salmon in autumn. At the base of the falls sits an attractive Cascadian style stone lodge, which holds a visitor center, restrooms, gift

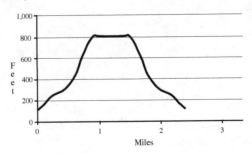

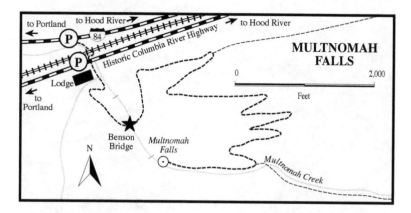

shop, snack bar, and restaurant. Multnomah Lodge complements the waterfall gallery and is on the National Register of Historic Places, as is the hike, the Multnomah Falls section of the Larch Mountain Trail.

You may access Multnomah Falls and Lodge either via the Multnomah Falls rest area on I-84 or via the Historic Columbia River Highway, 3.2 miles east of Bridal Veil Junction, 3.4 miles west of Ainsworth State Park.

The trail offers waterfall viewing from the terraced viewing deck at the lodge, the stone bridge (Benson Bridge) that spans Multnomah Creek between the two falls segments, and the upper viewing platform. On the terraced deck, the all-ability access ramp allows everyone to take in the view, feel the mist, hear the whoosh, and search for salmon in the creek. Reach both the terrace and the hiking trail from the east side of the lodge/visitor center.

Pick up the hiking trail on the west side of the terrace. The path is paved and ascends in switchbacks, tracing the western flank of the falls cliff toward the bridge. Maple, fern, and moss decorate the steep slope. Retaining features hold back the falling rock. At 0.2 mile is Benson Bridge, with its head-on view of the upper falls and an overlook of the lower falls and creek as it races toward the Columbia River. The vertical cliff is decorated in moss, lichen, and moisture-loving plants and has its own beauty with worn ledges and a columnar basalt rim.

At 0.4 mile, turn right to continue the climb to the platform at the head of the falls; straight is the Gorge Trail. Switchbacks carry the trail skyward. Gorge views, moss- and fern-capped rocks, spring wildflowers, and the classic Gorge forest keep hikers engaged until the upper falls view. At 0.9 mile, the trail reaches the high point crossing into the canyon of upper Multnomah Creek.

Multnomah Falls, Mount Hood National Forest, Columbia River Gorge National Scenic Area

Just ahead turn right off the Larch Mountain Trail, descending along the creek to the upper vantage. There gain a heart-thumping sense of the enormous plummet and admire the Gorge setting. You will also discover an attractive upper canyon falls, 12 to 15 feet high, in a bowl-like setting. Backtrack for encore views.

Tip: On the Oregon side of the Gorge, seventy-seven waterfalls trace the steep basalt walls; the most famous one, Multnomah Falls, is classified as a plunge waterfall and spills as a veil. Elsewhere discover horsetail, block, fan, and punchbowl falls. A horsetail falls resembles its namesake and drops vertically while maintaining contact with the cliff. A block falls spreads the breadth of a wide stream, a fan falls broadens at the base, and a punchbowl falls spills through a cleavage to an awaiting pool.

34. TRIPLE FALLS

Features	▪	Trio of side-by-side falls
Distance	▪	4.2 miles round trip
Elevation change	▪	500 feet
Difficulty	▪	Moderate
Season	▪	Year-round
Maps	▪	Green Trails: Bridal Veil 15' series; USFS Columbia River Gorge National Scenic Area
Information	▪	Columbia River Gorge National Scenic Area

This is a pretty sampling of the Gorge waterfall walks. It carries you back into a side-canyon crease of the Gorge where this picturesque waterfall carves three deep channels into a bulging cliff on Oneonta Creek. The hike begins at the acclaimed Horsetail Falls (arguably the prettiest of the Gorge waterfalls), passes behind Ponytail Falls, and crosses a bridge at the upper cascades and head of Oneonta Falls before reaching its destination. If still unimpressed, a steep side spur descends to unmask a hidden falls on Oneonta Creek. So, if tumbling waters appeal to you, strap on your boots and come along.

Start at Horsetail Falls on the Historic Columbia River Highway, 0.9 mile east of Multnomah Falls and Lodge and 1.5 miles west of I-84 exit 35, indicated for Dodson, the historic highway, and Ainsworth State Park. Be careful when crossing the historic highway to ascend the trail heading east from the picnic tables at the base of Horsetail Falls.

The switchback-ascending trail travels fern- and wildflower-decorated rocky slopes, lifting out of the bigleaf maple–dominated lower slope into the Douglas fir setting. The trail is wide and well-maintained but can be rocky. Exercise care and supervise children on side spurs.

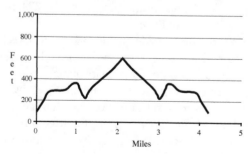

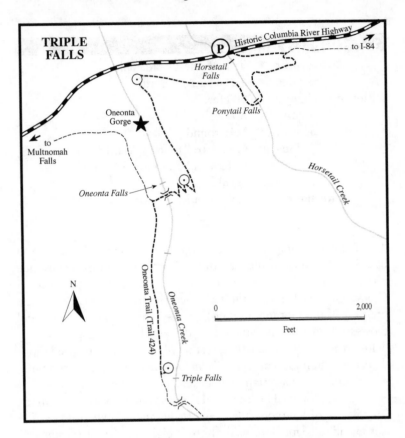

TRIPLE
FALLS

Historic Columbia River Highway

to I-84

Horsetail
Falls

Ponytail Falls

Oneonta
Gorge

Horsetail Creek

to
Multnomah
Falls

Oneonta Falls

N

Oneonta Trail (Trail 424)

Oneonta Creek

0   2,000

Feet

Triple Falls

In 0.2 mile, turn right upon meeting the Gorge Trail and continue to climb. At 0.3 mile, the trail swings through the eroded cliff hollow behind Ponytail Falls. This aptly named chutelike falls delights as it strikes its plunge pool. The creek calmly slips away, never betraying the much larger Horsetail Falls downstream. At 0.7 mile, spurs lead to the slope edge for Gorge views. Spy Washington's Beacon Rock and Hamilton and Archer Mountains, the upstream canyon, and the Columbia River floodplain, but stay back from the edge.

The trail then turns into the side canyon of Oneonta Creek, passing a weeping wall before descending to the bridge at the head of Oneonta Gorge and the abrupt dropaway of the primary plunge of Oneonta Falls. Oneonta Gorge is a richly vegetated slit canyon traced by the creek. As you peer out the chasm, sight in on Archer Mountain. From the bridge, the rock bowl of the upper falls vies for attention.

After crossing the bridge, reach a trail junction and turn left on

Lady ferns on Oneonta Creek Trail, Mount Hood National Forest, Columbia River Gorge National Scenic Area

the Oneonta Trail (Trail 424), continuing upslope above Oneonta Creek. Although the hike offers looks at the creek canyon, the water is kept secret. At 1.5 miles, locate the steep secondary trail to the hidden falls; this is one for the sure-footed. At 2.1 miles, view Triple Falls. Here, steep spurs descend to a cliff terrace for viewing, but watch your footing. Besides the 100-foot triplet streamers of white water, admire the lovely creek canyon with its upstream footbridge and water sheeting over angled cliff. Backtrack when ready.

35. ELOWAH AND UPPER McCORD CREEK FALLS

Features	A pair of exciting waterfall destinations
Distance	3.2 miles round trip
Elevation change	500 feet
Difficulty	Moderate
Season	Year-round
Maps	Green Trails: Bonneville Dam 15' series; USFS Columbia River Gorge National Scenic Area
Information	Columbia River Gorge National Scenic Area

This forked trail has a double punch leading to two waterfalls on McCord Creek. Elowah Falls, the lower falls, is an elegant waterfall spilling as a graceful plume from a cleft in the cliff. Upper McCord Creek Falls typically divides into a pair of white streamers tracing a broad broken-ledge cliff; high waters can transform Upper McCord into a wall of water. Elowah Falls is in the 100-foot-plus class of falls,

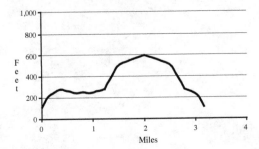

while Upper McCord is about half as tall. The cliff sections of the upper trail are worthy of a look in their own right.

The trail starts at Yeon State Park. Eastbound traffic on I-84, take exit 35, the Dodson exit, and head 2 miles east on frontage road to the park and trailhead. Westbound on I-84, take exit 37, the Warrendale exit: crossing under the interstate at 0.3 mile, head left on frontage road another 0.3 mile to the park and trailhead.

The trail enters the classic deciduous-fir mix of the Gorge forest, working its way upslope. A few dogwoods appear in the canopy, and thimbleberry, fern, and wildflowers decorate the slope. Travel is on a wide, graveled trail with some protruding rock. Early on, pass the Nesmith Point Trail, continuing toward Elowah Falls. The Elowah Falls Trail is part of the greater Gorge Trail, which traverses the front wall of the Gorge stringing between attractions. At 0.4 mile, reach the decision fork. Left leads to Elowah Falls; the trail that hooks back to the right leads to Upper McCord Creek Falls.

From the junction, it's 0.4 mile to Elowah Falls. Attractive McCord Creek becomes part of the hike setting as the trail descends via switchbacks. The stop sign for this tour is the waterfall view where the

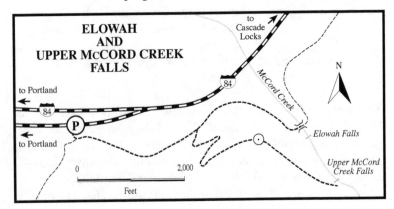

Columbia River view from McCord Creek Falls Trail, Yeon State Park,
Columbia River Gorge National Scenic Area

trail crosses the footbridge at the face of the falls. Beyond the bridge is
the continuation of the Gorge Trail. Mist carries to the bridge and
decorates the amphitheater bowl in green. Be careful on the wet bridge,
while admiring the falls. Parts of the basalt cliff are plastered in yellow
lichen. Altogether it's a lovely combination of rock, falling water, and
greenery. Backtrack to add the upper falls.

On the 0.8-mile stretch to the upper falls, the trail climbs and narrows. When not traveling the forest slope, you will traverse picturesque
slopes of rock and scree softened by mosses and ferns, pass beneath a
rock outcrop, and round a vertical rock wall. Watch youngsters along
the cliff stretches. Views include McCord Creek Canyon, a variety of
Columbia River images, Mount Adams, and the top of Elowah Falls.
Remnants of a rusting riveted pipeline cross course with the trail.

Obtain views of Upper McCord Creek Falls along the final 0.1 mile.
Taking the trampled bypass around the old-growth log at the end of
the trail puts you at creek level just above the falls. On the creekbed
here, discover a broad, bumpy angled cliff traced by a 6-foot-long
waterslide. Be careful when taking the bypass, it can be slippery. Backtrack when ready.

36. WAHCLELLA FALLS

Features	■	Picturesque 50-foot waterfall
Distance	■	2 miles round trip
Elevation change	■	300 feet
Difficulty	■	Easy
Season	■	Year-round
Maps	■	Green Trails: Bonneville Dam 15' series; USFS Columbia River Gorge National Scenic Area
Information	■	Columbia River Gorge National Scenic Area; Northwest Forest Pass

This comfortable hike—a rarity in the steep Gorge terrain—carries you to a lovely waterfall. On Tanner Creek, this falls plummets about 50 feet, fanning at the bottom and creating whitecaps on its plunge pool. High vertical basalt cliffs fashion the stirring waterfall bowl. A lush adornment of moss, fern, and other flora enhance the stage. A smaller upper falls can be detected, along with a seasonal side-stream falls that traces the east wall of the upper canyon.

Tanner Creek, Mount Hood National Forest, Columbia River Gorge National Scenic Area

From I-84, take the Bonneville Dam exit (exit 40) to find the trail's well-marked parking lot on the south side of the freeway. Ascend the gated dirt road.

This rolling hike follows scenic, clear-tumbling Tanner Creek upstream; maples and alders grace and drape the creek. Rocks in the stream create mini rapids. Away from the creek travel in a Douglas fir–mixed forest. Where the trail replaces the road at 0.3 mile, glimpse a small waterfall. Basalt cliffs loom overhead and frame travel. The trail climbs for the next 0.3 mile; keep right for the falls.

The trail then dips to cross Tanner Creek at 0.8 mile. Breakaway basalt boulders that fell from the cliffs came to rest here. At 1 mile

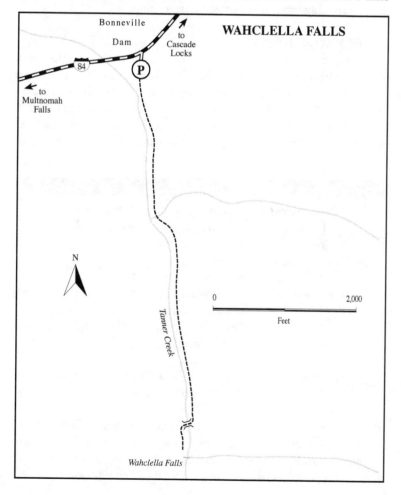

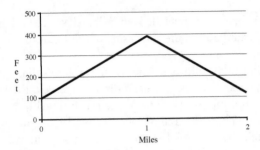

cross back over the creek, coming to the waterfall view and the trail's end. The waterfall is a dazzler and a favorite with photographers, so you'll probably want to linger before returning.

OF SPECIAL INTEREST

Tanner Creek wears the name of a pioneer who settled on a donation land grant near here; the falls takes its name from a Native American site near Washington's Beacon Rock. According to geographer Lewis A. McArthur, there was no historical connection between the Native American site and here, but the 1915 naming committee felt "Wahclella" had a pleasing sound that suited this picturesque falls.

37. EAGLE CREEK

Features ■	Premier canyon, waterfalls, wildflowers
Distance ■	7.1 miles round trip including Lower Punchbowl spur
Elevation change ■	600 feet
Difficulty ■	Moderate to difficult
Season ■	Year-round; in winter and spring, beware of slide danger
Maps ■	Green Trails: Bonneville Dam 15' series; USFS Columbia River Gorge National Scenic Area
Information ■	Columbia River Gorge National Scenic Area; Northwest Forest Pass

Built in the 1900s, this premier hiking trail—the most popular trail in the Gorge—journeys up picturesque Eagle Creek Canyon visiting a handful of the eleven waterfalls marking the creek. On this hike, you will visit the 150-foot Metlako Falls (named for the Native American goddess

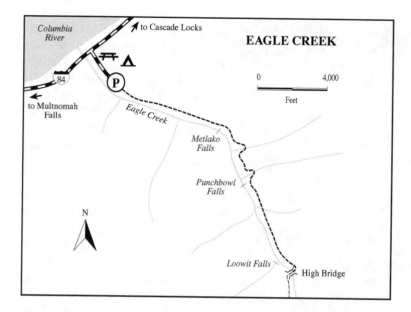

of salmon), the acclaimed Punchbowl Falls, and the horsetail plummet of Loowit before turning around at High Bridge. From High Bridge, observe where Eagle Creek tumbles through a rock fissure. The historic salmon runs in the creek attracted a following of eagles; hence the creek's name. Each fall, a few salmon still spawn here, delighting onlookers.

From I-84 eastbound, take the Eagle Creek exit, exit 41. If westbound, take the Bonneville Dam exit (exit 40) and then get back on the freeway heading east on I-84 to exit 41. Take the road into Eagle Creek Recreation Area, following it upstream to where it dead-ends at the trailhead. On summer weekends, both the campground and the trailhead parking lots can fill. Midweek and off-season visits are more tranquil.

As it enters the rich, green canyon, this hiker-only trail traces the east canyon wall quickly climbing above sparkling Eagle Creek. Wildflowers accent the weeping vertical rock walls that abut the trail. Cross-canyon views are of the forested west slope. Lovely bigleaf maples, a few old-growth Douglas fir, and the midstory hazel complement travel. The natural wealth and scenery of the canyon are first-rate.

The trail is straightforward, defined by the narrow canyon. It has an easy to moderate ascending grade. The trail alternates between forest stretches and cliff openings. Oaks claim the drier, exposed slopes. Where the trail narrows along cliffs, find guidewires but not handrails. Take children by the hand and shorten leashes.

Eagle Creek, Mount Hood National Forest, Columbia River Gorge National Scenic Area

At 1.5 miles, past a small trampled hemlock flat, find the best of several spurs to a guide-wire-fenced overlook of Metlako Falls. There is a sign and a log bench at the turnoff. Metlako is a lovely canyon adornment, arriving at an angle and spilling as a scenic chute.

After crossing Sorenson Creek on sidewalk disks, come to the Lower Punchbowl Trail. It descends to the head of Lower Punchbowl Falls, which graces an arched cliff in the streambed. The falls is about 12 feet wide and equally tall. The outcrop and a gravel bar downstream offer views; be careful on the wet rock. During low water, an upstream bar offers a glimpse at Punchbowl Falls through folded cliffs.

Return to the primary trail at 2.2 miles, coming to the Punchbowl Falls overlook in another 0.1 mile. The head of this falls emerges from an eroded pothole; the bowl-like canyon cupping the falls suggests the name. Ahead, bridges span tributaries, and talus slopes vary viewing.

At 3.7 miles, discover Loowit Falls as it traces the west canyon slope, dropping to Eagle Creek. It exceeds 200 feet in length and undergoes several character changes. Between its horsetail drops, find a broad skipping stretch. A dark narrow chasm and an intermediate plunge pool further add to its charm. Downstream from the confluence is an unnamed falls on Eagle Creek.

Next, overlook a gorge on Eagle Creek before reaching High Bridge (3.8 miles), the hike's turnaround. The trail, though, continues into the Mark O. Hatfield Wilderness Area. At the bridge, find boulder seating for admiring a cliff and scree slope and ragged canyon skyline. When ready, backtrack 3.3 miles on the primary trail.

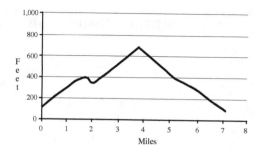

OF SPECIAL INTEREST

The Eagle Creek Trail leaves from Eagle Creek Recreation Area, which holds the distinction of being the first campground in the nation's forest system. The Civilian Conservation Corp structures are circa 1930s. The canyon geology is known as the Eagle Creek Formation, which is some 20 million years old.

38. WAHTUM LAKE–CHINIDERE MOUNTAIN

Features ▪	Wilderness lake, 360-degree summit panorama
Distance ▪	4.7 miles round trip
Elevation change ▪	1,000 feet
Difficulty ▪	Moderate
Season ▪	Spring through fall
Maps ▪	Green Trails: Bonneville Dam 15' series; USFS Columbia River Gorge National Scenic Area
Information ▪	Hood River Ranger District; Northwest Forest Pass, wilderness permit

At the backdoor to the Gorge, this hike ventures into the Mark O. Hatfield Wilderness Area, traveling to two splendid attractions, Wahtum Lake and Chinidere Mountain. Wahtum Lake is a prized big mountain lake nestled in an old-growth forested bowl at the edge of the wilderness. Chinidere Mountain is a rocky-topped peak that unfolds a wild 360-degree panoramic view. Overlook Waucoma Ridge, the Eagle and Herman Creek drainages, Wahtum Lake, and the forested drainage-ridge pattern of the wilderness. Mount Hood is nicely framed by the folded flank of Waucoma Ridge. Clear days offer seven-volcano viewing.

This hike is a bit tricky to reach but well worth the drive. From

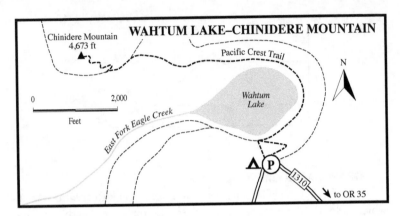

OR 35, about 14 miles south of the town of Hood River and 0.5 mile north of the community of Mount Hood, turn west on Woodworth Road, following it to Dee Highway in 2.1 miles. Turn right to reach Dee in 4 miles and from there, follow Lost Lake Road/FR 13 toward Lost Lake Recreation Area. After about 5.5 miles on FR 13, you'll come to where it forks forming a loop; turn right for Wahtum Lake. Go 4.3 miles and then head right on FR 1310, a paved single-lane road with turnouts. In another 6 miles arrive at the trailhead parking area and primitive campground.

Descend north from the parking area toward Wahtum Lake. You may choose either the Express Trail or the horse trail for this descent; the Express Trail offers a steeper, more direct route advanced by stairs. The trails merge just before meeting the Pacific Crest Trail (PCT) at 0.2 mile. Tall straight firs and varied flora dress the slope. The hike then follows the PCT to the right (northbound), but first, Wahtum Lake will likely call you aside with its blue-green waters and scenic basin. Respect any closures for shoreline rehabilitation. Over its narrow outlet end, you can spy the rocky top of Chinidere Mountain, the next destination. Huge firs contribute to the shoreline.

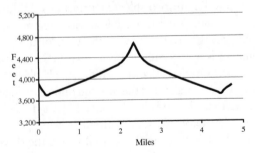

This stretch of the PCT extends one of the most comfortable climbs you will ever take. It journeys up and around the lake basin, rounding the southeast, east, and north slopes. The path is picturesque, rolling out as a brown ribbon through the diverse green understory. Even untrained eyes can count dozens of floral species, many of which bloom. Wonderful big trees add to the hike's charm. Where the trail lifts out of the lake's influence, find a Pacific silver fir–beargrass plateau. Forest sounds may include owl, woodpecker, and a deer in the bushes.

At 1.8 miles, the Herman Creek Trail angles in on the right; afterward, pass a left spur descending toward the Wahtum Lake outlet. Next up is the trail branch to Chinidere Mountain, on the right at 2 miles; it strikes uphill with decided intent—a dramatic contrast to the section of PCT just walked. Pass among high-elevation fir, tall meadow

Herman Creek drainage view, Mark O. Hatfield Wilderness, Mount Hood National Forest

flora, and rock ledges and slab scree to arrive at the rock and alpine flora of the summit (2.3 miles). Clear-day views are sensational but even when conditions are hazy, the wilderness stage is grand. The summit itself is attractive with rock ledges and an adornment of succulents, phlox, heather, and gentian. But keep off the rocky pedestals; they are highly fractured and dangerous.

Retrace your steps. When back at Wahtum Lake, for an extra 0.1 mile, the horse trail offers the more comfortable ascent to the trailhead, bringing the round trip to 4.7 miles.

CASCADES

The Oregon Cascades are a premier playground for the state, encouraged by their proximity to the I-5 metropolitan corridor and the mountain range's outstanding scenic and recreational offering. Hikers are blessed with a diversity of discovery from lofty summits to sparkling lakes, streams, and waterfalls to magnificent untouched forests. A historic segment of the Oregon Trail (Old Barlow Road), a hot springs, a buried forest, and glaciers up the ante.

Two stages of volcanic activity shaped this range, with the older volcanoes in the west, the younger ones in the east. Although the Oregon volcanoes have been silent in recent years, the westward migration of the North American plate over the seafloor continues to create a reserve of magma, which geologists say will fuel future activity.

In 1792, the Vancouver Expedition first recorded the Cascade Mountain Range, which separates the verdant Willamette Valley from the semiarid Columbia Plateau and desert plains. In 1805, Lewis and Clark sighted this range from Hat Rock. By the mid-1800s, Barlow Road represented the final obstacle to the 2,000-mile overland journey of the Oregon Trail. It was noted botanist David Douglas, who first dubbed this range the "Cascade Mountains."

Vegetation varies with elevation, latitude, and longitude. Generally, Douglas fir, western red cedar, and western hemlock dominate the western slope. Ponderosa and lodgepole pines and western larch prefer the eastern slope. Regional differences introduce other varieties. Rhododendron, huckleberry, bigleaf maple, vine maple, sword fern, Oregon grape, and vanilla leaf are common understory plants on the western slope, with bunchgrass and sagebrush on the drier eastern slope. Although the majority of hikes in this book keep to the western Cascade reaches, a few trails that start in the Willamette River watershed do carry you over the crest and into the eastern realm.

Common bird sightings include Clark's nutcrackers, Steller's and

Alder Flat Trail, Clackamas Wild and Scenic River, Mount Hood National Forest

gray jays, woodpeckers, bluebirds, flickers, and a variety of songbirds. Any hiker who has opened a sandwich bag can cite the larceny of the gray jay. Golden-mantled ground squirrels and pikas are among the small animal sightings. Larger animals are typically scarce except in the early morning and evening hours, but tracks and other signs betray their presence.

The lowest elevations of the Cascades offer year-round hiking, with the higher reaches typically open summer into fall. Summers offer mild temperatures and long days for maximum enjoyment of the trails and their offerings.

Four major river drainages partition the Northwest Oregon Cascades. They are the Clackamas, North Santiam, McKenzie, and Middle Fork Willamette. They define our subregions for grouping the hikes.

What you should know, if you go: When traveling to mountain summits, be aware of the danger of afternoon thunderstorms. Plot your time, keep an eye on the weather, and revise or abort your hike if necessary to avoid the risk. Also, carry something for warmth. Temperatures drop at higher elevations and summits are often windy. It'd be a shame to get chased off the summit before you can relish in your accomplishment and fully enjoy the view.

Of all the geographic areas described in the book, this is the one where mosquitoes can be most troubling, but it has slap-free reaches as well. Mosquito numbers tend to be greatest near snowmelt ponds, meadows, and the crest. Lower elevations are generally peaceful. If you are headed anywhere near the mountain lakes or the crest, be sure to carry ample bug juice and netting. Conditions typically improve by fall.

MOUNT HOOD–
CLACKAMAS RIVER AREA

(ACCESS ROUTES OR 35, US 26, OR 224)

Timberline Lodge, Mount Hood National Forest

39. LAKESHORE TRAIL, LOST LAKE

Features	■	Scenic lake, marsh, ancient trees, Mount Hood view
Distance	■	3-mile loop, nearly half is boardwalk or wheelchair-accessible
Elevation change	■	Minimal
Difficulty	■	Easy
Season	■	Midsummer through early fall
Map	■	USFS Mount Hood National Forest
Information	■	Hood River Ranger District; Northwest Forest Pass

Lost Lake is about as pretty as they come. This 290-acre triangular-shaped indigo lake at the northwestern foot of Mount Hood is the shimmering centerpiece to both the surrounding recreation area and

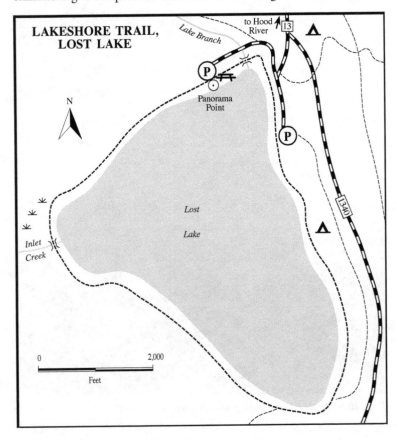

Mount Hood and Lost Lake canoe, Mount Hood National Forest

this hike. Its shoreline loop passes through marsh, old-growth splendor, and rhododendron-huckleberry wilds. Views spotlight Lost Lake Butte to the east and Mount Hood to the south, best seen from Panorama Point. A popular forest service campground and a rustic resort serve area visitors and provide access to other recreational opportunities.

Lost Lake Recreation Area is about 35 miles southwest of Hood River. From OR 35, about 14 miles south of the town of Hood River and 0.5 mile north of the community of Mount Hood, turn west on Woodworth Road, following it to Dee Highway in 2.1 miles. Turn right to reach Dee in 4 miles, and from there keep left to follow Lost Lake Road/FR 13 toward Lost Lake Recreation Area. Reach Lost Lake in another 13.4 miles. The hike begins at Panorama Point on the north shore; follow signs through the recreation area to its parking lot.

At Panorama Point, locate the Lakeshore Trail as it enters the woods to the west and follow it for a counterclockwise tour. An ancient forest of large-diameter Douglas and Pacific silver fir, western hemlock, and western red cedar shrouds the trail in mystical beauty. Gaps in the tree cover offer teasing peeks at Mount Hood. In summer, bunchberry, vanilla leaf, queen's cup, and parrot's beak sprinkle the forest in

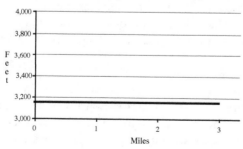

143

wildflower splendor. At 0.6 mile, a 0.25-mile boardwalk traverses the marsh of Inlet Creek and its associated springs. The rare cutleaf bugbane grows here and nowhere else. At 1.3 miles an open talus passage interrupts the rolling forest-shore trip. Be careful on rocks but enjoy the lake view; mergansers are common.

Hike past the Huckleberry Mountain Trail to swing around the lake's southern tip, passing below the camp. Views of Lost Lake Butte and stands of stout cedar bring pleasurable discovery. Much of the trail along the east shore is either on boardwalk or shows a wheelchair-accessible width. Admire the lake platter and its forested rim.

Hike past the Old-Growth Barrier Free Trail (a splendid big tree–rhododendron walk), a couple of platforms for lake access and viewing, and the public boat ramp. Beyond the resort area, the trail crosses the Lake Branch bridge for the return leg along the north shore, skirting below the picnic area. Capping off the trip is Panorama Point with its impressive view of Mount Hood above Lost Lake. The clicking of camera shutters will signal you're there. Ascend the stairs to return to parking.

OF SPECIAL INTEREST

Rumors of the existence of this beautiful isolated lake caused a party from Hood River to set out in search of it in August 1880. The search was filled with missteps and confusion, but the party eventually came upon the so-called lost lake. Even though roads now lead the way, it's still a bit of a treasure hunt to reach Lost Lake, today.

40. LOST LAKE BUTTE

Features ▪	Summit panorama of peaks and water
Distance ▪	4.5 miles round trip
Elevation change ▪	1,300 feet
Difficulty ▪	Moderate to difficult
Season ▪	June through September
Map ▪	USFS Mount Hood National Forest
Information ▪	Hood River Ranger District; Northwest Forest Pass

On the east shore of Lost Lake, Lost Lake Butte is a rather modest Cascade feature, but it bids hikers skyward, as it has done for more than a century. The trail ascends from the old growth and rhododendron at the base of the mountain up through a huckleberry-crowded mid-elevation forest to claim the summit opening (elevation 4,468

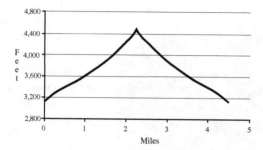

feet). Views take in the icy grandeur of Mounts Adams and St. Helens in Washington and Mounts Hood and Jefferson in Oregon, the sparkling jewel of Lost Lake in the basin below, and the upper Hood River drainage. A popular forest service campground and a rustic resort serve area hikers who choose to linger a spell.

Lost Lake Recreation Area is about 35 miles southwest of Hood River. From OR 35, about 14 miles south of the town of Hood River and 0.5 mile north of the community of Mount Hood, turn west on Woodworth Road, following it to Dee Highway in 2.1 miles. Turn right to reach Dee in 4 miles. From there, keep left to follow Lost Lake Road/FR 13 toward Lost Lake Recreation Area. Reach Lost Lake in another 13.4 miles. The hike begins where the recreation area road arrives and forks at the lake. But because there is no immediate parking here, you may choose to park and start instead where the trail crosses FR 1340, shaving 0.2 mile each way.

The signed trail ascends from the east side of the recreation area road, crossing both the Lakeshore Express Trail and FR 1340. It then swings left contouring above the campground before turning uphill and crossing swords with the Old Skyline Trail. The rock-studded butte trail offers a comfortable gradient for the climb. Travel is mainly in a

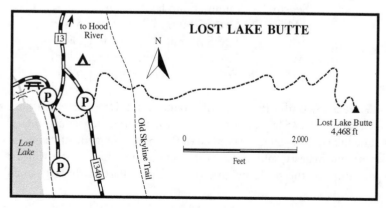

mid-elevation mixed-conifer forest, where the tree trunks of the Douglas fir are hairy with lichen. Rhododendron and beargrass contribute to the huckleberry understory. The rhododendron belt about midway is showy when blooms arrive in early summer.

Mount Hood from Lost Lake Butte, Mount Hood National Forest

Switchbacks help moderate the steep climb along the final 0.7 mile. At 1.9 miles attain the upper butte reaches for the first volcano views, with Mounts Adams and St. Helens to the north. In June, snow patches can linger in the trail. At the top, Mount Hood boldly salutes hikers, while Mount Jefferson can be seen peeking over the distant ridges. Rounding out the view are the community of Dee, the West Fork Hood River drainage, and Hickman Butte Lookout. Lost Lake shimmers in the basin below, bidding you to return. Just below the butte's summit rest the remains of a former lookout. Backtrack when ready.

41. TIMBERLINE TRAIL: COOPER SPUR SHELTER SEGMENT

Features	▪	Mount Hood views, timberline discovery
Distance	▪	2.8 miles round trip (3.2 miles if you explore)
Elevation change	▪	800 feet
Difficulty	▪	Difficult
Season	▪	Summer into fall
Maps	▪	Green Trails: Mount Hood 15' series; USFS Mount Hood National Forest
Information	▪	Hood River Ranger District; Northwest Forest Pass and wilderness permit

While many trails offer views of Mount Hood, Oregon's tallest peak (elevation 11,235 feet), this trail puts Mount Hood beneath your feet. The hike draws you into the spell of the mountain, with all its fierceness and majesty, and awakens the senses. The bite of the wind, a signature of the peak, heightens awareness. Part of the acclaimed

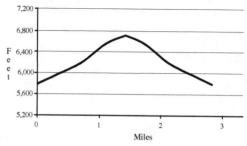

Timberline Trail, which encircles the mountain, this hike travels at the 6,000-foot elevation at the margin between tree line and the rock-and-snow glory. Passing between Cloud Cap and the Cooper Spur shelter, you will gather spectacular Mount Hood views. From this proximity, the mountain looms large, the detail is unsurpassed. The shelter has a defiant charm standing against the elements and offers a grand final impression of Mount Hood and Eliot Glacier.

From OR 35 about 23 miles south of Hood River, turn west on Cooper Spur Road. Go 2.3 miles and turn left on FR 3512 toward Cloud Cap opposite Cooper Spur Inn. Proceed forward past Tilly Jane Sno-Park, now on gravel road. At the T-junction in 9.6 miles, head right 0.6 mile to Cloud Cap Saddle Campground and trail parking. Expect some washboard, but generally the road is fine for passenger vehicles with normal clearance.

Wear boots, carry plenty of water, and be sure to wear sunglasses. The hike's upper elevation and the light color of the ash and rock as well as the snow and ice are menacing to unprotected eyes.

Hike up through the campground on a wide grade and bear left to locate the Timberline Trail and a register. On the Timberline Trail, head left. This hike is strenuous but worth every difficult step. It introduces the upper reaches of Mount Hood at a point where climbing routes take the baton. On this trail, you can better appreciate the volcanic power of the mountain, the erosive power of ice, and the struggle of the trees and snags just to stand here. Lupine, red-leaf dogbane, phlox, heather, monkeyflower, and alpine annuals and grasses decorate the stage.

Traverse dry ashy slopes and picturesque stands of short, stout true fir, mountain hemlock, and whitebark pine. At 0.5 mile reach the volcanic canyon drainage of Tilly Jane Creek. It holds the first view. Admire the drainage gouge, the thin green ribbon of the headwater, the dramatic canyon headwall, and Mount Hood. The headwall is a moraine, a wall of boulders pushed up by the advance and retreat of a glacier. Large cairns with protruding posts dot the route, but are unneeded if the trail is snow free. Mount Hood continues to add to viewing.

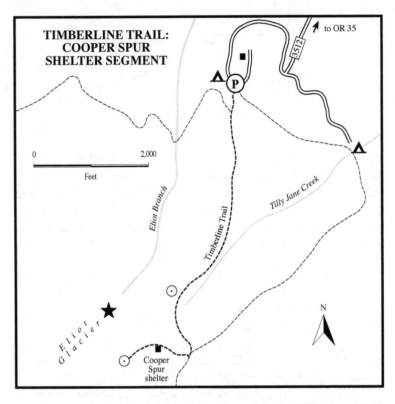

TIMBERLINE TRAIL:
COOPER SPUR
SHELTER SEGMENT

to OR 35

0   2,000
Feet

Eliot Branch

Timberline Trail

Tilly Jane Creek

N

Eliot Glacier

Cooper Spur shelter

At 1.2 miles is the four-way junction with the Tilly Jane Trail. Here, depart the Timberline Trail, heading uphill to the right to Cooper Spur shelter. An unbroken 0.2-mile climb leads to the shelter turnoff. This sturdy, windowless, boxlike stone shelter stands in plain view of Mount Hood. It has a dirt floor, rustic fireplace (fire ring and chimney), and a sound roof. A heavy rubber mat shuts out the wind. The shelter sits in an alpine meadow punctuated by pinkish beige boulders and clusters of stunted whitebark pines.

Once your respiration has slowed and the call to explore kicks in, locate a path at the back of the shelter; it leads to views that up the ante. In 0.1 mile, discover both a bigger relief of Mount Hood and a greater length of Eliot Glacier. The moraine and ashy canyon walls scoured by the glacier add to viewing and beckon you on. By going another 0.1-mile to the edge of the canyon and up the next ashy ridge; the scene jumps exponentially in scale and impact. The loose ash is leg-working but the climb is short.

The top of the lateral moraine reveals the full extent of Eliot Glacier. Parts of the glacier are blue ice but much is covered in rock

Mount Hood and Cooper Spur shelter, Mount Hood Wilderness, Mount Hood National Forest

and dirt (glacial till). Water melting under the ice lends an anonymous voice. Mount Hood with the flanking features of Cooper Spur and Upper Langille Crags commands eyes skyward. Views north are of the Hood River Valley, the clouds of the Gorge, and Washington beyond. Return as you came.

OF SPECIAL INTEREST

Mount Hood, which is the highest peak in Oregon, is the fourth tallest peak in the string of Cascade Mountain volcanoes that stretch south from Mount Garibaldi in British Columbia to Mount Lassen in Northern California. Eleven glaciers grace Mount Hood, including Eliot Glacier on the north slope. Together the glaciers and named snowfields cover approximately 80 percent of the cone above 6,800 feet.

42. TAMANAWAS FALLS

Features	▪	Superb 100-foot waterfall
Distance	▪	4 miles round trip
Elevation change	▪	400 feet
Difficulty	▪	Moderate to difficult
Season	▪	Late spring through fall
Maps	▪	Green Trails: Mount Hood 15' series; USFS Mount Hood National Forest
Information	▪	Hood River Ranger District; Northwest Forest Pass

This hike pursues the west bank of the East Fork Hood River downstream before following Cold Spring Creek upstream to its attractive

149

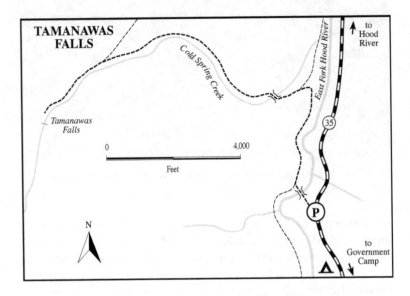

waterfall feature. Named for the Chinook Indians' "Guardian Spirit," Tamanawas Falls is an elegant broad waterfall cascading in lacy streamers over a black basalt cliff. It is an estimated 100-feet tall and 40-feet wide. The imposing cliff signals an abrupt end to the hike but the attraction more than satisfies seekers.

For this hike, start at the OR 35 trailhead that is just 0.25 mile north of Sherwood Campground. You will find the trail parking lot on the west side of the highway, 14 miles north of the US 26–OR 35 junction or about 25 miles south of the town of Hood River.

Cross over the East Fork Hood River on the 125-foot-long single-log bridge—one of the longest of its kind in the Northwest. Once across, turn right on the East Fork Trail and follow the river downstream for the next 0.5 mile. The East Fork races past milky green in color, betraying its glacial origin—born on the flank of Mount Hood. Mixed

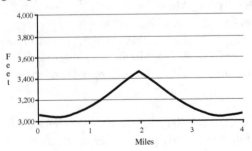

conifers shape the forest, which has an open spacing. Among the patchy ground flora, find prince's pine, twin flower, bunchberry, and vanilla leaf. Meet the Tamanawas Falls Trail; turn left on it, crossing a foot-bridge over Cold Spring Creek; and head west upcanyon.

Along Cold Spring Creek, the setting is engaging. Cliffs frame the canyon, while a rich forest of Douglas and Pacific silver fir, hemlock, and deciduous trees and shrubs envelop the way. The ground flora is verdant, lending bloom are currant, gooseberry, trillium, columbine, and lily. Draped by alders, sparkling Cold Spring Creek reveals pictur-esque pools and swirling cascades and is seldom far from the trail.

Where the Tamanawas Tie Trail arrives, continue along the north shore, crossing a talus (rock and boulder) field, to arrive at the falls. The old trail, which turned left at the junction now requires two

East Fork Hood River, Mount Hood National Forest

fordings to reach the falls. Although plans call for the construction of a tread across the talus, until then hikers must choose between scrambling across the open talus field or getting their feet wet taking the old trail. When crossing on talus, beware of the shifting, unstable rock and wear boots.

The stunning waterfall and its imposing cliff cause you to stop in your tracks at 2 miles. The jet black boulders at the base of the falls are pounded by the 100-foot drop. Behind the shimmery curtain of white water sits a black hollow. Tree roots and boulders offer audience seating, and two amazing stout conifers offer shade.

43. LOST CREEK

Features ■	Scenic creek through volcanic mudflow, buried forest
Distance ■	0.5-mile all-ability loop
Elevation change ■	Minimal
Difficulty ■	Easy
Season ■	May to October
Maps ■	Green Trails: Government Camp 15' series; USFS Mount Hood National Forest
Information ■	Mount Hood Information Center; Northwest Forest Pass

Too often, recreation sites for the physically challenged have been an afterthought, but not here. The recreation complex of Lost Creek Campground and Nature Trail was conceived and fully designed for catering to wheelchair-bound and physically challenged outdoor enthusiasts. The nature trail's overall ease and sensory-rich setting appeals to others as well. Its loop travels the low forested bluff of Lost Creek, passing in the

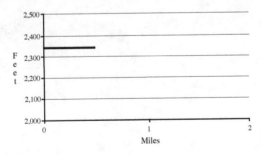

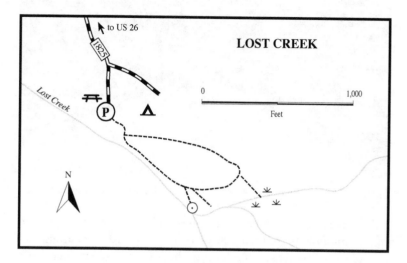

shadow of attractive mountain hemlock, western red cedar, and Douglas fir. Alders dress the creek, and rhododendrons in early summer bloom add a lively forest flare. The ashy terrain of the creek channel and the remnants of a buried forest reveal you are in the midst of a volcano—Mount Hood.

From US 26 at Zigzag, head north on FR 18 (Lolo Pass Road) for 4.2 miles and turn right on FR 1825. Follow it for another 2.7 miles, finding the entrance to Lost Creek Campground, which holds the trailhead. Park in the designated day-use sites; the trail starts in the campground opposite the day-use parking.

The nature trail consists of a loop, plus three round trip spurs. Interpretive panels along the paved trail relate the natural history, provide fun facts, and use quotes of the famous to inspire reflection. Booklets in braille that correspond to the trail may be borrowed from Mount Hood Information Center. Memorial benches invite pause. You might come upon some buckled pavement here and there, but otherwise travel is carefree.

Explore the low bluff above pretty Lost Creek, with its cobble and ash bottom, small rocky bars, and fanning vegetation. In the late 1700s, hot mud from Mount Hood's last eruption blanketed this area. Over the ensuing years, Lost Creek, born at the base of Reid Glacier, has cut a deep gouge into the soft, ashy deposit.

At the loop junction in 0.1 mile, bear right for a counterclockwise tour. At 0.2 mile, a pair of right spurs lead to a creek overlook and a fishing platform. From the viewing deck, admire the creek, its ashy

Viewing platform along Lost Creek Nature Trail, Mount Hood National Forest

bank, and a line-up of five huge stumps—relics from the forest buried in the mudflow more than 200 years ago. A boardwalk through an area of dense riparian shrubs leads to the fishing platform. Beware of the stalks of nettles and devil's club that can droop into the pathway. Old-growth trees and a pileated woodpecker may suggest you pause.

The counterclockwise loop then continues toward Beaver Pond Viewing—the third spur, also to the right. The pond is now reclaimed by meadow vegetation, save for a small pool that is deep enough for trout and draws wildlife. Close the loop at 0.5 mile and return to the trailhead.

44. RAMONA FALLS

Features	Outstanding waterfall, mudflow, Mount Hood views
Distance	7.3 miles round trip
Elevation change	1,000 feet
Difficulty	Difficult
Season	Late spring into early fall
Maps	Green Trails: Government Camp 15' series; USFS Mount Hood National Forest
Information	Mount Hood Information Center; Northwest Forest Pass, wilderness permit

Ramona Falls has become a signature feature and one of the most popular hikes in the Mount Hood Wilderness. Because of this, mid-week visits are more satisfying, and your best hiker manners are mandatory. The trail parallels the Sandy River upstream to the waterfall

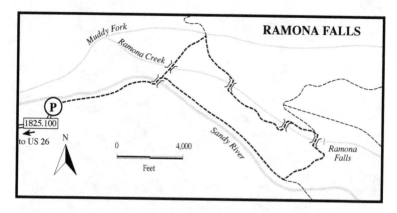

loop, where Ramona Falls is centerpiece. Along the Sandy River, the hike follows the lahar of Old Maid Flat, a volcanic flow of mud and debris deposited here more than years ago in Mount Hood's last eruption. Ramona Falls is a stunner, cascading in skips over the mossy ledges of a basalt cliff. An arid conifer forest vegetates the flow; waters along the trail are of glacial origin and fast racing.

To reach this wilderness attraction, from US 26 at Zigzag, head north on FR 18 (Lolo Pass Road), go 4.2 miles, and turn right on FR 1825. Follow FR 1825 for 2.4 miles and turn left onto FR 1825.100. Reach the large dirt parking area at road's end in 0.5 mile. Find the trail at the upper end of the parking lot.

The hike is lasso-shaped. A 1.4-mile trail leads to the waterfall loop, which swings between the main stem and Muddy Fork of the Sandy River. The first leg of travel as far as the river crossing is open to shared-use, but only hikers and horses may continue—wilderness lies beyond. On Ramona Falls Loop, hikers alone are allowed on the Ramona Creek side of the loop; on the loop's Sandy River side, horses share the way.

From trail parking, follow the wide sandy path paralleling the

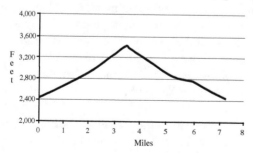

Ramona Falls, Mount Hood Wilderness, Mount Hood National Forest

Sandy River upstream. The forest consists of small hemlock, lodge-pole pine, and fir. Boulder arrays and mosses and kinnikinnick add to viewing. Find an early view of Mount Hood at Sandy River overlooks. The cloudiness of the river hints at its glacial origin, while its scoured channel reveals the volcanic nature of the lahar on which you are traveling. Popularity can make the meandering ascent dusty, yet orchids find a foothold in the harsh, dry volcanic soil; look for an August bloom.

Side-stream crossings after a mile require stone hopping or wading early in the season. Ahead follow a rock-lined path and cairns to the site of the river crossing via rocky bars and seasonal bridge spans. Because the crossing placement can vary from year to year in response to river changes, be alert for the trail markings pointing the way. A regal upstream view of Mount Hood greets you at the crossing and suggests you take your time. About 0.1 mile past the crossing, locate the loop and the wilderness register.

A clockwise tour of the loop begins to the left, passing through similar forest. En route to the falls, the trail parallels and crisscrosses Ramona Creek. Find views of the stark pinkish-gray cliffs, clear-spilling water, and mottled moss-and-lichen carpet of the forest floor. Ramona Falls captivates onlookers with its fanciful cascading beauty. Its series of bouncing white streamers trace the broken cliff face, descending in irregular, short splashing drops.

Upon departing the falls, travel the hiker-horse stretch of trail, passing through lodgepole pine forest, uncharacteristic of the western slope of the Cascades. Where the trail passes alongside the Sandy River canyon, return to a more mixed forest and better shade. Close the loop at the river crossing, with an encore view of Mount Hood, and backtrack the first 1.4 miles.

45. WILDWOOD WETLAND

Features ▪	Cascade Mountains wetland, Salmon River, wildlife watching
Distance ▪	0.9 mile round trip
Elevation change ▪	Minimal
Difficulty ▪	Easy (all-ability, traveling paved and boardwalk stretches)
Season ▪	Spring into fall; daylight hours
Map ▪	BLM Wildwood Wetland Trail brochure
Information ▪	Salem District, BLM; fee

In the Wildwood Recreation Site near Welches, this trail welcomes with its ease and natural offering and is ideal for unhurried travel. This short interpretive trail meanders through picturesque habitats, while an interpretive brochure and attractive plaques discuss the natural processes and identify the common wildlife. The trail's highlight is the boardwalk stretch through a Cascade Mountains wetland—a rarity. Here, bog, pond, and marsh secret signature species of aquatic and terrestrial plants and animals. Birders can enjoy the trail, looking for

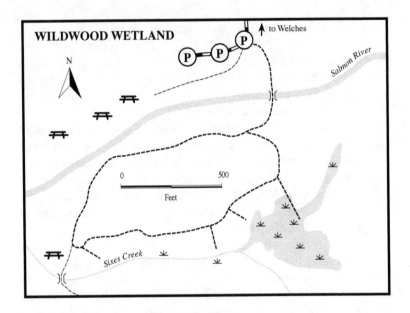

some seventy species of bird that reside or frequent the area. At the Salmon River crossing, look for spawning salmon and steelhead in the fall and winter.

To reach this trail from US 26, 14.5 miles east of Sandy and 1.3 miles west of Welches, turn south entering the Wildwood BLM Recreation Site. Follow the signs to the trailheads and Cascade Streamwatch. You will find the marked trail as it enters the woodland on a wide paved path, left of the interpretive kiosk (past the restrooms). Brochures are available at the kiosk. This trail also launches the Boulder Ridge Trail, a hiking trail.

The nature trail is immediately engulfed in a welcoming bower of bigleaf maple and Douglas fir before reaching the scenic long, broad span over the Salmon River. From the bridge, enjoy both upstream

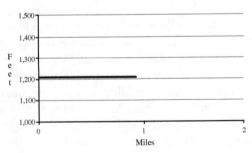

Salmon Wild and Scenic River, Wildwood Recreation Area

and downstream viewing. Tranquil bends, boulder bars, framing alder and cedar, and multicolor rocks in the riverbed add to the shimmering beauty of the river. Upon crossing remain on the wide surfaced trail; stairs descend left.

The loop junction is just ahead; turn left, remaining on paved trail; the gravel trail on the right is the return. Benches dot the way, allowing for stopping and birding. Where boardwalk advances the trail, you might notice a variety of surfaces being tested for their durability and finish. The trail's wildlife plaques have interpretive notes in type and braille, raised images of the species, and the imprints of their tracks.

From the shady realm with huge cottonwoods and phantasmagoric mossy vine-maple tangles, the trail enters wetland and changes to board-walk. Along it four spurs branch left to special attractions. View slicks of methane gas on the black water; gnawed or drowned stumps; cattails, sedges, and reeds; and red-winged blackbirds, water snakes, and newts. Young coho salmon live in the nutrient-rich wetland before migrating to sea. A great blue heron, rare red-legged frog, or aquatic mammal may add surprise.

Where the boardwalk ends at 0.5 mile, find the gravel return head-ing right. To the left leads to a lovely covered picnic site and just beyond it, the bridge over Sixes Creek, the start of the Boulder Ridge Trail, and a pair of unusual cedar stumps. Some travelers may choose to backtrack rather than complete the gravel stretch of the loop. The gravel return tours a visually compelling forest. Where it nears the river, snare a few river glimpses and pass some impressive-size cedar stumps. Either way, conclude retracing the bridge back to the trailhead.

If time allows, you might want to tour the site's other acclaimed trail, the Cascade Streamwatch Trail, a 0.75-mile loop. It journeys to an underwater anadromous fish viewing site and along the river. It, too, is all-ability, but buckling in the pavement and some steeper stretches make it more difficult for wheelchair use.

OF SPECIAL INTEREST

Recognized for its beauty and its anadromous fish runs, the Salmon River is protected as a National Wild and Scenic River for its entire 33-mile length from its headwaters on Mount Hood to its confluence with the Sandy River. Such full-length river protection is a rarity in the Lower 48.

46. BURIED FOREST

Features ▪	Mount Hood views, buried forest, alpine wildflowers
Distance ▪	1.2 miles round trip
Elevation change ▪	200 feet
Difficulty ▪	Moderate
Season ▪	Summer into fall
Maps ▪	Green Trails: Mount Hood 15' series; USFS Mount Hood National Forest
Information ▪	Mount Hood Information Center; Northwest Forest Pass

If you're in the mood for big views and lofty perspectives, this Mount Hood hike will put your yearnings to rest. It follows an overlapping section of two premier trails: Timberline and Pacific Crest (PCT). At timberline and alpine heights, the hike travels east from Timberline Lodge (on the National Register of Historic Places) to the Buried Forest/White River Canyon overlook. Mount Hood looms supreme over your left shoulder. The discovery is one of striking juxtapositions: the harsh volcanic landscape and the tenuous alpine flora, the colorful wildflowers and the stark ash, and fire and ice—the volcanic and glacial legacies. At White Canyon, the tops of dead trees buried

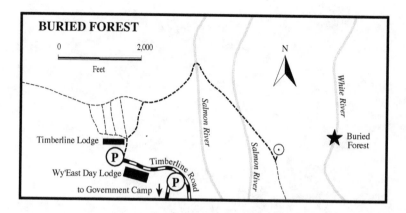

by the last eruptions have worn free, seeing the light of day after two centuries of entombment in rock, mud, and ash.

To take this hike, from US 26 east of Government Camp, turn north on Timberline Road and proceed 5.2 miles to Timberline Lodge and ample parking.

At the east side of the lodge, begin the hike by following the service road heading uphill toward Silcox Hut. Ahead, turn east on a rock-lined path, crossing a snowmelt drainage to reach the Timberline/PCT. The sign shows "Canada, 498 miles; Mexico, 1,852 miles." Point your toes toward Mexico, taking the PCT to the right. A mountaineer trail leads to the hut.

On the selected hike, you will pass through patchy, snag-pierced alpine forest and open wildflower-dotted slopes, crossing the headwater drainages of the Salmon River before reaching the canyon overlooks. Mountain hemlock and whitebark pine are among the trees. Lupine, phlox, yellow buckwheat, aster, Indian paintbrush, penstemon, and dwarf star-tulip are but a few of the blooms on the open slope. In all directions the viewing is captivating. From the icy summit to its forested wilderness

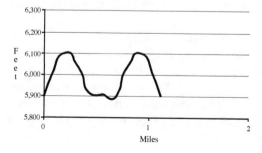

White River Canyon and Mount Hood, Mount Hood National Forest

skirt, Mount Hood looms grand. Trillium Lake and Mount Jefferson turn eyes south.

Upon exiting the Salmon River Canyon, a left spur leads to the destination, Buried Forest Overlook (elevation 5,900 feet). The entombed ancient forest sits below White River Glacier in the deep furrowed gouge of White River Canyon. The canyon appears wild and desolate, almost lunarlike, with its massive ridges of rock and sand and the tips of trees hinting at the buried forest. Uncovered bits of roots, logs, and limbs at the exposed former soil line are other clues to the long-ago forest. Usually you can detect the forest by scanning the east wall; but flooding can rewrite the canvas. For the 1.2-mile round trip, backtrack to the lodge.

To extend the trip, you may continue on the PCT, descending an additional 0.5 mile along the dividing ridge between the Salmon and White River drainages to conclude this hike at a broad plateau where the PCT drops steeply away. The loose sand on this stretch can tire leg muscles, especially on the uphill return. From the lower canyon vantage, you can gather a better impression of the headwater bowl of White River Canyon. Return as you came.

OF SPECIAL INTEREST

Mount Hood ("Wy'East" to the Northwest Indian tribes) is one of the most climbed glaciated peaks in the world and most climbed peak of its kind in the United States. Climbing spurs branch off the 40.7-mile Timberline Trail. The first full ascent came in 1845.

47. LITTLE ZIGZAG FALLS

Features	▪	Attractive waterfall and creek canyon
Distance	▪	0.6 mile round trip
Elevation change	▪	100 feet
Difficulty	▪	Easy
Season	▪	April through October
Maps	▪	Green Trails: Government Camp 15' series; USFS Mount Hood National Forest
Information	▪	Mount Hood Information Center; Northwest Forest Pass

This is a nice little trail either for breaking up your drive on US 26 or extending a discovery trip in the Mount Hood area. It sits just outside Mount Hood Wilderness and traces a parallel course to the clear-spilling Little Zigzag Creek, one of the many glacial waters draining from Mount Hood. The narrow corridor of this hiker-only trail packs a lot of wallop for its size—with tall conifers, scenic snags, a weeping and moss-coated slope wall, and the stairstepping creek. Little Zigzag Falls adds the exclamation point. Postcard pretty, it's about 60- to 80-feet high, pleated by a protruding section of cliff.

This family trail is reached off US 26, 22.8 miles east of Sandy and 4.5 miles west of the Government Camp turnoff. Turn north on Road 39 (also referred to as FR 2639), following it 2.3 miles to the road's end and the large parking/turnaround area.

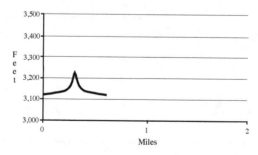

Little Zigzag Falls, Mount Hood National Forest

This wide gravel trail leaves the upper end of the parking lot, pursuing Little Zigzag Creek upstream to the falls. The lovely creek flows clear and fast, offering continuous views with one scenic image after another. The movement of the water fans the creekside vegetation. Tall Douglas and Pacific silver fir, western hemlock, and western red cedar edge the trail as its passes between canyon slope and creek.

The trail gradually grades higher and shows few obstacles, mainly a couple of puddles when wet. At 0.25 mile, reach the base of the falls

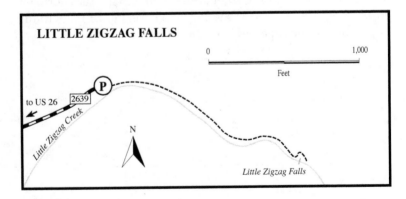

for a full-falls image; a scenic memorial bench invites repose. The racing water of the falls has carved two deep chutes along either side of the bulging cliff, shaping an island in the upper flow. Wonderful mossy banks, the washed red-and-black cliff, the rush of falling water, and the chill breeze contribute to the falls' beauty and excitement.

Hikers may choose to take the switchback uphill from here to the top of the falls (0.3 mile). The climb gives you a better sense of the height of the falls. Viewing is primarily of the creek and the bubbling fury at the head of the plunge. Do not attempt to peer down the falls. Because the trail beyond the upper vantage deteriorates and dead-ends, return as you came.

48. "OLD" SALMON RIVER TRAIL

Features ■	Wild and scenic river, old-growth gallery
Distance ■	5.2 miles round trip
Elevation change ■	200 feet
Difficulty ■	Moderate
Season ■	Much of the year when clear of snow
Maps ■	Green Trails: Government Camp 15' series; USFS Mount Hood National Forest
Information ■	Mount Hood Information Center; Northwest Forest Pass

Away from the hectic bustle of the Mount Hood recreation core, this shuffle through nature rolls out a sensory-rich experience along the Salmon River. The river's entire 33-mile length is federally protected for its wild beauty and specialness; anadromous fish run the river. This hike pairs up with the Salmon Wild and Scenic River as it emerges from Salmon-Huckleberry Wilderness; the milder terrain outside the wilderness area allows for an easy acquaintance. Travel is in an engaging

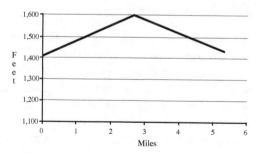

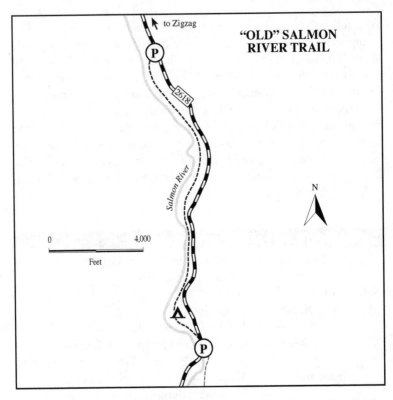

setting of ancient forest with interruptions of shrub-woodland. The close presence of lightly traveled Salmon River Road alone disrupts the natural sojourn, but mostly the road is a quiet neighbor.

Access this hike by turning south off US 26 at Zigzag onto Salmon River Road/FR 2618. Follow it about 2.5 miles to the marked lower trailhead and roadside parking, 4.5 miles to Green Canyon Campground (on the right), or 4.8 miles to the upper trailhead at the wilderness outskirts. A more challenging trail into the wilderness heads upstream from the upper trailhead.

This lightly tracked casual trail pursues the east bank of the Salmon Wild and Scenic River passing between the upper and lower trailheads. It offers a rolling excursion in the rich, cool darkness of a lush old-growth setting, contrasted by short spells in alder-salmonberry woodland. In the bountiful green forest understory, plants can mask or drape into the path. The large-diameter trees can put a crimp in your neck as your eyes follow the trunks skyward.

Enjoy nearly continuous river views. The clear water alternates from smooth to churning and shows gravel bars, mossy banks, and

Forest along "Old" Salmon River Trail, Salmon Wild and Scenic River, Mount Hood National Forest

cascading side streams. During winter and spring, be prepared to ford tributaries. Where the road and river become pinched together, the trail is briefly pushed out onto Salmon River Road. Turn around here and return to trailhead for a 5.2-mile round trip.

49. MIRROR LAKE

Features ■	Reflection lake, Mount Hood view
Distance ■	3.2 miles round trip
Elevation change ■	650 feet
Difficulty ■	Moderate
Season ■	June to October
Maps ■	Green Trails: Government Camp 15' series; USFS Mount Hood National Forest
Information ■	Mount Hood Information Center; day-use fee or Northwest Forest Pass

Although many places in the country have Mirror Lakes that are choice destinations, this hike ups the ante. This trail takes you to a lovely dark-blue mountain lake in the basin of Tom Dick and Harry Mountain, with a wonderful cross-lake view of Mount Hood from the south shore—and oh, lest I forget, great reflections. But such a prize has a

Mount Hood view from Mirror Lake, Mount Hood National Forest

cost—popularity. Your boots likely will have company thumping up the trail. The beloved lake also requires a bit more effort on the parts of all hikers to keep it pristine. Use your best leave-no-trace manners, limit your party size and length of stay, and take away great memories and photographs so you don't have to return so often. Besides the engaging lake, forest, rock, and meadow habitats await.

Reach this highly popular trail on the south side of US 26, 26.1 miles east of Sandy and 1.2 miles west of the Government Camp turnoff. Despite the large roadside head-in parking area, the lot frequently fills, with parking spaces hard to find midday. For safety, park only in the parking lot.

Cross the footbridge over Camp Creek, and take the wide hiking trail to the right and begin ascending. True fir, mountain hemlock, cedar, and Douglas fir fashion the forest. At the upcoming bridge, you might spy notched cedar stumps from the days of springboard logging. With their big radial leaves and seasonal blooms, rhododendrons shape a charming travel aisle before being displaced by salal.

The rapid wing-flap of a startled grouse or the high-pitched "eek" of a pika in the talus can stir you from your musings. The talus slope at 0.5 mile opens a narrow gap in the forest for a northern view. Be

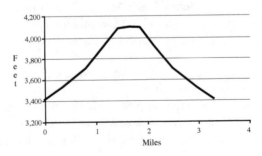

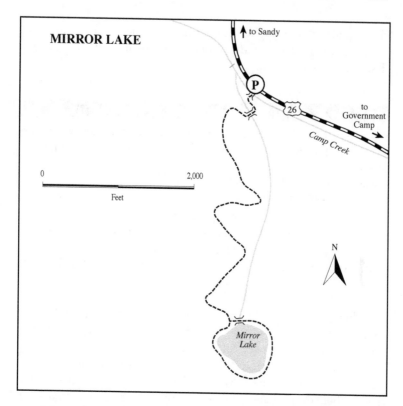

MIRROR LAKE

↑ to Sandy

P

26

to
Government
Camp →

Camp Creek

0   2,000
Feet

N

Mirror
Lake

careful on this rocky crossing. Switchbacks and broadening views follow as the route climbs to the lake loop junction (1.4 miles). The forks straight and to the left shape the loop. For this hike, continue forward (bear right) on the primary trail to Mirror Lake and Tom Dick and Harry Mountain.

Mirror Lake is a small to midsize mountain lake with glassy surface and log-strewn outlet. Its upper edge is framed by a textured meadow of grasses, wildflowers, and shrubs. Forest rings the basin and Tom Dick and Harry Mountain cups the entire scene, adding its reflection to the lake. Rounding the lake, pass a few approaches to shore before bearing left on the lake loop. The trail to the right continues to the tri-summit ridge of Tom Dick and Harry.

As you cross the meadow on a plank walk, find views and reflections of Mount Hood. Lupine, fireweed, Queen Anne's lace, aster, coneflower, and monkeyflower dress up the meadow. Among the shrubs are black twinberry, mountain elder, salmonberry, and small alder. The meadow alone would slow strides. Where the trail returns to forested shore, find a stone-stepping crossing of a tiny inlet stream followed by a sagging log bridge over the outlet. Close the loop at 1.8 miles and descend to the trailhead.

50. OLD BARLOW ROAD

Features ▪	Oregon Trail, historic gravesite, wagon ruts
Distance ▪	2 miles round trip or 1-mile downhill shuttle
Elevation change ▪	500 feet
Difficulty ▪	Difficult
Season ▪	Late spring into fall
Maps ▪	Green Trails: Mount Hood 15' series; USFS Mount Hood National Forest
Information ▪	Hood River Ranger District; Northwest Forest Pass

This hike, a step into the past, shows you the route of the Oregon Trail pioneer and provides a sense of the encountered hardship. It is no simple walk in the park; fallen trees and scruffy trail lead the way. The opening of the Barlow Toll Road in 1846 provided pioneers with an overland route around Mount Hood to the Willamette Valley, sparing them the perilous raft trip down the unbridled Columbia River. But the overland route was not without danger; the season was short and the terrain grueling. This hike unveils the 1-mile stretch of the over-land route between Barlow Pass (elevation 4,157 feet) and the Pioneer Woman's Grave. Even if your hiking ability prohibits walking this stretch of toll road, almost everyone can peek in the door at its two trailheads.

Both trailheads are reached off OR 35. Find the upper trailhead at Barlow Pass Sno-Park: Near milepost 60 (2.4 miles north of the

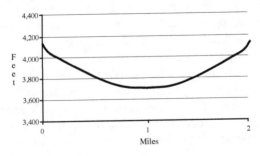

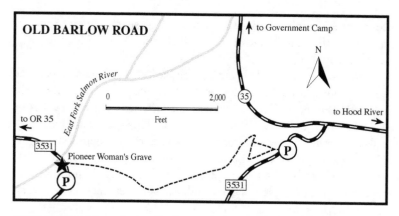

US 26–OR 35 junction), take FR 3531 east off OR 35, and follow it to the trail and sno-park parking on the right. For the lower trailhead, Pioneer Woman's Grave, turn east off OR 35 onto FR 3531 near milepost 58, 0.4 mile north of the US 26–OR 35 junction. Locate the grave in 0.3 mile with parking just beyond.

This hike alternately traces the original wagon route or the switchback-improved post-emigration section of the Barlow Road, used as a market route between 1860 and 1924. Round-trip hikers have a choice of trailhead. Shuttle hikers typically opt for downhill travel. Either doorway offers a glimpse at the original trail. In places, ruts are 5 feet deep.

From the upper end of the upper trailhead parking area, descend west finding a split-off in 100 feet. Descend on either the steep historic trail used by horses, mules, oxen, and foot-sore pioneers or the switchbacking route of the updated dirt market road to its left. Taking the untamed original wagon road requires a bit of scrambling around or over logs, but even the newer stretch is not obstacle-free. Where necessary, well-tracked bypasses guide you around obstacles.

The hike mostly keeps to the market route, which incorporated portions of the original trail. At times, you might see hints of the un-swerving line of the pioneer route disappearing into forest. As you curse the downfalls, consider the challenge of the pioneers who had already walked 1,900 miles and needed to get a loaded wagon through here.

True fir and mountain hemlock cloak the upper slope. Midway, Douglas fir, western red cedar, and western hemlock displace the higher elevation forest. The spare flora is replaced with patches of greenery. At 0.6 mile a clearcut to the west admits more light, and a walk to its edge adds views of Mount Hood. Rhododendron bushes color parts of the forest away from the trail. After parallel logs span a soggy tributary, look left. The deep gouge of the original trail is now beside the path; a ski-and-foot trail arrives on the right.

Remain on the market route of the Barlow Road, passing parallel to the pioneer trail. Again view the original wagon ruts on a flat near FR 3531. Here, the deep-worn ruts are softened by greenery. Cross FR 3531 to the Pioneer Woman's Grave. This quiet landmark signals either the stop or your turnaround. A cairn and memorial plaque honor the unknown woman. Crosses fashioned of twigs and needles, stones, and other tributes are placed at the site, but do not pick the wildflowers. The grave has been a pilgrim site ever since its discovery in the 1920s.

OF SPECIAL INTEREST

In building Mount Hood Highway, which replaced the market route, road crews discovered what is now known as the Pioneer Woman's Grave. The discovery consisted of the old wagon tongue used as the grave marker and the wooden wagon box that served as the casket. Helping substantiate that the grave belonged to an Oregon Trail pioneer were the recollections of a Barlow Toll Road superintendent's son. He recalled hearing in his youth about a pioneer woman who had died of illness and was buried by her husband and children in just such a way.

Barlow Road sign, Mount Hood National Forest

51. ALDER FLAT

Features	▪	Old growth, Clackamas River
Distance	▪	1.8 miles round trip
Elevation change	▪	100 feet
Difficulty	▪	Easy
Season	▪	Year-round
Maps	▪	Green Trails: Fish Creek Mountain 15' series; USFS Mount Hood National Forest
Information	▪	Clackamas River Ranger District; Northwest Forest Pass

This trail wins over travelers with its overall package. The trail journeys through a beautiful cathedral forest with an understory bursting in green and skirts meadow and wetland habitats before arriving at a picnic/camp flat at the Clackamas River. Towering alders edge the flat, suggesting the trail's name. Cobble bars distance the flat from the river. On this beautiful, roadless winding stretch, the wild and scenic river shows cascades, mirror-still segments, and racing water. Together, the flat and river shape a great spot to lull away part of a day.

Near the southeast end of OR 224, about 24.5 miles southeast of Estacada and 0.2 mile north of Ripplebrook Ranger Station, find the gravel loop of the trailhead parking lot.

The trail descends into the spell of the multistory old-growth forest of Douglas fir, western hemlock, and western red cedar. The big trees exceed 250 years in age and stretch 150 feet skyward. Bountiful vine maples fashion a showy midstory, while the leafy understory engages with a variety of shades and shapes. The forest richness soothes the civilized soul.

As the comfortable trail wraps along the slope, hikers may detect a meadow beyond the immediate silhouette of trees. Soon after keep

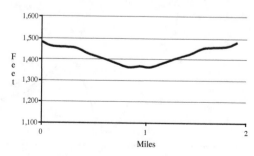

Frog on Alder Flat Trail, Clackamas Wild and Scenic River, Mount Hood National Forest

right, passing to the river side of the slope away from OR 224. The river's voice immediately adds to impressions.

Small birds and wildlife engage visitors. Musings may be interrupted by the noisy pecking of a pileated woodpecker. As the trail wraps and descends the slope, overlook a drainage bottom with skunk cabbage, mossy logs, rich ferns and wetland grasses, and perhaps muddy animal tracks. The solitude and sense of isolation surprise, especially given the trail's shortness, its river access, and its convenient trailhead off a state highway.

On the lower slope, bigleaf maple and cedar vary forest viewing. At the base of the slope, rustic footbridges and earth-covered boardwalks traverse the drainage wetland for closer discovery. Polliwogs and water striders ripple the small pools. At the small primitive walk-in

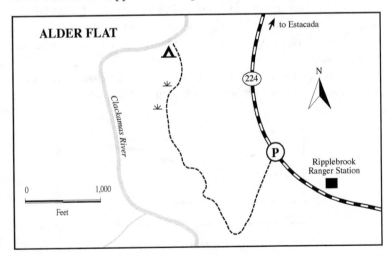

picnic/camp flat (no developed water, no toilets), keep right for the most straightforward river access. It comes out at a small beach below a modest landslide (0.9 mile); larger slides mark the slope at the river bend. Picturesque cedars dot the flat.

This short stretch of river is packed with personality. Knobby volcanic boulders lend visual interest and launch cascades and ripples. Ospreys soar overhead, and for the sure-footed, the gravel bar upstream usually allows another 0.1 mile of riverside exploration, depending on river level. When ready, return as you came.

52. BAGBY HOT SPRINGS

Features ■	Magnificent old growth, rustic hot spring tubs and baths
Distance ■	3 miles round trip
Elevation change ■	200 feet
Difficulty ■	Easy to moderate
Season ■	Spring through fall
Maps ■	Green Trails: Battle Ax 15' series; USFS Mount Hood National Forest
Information ■	Clackamas River Ranger District; Northwest Forest Pass

In a magical forest setting along the Hot Springs Fork of the Collawash River just outside of Bull of the Woods Wilderness, Bagby Hot Springs has been a regional draw since the 1880s. Today, the hot springs site includes a rustic bathhouse, dugout-style cedar tubs for personal use, and round communal tubs. The trail bustles with the feet of day hikers, wilderness backpackers, and bathers, but midweek and morning visits tend to be quieter. In choosing whether this destination is appropriate for you and your family, know that clothing is optional here.

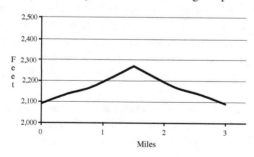

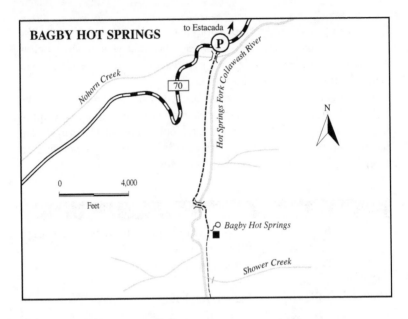

To reach the Hot Springs trailhead, from Estacada follow OR 224 southeast 25 miles to where it ends at the FR 57–FR 46 split. Head right on FR 46 for 3.5 miles, taking a right on FR 63. Follow FR 63 another 3.5 miles, then take FR 70, 6 miles west to the trailhead. It is left off FR 70, 0.5 mile past Pegleg Falls Day-Use Area. The ample parking lot is seldom empty.

The comfortable, well-maintained trail crosses Nohorn Creek to pursue the Hot Springs Fork Collawash River upstream, passing beneath towering old-growth trees. The Hot Springs Fork is another of Oregon's stunning waterways; enjoy frequent looks at the clear tumbling water. Some rhododendron and vine maple, along with a lush understory, dress the ancient Douglas-fir complex. The girths and heights of the big trees amaze.

At 1.2 miles, cross the footbridge over the Hot Springs Fork, spying its picturesque carved bowls, pools, side gorges, cascades, and reunion waters. Then, at 1.5 miles, cross Peggy Creek to arrive at the rustic hot springs complex. The structures of hand-hewn cedar blend with the natural stage. A historic 1913 Forest Service log cabin sits among them.

The hot springs consists of an upper and lower springs with their associated tubs and communal pools. Wooden flumes carry hot (135-degree) mineral water and cool freshwater to the tubs, allowing visitors

Hot Springs Fork Collawash River, Mount Hood National Forest

to adjust the comfort level of the bathing waters. The soothing steamy waters and open-air pools with forest views are hard to pass up. In summer you may have a bit of a wait to claim a pool. Nudity is only allowed in the tub area, not on the grounds. Gray jays, nuthatches, sounding grouse, and plaintive ravens add amusement.

A meadow to the east of the hot springs is open to picnicking. Shower Falls, 0.25 mile past the complex, offers a cold water rinse off. This 100-foot falls spills over mossy rock terraces, dropping from the lowest shelf as a rain shower. A platform sits beneath the falls allowing hikers to easily soak their heads. The return is as you came.

OF SPECIAL INTEREST

The hot springs were used by Native Americans long before their discovery by Robert Bagby in the 1880s. According to Native American oral history, the visiting tribes would lay down weapons at the springs, which were considered a place of peace.

MOUNT JEFFERSON – NORTH SANTIAM RIVER AREA

(ACCESS ROUTE OR 22)

Fish Lake, Olallie Lake Scenic Area, Mount Hood National Forest

53. OPAL CREEK

Features	■	Exceptional old-growth, pristine creek and river, historical sites
Distance	■	7 miles round trip to Opal Pool
Elevation change	■	200 feet
Difficulty	■	Moderate to difficult
Season	■	Spring through fall
Maps	■	Imus Geographics: Bull of the Woods Wilderness–Opal Creek Wilderness; USFS Willamette National Forest
Information	■	Detroit Ranger District; Northwest Forest Pass

This is one of Oregon's truly special sites that is now protected for posterity. Opal Creek is one of the last intact uncut drainages in the lower Cascades, which means big trees, thriving multistory vegetation, and some of the clearest flowing waters anywhere. The trail pursues the Little North Santiam River upstream to its headwaters, where it then follows Opal Creek. The picturesque river and creek captivate with their emerald pools, cascades, waterfalls, gorge features, and see-through blue-green water. The route passes through historic Jawbone Flats, a mining camp, now a place of staff residences, environmental education, and an interpretive stop. The area mines produced copper, lead, cadmium, and zinc.

To reach this special place, at Mehama (23 miles east of Salem), turn north off OR 22 onto North Fork Road, heading toward Little North Fork Recreation Area. Pavement ends after 15.1 miles. At the fork at 16.4 miles, head left on FR 2209. Expect a few potholes, ruts, and traffic. Reach the trailhead in another 4.2 miles. The parking area can fill on summer weekends, when the cool waters are most inviting.

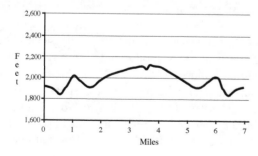

Opal Creek, Opal Creek Scenic Recreation Area, Willamette National Forest

On its upstream journey, the trail traces the old road to the mining camp and then follows foot trail. Only the old-road section is open to mountain bikers as well as hikers; after that everyone is on foot. The tree-framed gravel road allows carefree strolling as it wraps along the north slope above the river. Enjoy a great diversity with big Douglas firs, cedars, and hemlocks surrounded by alder, vine maple, bigleaf maple, hazel, and the occasional rhododendron or dogwood. The route advances with gentle inclines and modest rolls. Enjoy river views where the road and stunning blue-green Little North Santiam are closely paired. Sides spurs sneak away to pleasant river spots.

Pass a giant 1,000-year-old Douglas fir (the Governor Gus Gibbs fir), cross the bridge over Gold Creek, and remain on road passing the Whetstone Mountain Trail. Rustic toilets tucked to the side of the

180

route help keep the area unspoiled; find them at 0.25 mile, 2 miles, and at Jawbone Flats. Where cliffs abut the road, hikers might spy some abandoned mine adits. Although of historical note, they are dangerous; keep out.

Look for the Merten Mill ruins and the spur to Sawmill Falls (also known as *Cascadia de Los Niños*, or Waterfall of the Children) on your right at 1.7 miles. Rusted equipment, part of the old steam mill structure, and the younger trees here all recall the former sawmill. Find the spur to the falls near an old storage structure. It descends hillside and outcrop to reach the falls viewing. The 30-foot waterfall is a beauty, spilling in lacy streamers over the bulging river outcrop. At the foot of the slope sits a small gravel beach and a mesmerizing deep emerald pool isolated from Sawmill Falls by an arm of the rock outcropping.

At 2 miles reach the Opal Pool Loop junction. Follow the road, returning via the river footbridge to the right. Then at 3.1 miles, enter Jawbone Flats and Opal Creek Preserve, finding an information station. Jawbone Flats was the original town for the miners and their families and consists of both old and new cabins. Here, you can view relics of the mining era, but respect the privacy of residents, heeding posted rules.

Next, follow the signs to Opal Pool. Head straight through the Flats, cross Battle Ax Bridge, and turn right, passing equipment sheds and a boneyard of mining machinery. Beyond a picnic shelter come to the foot trail to Opal Pool (a right). At the Opal Creek footbridge, view a splendid creek stretch with serial stepped falls and a gorge. Spurs access the creek.

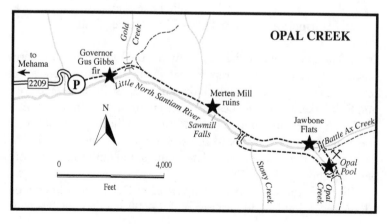

Opal Pool is just downstream from the crossing; reach it on the west shore via either the Opal Creek Trail or a creekside spur. The deep slot pool sits where the gorge broadens; mossy rock cliffs add to viewing. For the return, either follow the Opal Creek Trail downstream to the bridge crossing at 2 miles or backtrack the way you came. The narrow foot trail is less refined, with roots and rocks, so watch your footing.

OF SPECIAL INTEREST

At the end of a long environmental battle, legislation created the Opal Creek Wilderness and Scenic Recreation Area in 1996, which encompass 35,000 acres of wonderful old growth and sterling waters. The Governor Gus Gibb fir, which stands 100 feet south of the trail at 0.2 mile, is 1,000 years old and 270 feet high; elsewhere trees exceed 500 years in age. The trail along Opal Creek is named the Kopetski Trail, honoring the legislator who fought for this wilderness protection in the U.S. Congress.

54. LOWER LAKE–FISH LAKE

Features	Mountain lakes, fall huckleberries and blueberries
Distance	3.2 miles round trip
Elevation change	500 feet
Difficulty	Moderate
Season	Late spring through fall
Maps	Green Trails: Breitenbush 15' series; USFS Olallie Lake Scenic Area
Information	Clackamas River Ranger District

In 11,000-acre Olallie Lake Scenic Area, you'll find lakes and berry bushes galore. This hike is representative of the bounty. It takes you to two charming lakes: Lower Lake, the deepest in the scenic area, and Fish Lake, an isolated beauty in a deep forested basin. The trail is ideal for families, and almost everyone can reach the long oval of Lower Lake. Because mosquitoes in the scenic area are menacing in the early part of the hiking season, late summer and fall promise a more leisurely appreciation.

To reach the scenic area from OR 22 at Detroit, head north on FR 46 for 22.3 miles and turn east on FR 4690 at a sign for the scenic

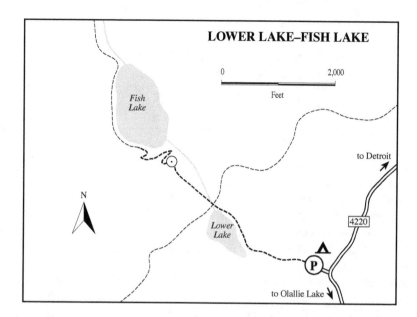

area. The well-traveled route begins paved but changes to dusty road with rough spots. At the T-junction with FR 4220 in 7.8 miles, turn right for the lakes. Find the turnoff for Lower Lake Campground and the trailhead in another 4.3 miles. A couple of parking spaces sit next to the trail in camp; do not block campsites. A couple more spaces are located on FR 4220 at the campground turnoff. The trail leaves from the upper end of the campground.

Travel through a picturesque setting of true fir, mountain hemlock, and lodgepole pine with true and dwarf huckleberry, arnica, lupine, and vanilla leaf coloring the floor. After rolling over a low divide arrive at Lower Lake (0.25 mile), a long, beautiful 16-acre blue lake below a low forested hill. Surprised ducks may run atop the lake in hurried take-off. As the trail hugs the shoreline, find convenient spots for lake admiration. Small alders, boulders, and beargrass accent the shore.

At the 0.6-mile junction at the far end of Lower Lake, the fork to the left leads to Averill and Red Lakes; the one to the right leads to Triangle Lake and Olallie Meadow; and the one straight ahead leads to the chosen destination—Fish Lake. Berry bushes abound at the junction, but when going off trail to pick them, watch out for yellow jackets.

Descend passing from a small-stature young fir forest into a lichen-dressed setting of more mature hemlock and fir. In places, shrubs can

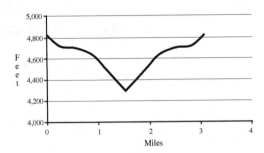

brush the legs as you follow the narrow, rock-studded forest path. At 0.9 mile, short spurs to the right lead to an outcrop edge and an over-look of Fish Lake cradled in its steep-sided basin. Glimpse Mount Hood beyond a conical butte to the north.

Switchbacks then ease the way downhill to lake level. With the descent come bigger and bigger trees and some rhododendron. Cross a rocky inlet drainage to arrive at Fish Lake and a junction. To the left is the primary trail that continues to Surprise and Si Lakes, and to the right find shoreline travel toward the scree slope below the outcrop vantage. The spur straight ahead presents the quickest lake view.

Fish Lake is pretty and round, with silver logs at its outlet. It possesses a wonderful sense of remoteness. Larcenous gray jays, a bombardier squirrel dropping cones from the treetops, and a knock-ing pileated woodpecker enliven the stage. Dipper, kingfisher, and merganser add to the lake's charm. When ready, return as you came or add another lake to the tour.

Huckleberry, Olallie Lake Scenic Area, Mount Hood National Forest

55. OLALLIE LAKE–MONON LAKE

Features	■	Picturesque mountain lakes, berries, Mount Jefferson views
Distance	■	Up to 8.4 miles round trip
Elevation change	■	Minimal
Difficulty	■	Moderate to difficult
Season	■	Late spring through fall
Maps	■	Green Trails: Breitenbush 15' series; USFS Olallie Lake Scenic Area
Information	■	Clackamas River Ranger District; Northwest Forest Pass

Olallie and Monon Lakes sit at the heart of Olallie Lake Scenic Area and steal the hearts of visitors. Their large irregular shorelines present changing views of the lakes and Mount Jefferson and Olallie Butte. Meadow, berry patch, forest, and fire zone vary lakeshore passage; stretches of raised planking span soggy reaches. *Olallie* is the Native American word for huckleberry, and the berries ripen from early to mid-September. In 2001, lightning strikes started the Paul Dennis Fire, which burned part of the forest and half of Peninsula Campground. The bronze needles add to the lakeshore mosaic and the process of renewal adds to discovery. Whether you walk snatches of the shorelines or the combined distance, you'll have a fine time.

To reach the lakes from OR 22 at Detroit, head north on FR 46 for 22.3 miles and turn east on FR 4690 at a sign for the scenic area. The well-traveled route begins paved but changes to dusty road with rough spots. At the T-junction with FR 4220 in 7.8 miles, turn right. Travel 5.2 miles to Olallie Lake Day-Use Area at the Olallie Lake Resort/Paul Dennis Campground turnoff. The Olallie Lake Trail begins at the far end of Paul Dennis Campground but because there is no day-use parking there, you must either hike into camp from the

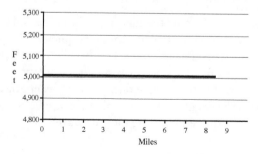

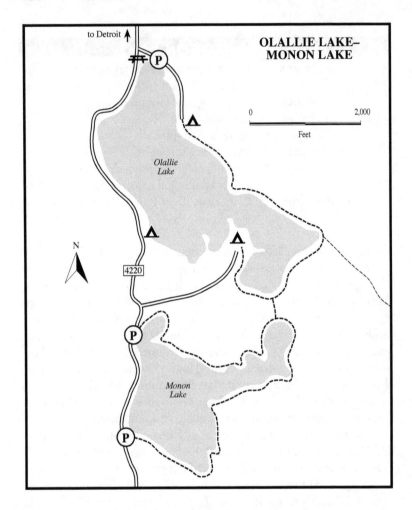

lake day-use area or be a Paul Dennis camper. The Monon Lake
trailheads are reached on FR 4220, at 1.5 and 1.8 miles past the Olallie
Lake turnoff; roadside turnouts provide trail parking. Monon Trail is
hiker-only because of its areas of raised planking.

Centerpiece to the hike are the amazing natural lakes. Olallie Lake
is the larger, more developed lake; Monon is quieter, but peaceful
retreats exist along each. The Monollie Trail bridges the two. Because
loop travel requires walking the active west-shore roadway, backtracking is best. Temporary closures may turn you back where the burn is
unsafe because of the danger of falling limbs or snags. Check with the
ranger district or at the resort before plotting travel.

Gray jay, Olallie Lake Scenic Area, Mount Hood National Forest

From the south end of Paul Dennis Campground, the Olallie Lake Trail travels the east shore of Olallie Lake, a big blue lake with soaring ospreys and quiet paddlers. The comfortable trail passes through a true fir–mountain hemlock–lodgepole pine forest with a huckleberry-beargrass understory. Enjoy great cross-lake views south of Mount Jefferson, with spurs leading to shore. In 0.2 mile, enter the first area of burn where the lake influence spared some of the shoreline trees. Deeper in the forest, lichen tresses still cling to blackened trunks. With the fire burning hit-and-miss, untouched forest reclaims the trail between the burn sites.

At 1 mile, hike past the spur heading left to Long Lake to round the southern end of Olallie Lake toward Peninsula Campground. At 1.4 miles is the 0.2-mile Monollie Trail turnoff, which crosses the neck of land between Olallie and Monon Lakes. It tags the Monon Lake Trail, 1 mile from the northern trailhead; 1.6 miles from the southern trailhead, for piecemeal travel.

The Monon Lake Trail hugs the shoreline, passing through mixed conifer forest, patchy meadows with berries, and more of the burn. Rhododendrons share space with the huckleberry bushes. Small peninsulas and coves reveal secret corners. Elsewhere, sweeping views of the broad open lake lend appeal. To the north, view Olallie Butte with its volcanic crest and crags, as well as its lake reflection. View Mount Jefferson to the south. Much of the east shore travel is through standing burned forest.

56. SOUTH BREITENBUSH GORGE

Features	▪	Engaging old-growth setting and gorge
Distance	▪	4 miles round trip or a 2 or 2.5-mile shuttle
Elevation change	▪	250 feet
Difficulty	▪	Easy to moderate
Season	▪	Year-round, except during low-elevation snow
Maps	▪	Green Trails: Breitenbush 15' series; USFS Willamette National Forest
Information	▪	Detroit Ranger District; Northwest Forest Pass

There is nothing better than pulling a rich blanket of old growth around you, and this national recreation trail (NRT) allows just that. The ancient forest of Douglas fir, cedar, and hemlock fashions a tranquil cathedral. A glorious textured mid- and understory completes the welcoming scene. For many, walking among the centuries-old trees has a spiritual quality. Areas of snapped trees and logs are a legacy of past winter windstorms and hold the story of forest renewal. The trail follows the South Fork Breitenbush River upstream to the gorge vista and picturesque Roaring Creek.

To reach the gorge from OR 22 at Detroit, head north on FR 46 for about 14 miles and turn southeast (right) on to gravel FR 4685. Find trailheads in 0.25 mile, 2 miles, and 2.5 miles.

Starting from the first (the lowest) trailhead, follow the connector spur south and turn left (upstream) upon meeting the South Breitenbush Gorge Trail. To the right leads to the confluence with the North Fork Breitenbush, an optional extension to the hike. The primary trail remains above the river in the enchanted forest, but the

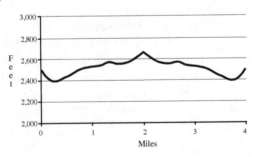

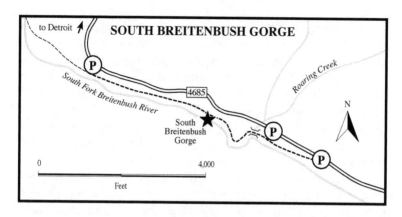

rush is constant and river glimpses are possible. Ahead, the rough, unofficial Emerald Forest Trail built by people at Breitenbush Hot Springs branches right to cross the South Breitenbush before journeying up and over Devils Ridge. It offers an opportunity to get a closer look at the river.

At 1.5 miles, take the spur descending right to South Breitenbush Gorge, a narrow chasm 300 feet long and 3 to 10 feet wide, where the deep clear waters reflect the dark cloak of the gorge. Mosses, ferns, and water-loving plants decorate the 30- to 40-foot-high walls. Logs crisscross over and dip into the chasm. The racing, tumbling waters and the inaccessible deep slot pools engage. Viewing is from the gorge rim.

Bunchberry along South Breitenbush Gorge National Recreation Trail, Willamette National Forest

Upstream, the NRT crosses Roaring Creek at 2 miles, which parts the forest with flare, racing down a steep section of creekbed. The excited waters brimming with bubbles spill around and over mossy rocks in an attractive cascading white ribbon. For round-trip hikers, the creek bridge signals a good turnaround point because the NRT then pinches toward FR 4685. For shuttle hikers, the 2-mile parking lot is just past the bridge. On the final 0.5 mile to the uppermost trailhead, drainages can muddy the path and the added light from the roadway steals from the old-growth mystery.

If you choose to add the side trip downriver to the confluence from the initial junction, it's about 1 mile round trip with an additional 200 feet in elevation change. Pass from old-growth splendor through a corridor of chinquapin, vine maple, and rhododendron to arrive at the alder-maple riparian setting of the river corridor. Footbridges span the braided water of the North Breitenbush. From the North Breitenbush, the trail then continues to FR 4600.050, but this stretch of trail mainly serves the Breitenbush Hot Springs guests who make the pilgrimage to the gorge.

57. TRIANGULATION PEAK

Features ■	Outstanding view of Mount Jefferson, wildflowers
Distance ■	4.4 miles round trip
Elevation change ■	700 feet
Difficulty ■	Moderate with a difficult 0.6-mile spur to peak
Season ■	Late spring through early fall
Maps ■	Green Trails: Mount Jefferson 15' series; USFS Willamette National Forest
Information ■	Detroit Ranger District; Northwest Forest Pass, wilderness permit

This hike into the Mount Jefferson Wilderness Area passes through high-elevation forest, tracing a ridgeline to the steep spur topping Triangulation Peak (elevation 5,484 feet). Wildflowers decorate the way. The former lookout site extends a fine 360-degree view featuring Mount Jefferson and the Cascade Crest's volcano lineup from Mount Hood to North and Middle Sisters. Mosquitoes can sometimes annoy; come prepared.

Mount Jefferson from Triangulation Peak, Mount Jefferson Wilderness, Willamette National Forest

From OR 22 just east of Idanha, head north on FR 2233 for 8.8 miles to the junction with FR 635. Travel is on a single-lane paved route with turnouts becoming gravel. Find the marked trailhead on the right at the junction, off FR 635.

On its ridgeline tour, the gentle rolling trail passes through a forest of mountain hemlock and true fir, shaggy with lichen. Beargrass (in bloom mid-July) and huckleberry (ripe in September) compose the primary understory. The moist drainages support trillium or shooting star, depending on season. Cascade lily, bride's bonnet, columbine, and fragile orchids are other floral discoveries. At 0.5 mile, a clearcut to the north opens views to Spire Rock, Olallie Butte, Mount Hood—and, oh yes, Triangulation Peak.

Impressive big trees and snags punctuate the forest, with a noteworthy 6-foot-diameter fir at 0.9 mile that calls for a doubletake. Where the trail crosses the foot of a scree slope, wildflower seekers can add penstemon to their list. At 1.4 miles, a sign on a trailside tree announces "Spire Rock," a basalt outcropping, seen through a gap in the tree cover with Mount Hood beyond. It's been strictly a forest tour since 0.5 mile. At 1.6 miles, find and take the spur to Triangulation

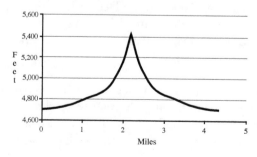

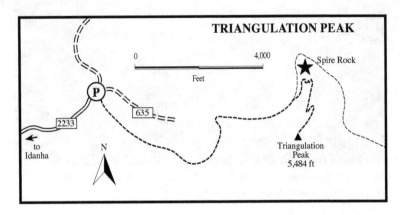

Peak; the primary trail continues below and to the left wrapping toward Spire Rock.

The summit spur climbs steadily, advanced by switchbacks. You will tag the Triangulation Peak–Spire Rock saddle before reaching the summit and finding open views of Mount Jefferson, Cathedral Rocks, Three Fingered Jack, Mount Washington, and Middle and North Sisters. Forested ridges spread away to the Santiam drainage. Two short spurs top the summit high points. The right top holds 360-degree viewing; the left one has a rocky protrusion and small spire feature and presents a bold unadulterated look at Mount Jefferson. Among the rocks grow succulents and other rock flora. Backtrack when ready.

58. COFFIN MOUNTAIN

Features	■	Summit lookout, views, beargrass
Distance	■	3 miles round trip
Elevation change	■	1,000 feet
Difficulty	■	Moderate to difficult
Season	■	Late spring through fall, daylight hours
Maps	■	Green Trails: Detroit 15' series; USFS Willamette National Forest
Information	■	Detroit Ranger District; Northwest Forest Pass

South of Detroit Lake, this hike climbs to the summit of a prominent, descriptively named skyline feature. The route passes through post-fire meadow and summit tree stands. In late July and early August, the summit ridge exhibits a spectacular beargrass bloom, saturating the mountain air with intoxicating perfume. At the fire lookout (staffed during summer months), summit views sweep the Cascade Crest spotlighting Mounts Jefferson, Hood, and Washington; the Three Sisters; and Three Fingered Jack. Olallie Butte, Detroit Lake, and a neighboring former lookout site, Bachelor Mountain, fill out the scene. Because the trail is demanding, dry, and exposed, carry plenty of water. *Water is not available from the fire lookout staff.*

This hike is reached off the Quartzville Back Country Byway. From OR 22 about 20 miles east of Detroit and 38 miles west of Sisters, turn south on Straight Creek Road/FR 11, the back country byway. Proceed 1.5 miles and bear left to remain on FR 11. In another 2.7 miles turn right onto gravel FR 1168. Go 3.8 miles and turn left on FR 450, finding the trail parking area in less than 0.1 mile. The turnout accommodates a handful of vehicles. This hike approaches the Coffin Mountain lookout from the south. A second route arrives from the north off FR 2236.137.

Pass through the boulder barricade entering a steep 0.1-mile climb on old road. It's the most difficult stretch of the trip, so hang in there if you're having second thoughts. The post-fire meadow shows young trees, silvered stumps and logs, and fireweed. Beargrass and other wildflowers dot the rocky and grassy slope. Find an early view of Coffin Mountain, but not its signature image. Also, view Bachelor Mountain and Mount Jefferson above the immediate patchwork slopes. The ascent is more measured after the footpath turns left off the road grade.

Ahead the trail tags the ridge only to proceed right, wrapping and switchbacking up the slope. It kisses the ridge several more times for

Coffin Mountain Lookout, Willamette National Forest

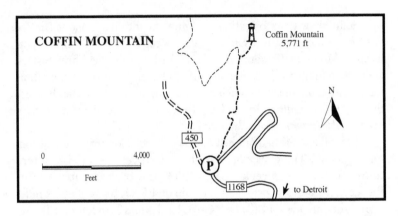

views before attaining and tracing the ridge north at 1 mile. Views build; admire Three Fingered Jack, Three Sisters, Mount Washington, the folded ridges stretching west to Detroit Lake, and both sides of this Coffin Mountain ridge. Ultimately the view stretches from Mount Jefferson south past Diamond Peak. The changing views and the sea of beargrass topped by pretty floral stalks in summer invite frequent pauses.

The rocky crest and summit lookout grow more impressive the closer you get. Mountain hemlock, noble fir, and creeping juniper variously edge the trail. An eerie patch of hanging blowdown (wind-snapped and semi-toppled trees) precedes the junction at 1.25 miles. Here the other summit approach arrives on the left. Where the trail pulls into the open, the tower looms ahead.

At 1.5 miles, the trail claims the summit (elevation 5,771 feet) for a grand look at the Detroit Lake area and the Cascade volcano lineup from Mount Hood to Diamond Peak. Impressive drop-away vertical cliffs claim the north and east sides of the lookout point. When ready to surrender the view, return as you came to FR 450, but be careful on the descent: the gravelly soil of the trail can cause skidding.

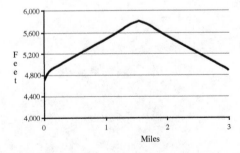

OF SPECIAL INTEREST

The paved Quartzville BLM Back Country Byway strings south between OR 22 and US 20. It rounds south of Coffin Mountain along Quartzville Creek and out past Green Peter Reservoir, coming out 5.5 miles east of Sweet Home. About midway it passes the historic Quartzville mining area (1863–1870). The town was named for the gold-bearing rock. Yellowbottom (BLM) Recreation Site offers camping along the route, with twenty-two sites.

59. MARION LAKE

Features ■	Large mountain lake, old growth, vistas
Distance ■	5.2 miles round trip
Elevation change ■	800 feet
Difficulty ■	Moderate
Season ■	Late spring into fall
Maps ■	Green Trails: Mount Jefferson 15' series; USFS Willamette National Forest
Information ■	Detroit Ranger District; Northwest Forest Pass, wilderness permit

This is a highly popular destination and for good reason—it's beautiful and provides an easy entry to Mount Jefferson Wilderness Area. The comfortable forest trail passes through old growth and visits smaller shrub-lined Lake Ann before reaching Marion Lake. Marion Lake is a large water body rimmed by forest with talus slopes dipping to the lake. Trails radiate out from the lake to peak and other lake attractions. The Marion Lake vistas feature Three Fingered Jack, Mount Jefferson, and Marion Mountain. Because of the site's popularity, respect all closures to restore vegetation and practice leave-no-trace travel.

From OR 22 at Marion Forks, turn east onto FR 2255 (Marion

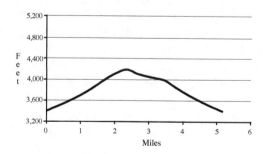

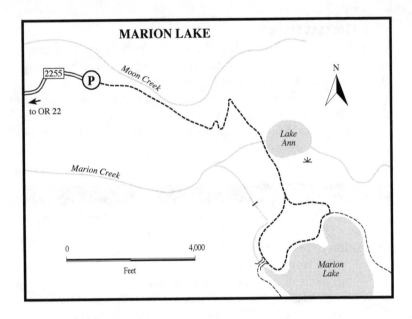

Road) and proceed 4.4 miles to the large trailhead parking area. The route is paved, becoming gravel; parking can fill on summer weekends. Hikers who plan midweek and off-season visits have greater peace on the trail and at the lake.

This hike rolls out a steady comfortable climb on a wide packed-earth trail. Pass through a multistory old-growth hemlock-fir forest with many tall, stout trees. Pacific yew and rhododendron lend interest, along with the classic mid-elevation Cascades forest flora. By 0.6 mile the setting loses some of the big trees, and after 1 mile find the route slightly steeper with more roots and rocks. The skirting of a talus slope precedes arrival at Lake Ann (1.4 miles). Pikas, rodents with high-pitched shrieks, may pop up between the rocks.

Lake Ann is a medium-size mountain lake rimmed by forest and a talus slope traced by the trail. Grasses pierce the watery edge, while alders and shrubs keep admirers at a distance. The ascent again eases as the trail climbs toward Marion Lake. Higher elevation species appear, including huckleberry and beargrass.

At 1.7 miles reach a fork; both the Marion and Outlet Trails lead to the lake. Together, they fashion a lakeside loop. Clockwise, ascend the Marion Trail, arriving at the large western lobe of this heart-shaped wilderness lake at 2 miles. A peninsula isolates the lobes. Spruce, mountain hemlock, and true fir add to the lakeshore forest mix. Keep to the

Three Fingered Jack and Marion Lake, Mount Jefferson Wilderness, Willamette National Forest

primary trail, bearing west (right), avoiding spurs to camp spots. The trail to the east offers additional shoreline discovery before branching off to other desirable wilderness spots.

While exploring along the northwest shore of Marion Lake, gather images of the open blue water, Three Fingered Jack, and Marion Mountain (2.8 miles away by trail). The trail crosses a small peninsula before reaching the lake outlet bridge at 2.7 miles. Take the Outlet Trail, heading north downstream for the return. Partway the trail trades images of scenic Marion Creek for forest travel as it curves back to the loop junction (3.5 miles). Backtrack to the trailhead, ending at 5.2 miles.

60. PYRAMIDS

Features	▪	Vista, wildflowers
Distance	▪	5.2 miles round trip to Middle Pyramid
Elevation change	▪	1,800 feet
Difficulty	▪	Difficult
Season	▪	Spring through fall
Map	▪	USFS Willamette National Forest
Information	▪	Sweet Home Ranger District; Northwest Forest Pass

With its steep inclines, this trail will give you a workout, but it carries you to the top of Middle Pyramid, the former site of Three Pyramids Lookout, for a grand view. The summit's 360-degree panorama includes a volcano view stretching from Mount Hood south past the Three Sisters. Plant societies take on the peak's challenge to admire the forest, meadow, and cliff wildflowers, which are showiest from late June through early July. The parade of blooms lasts through much of the hiking season. Even the untrained admirer can identify scores of blooming species. Old growth, a meadow basin, a cliff bowl, high-elevation forest, and building views keep the discovery new and the anticipation high.

Find the turnoff for this trailhead off OR 22, 26.5 miles south of Detroit and 2 miles north of Maxwell Butte Sno-Park. There turn west onto FR 2067, go 4.1 miles, and turn right on FR 560. At the junction in 2.9 miles, continue straight on FR 560 for the selected hike; to the left is South Pyramid. Reach the trailhead and parking at road's end in 0.6 mile.

The trail crosses the footbridge over a tributary of North Fork Parker Creek and heads right to travel through a prized area of old growth. A continuous climb stretches before you, below is the rushing tributary. After a set of switchbacks, glimpse a pair of waterfalls, the first accents a narrow green canyon; avoid trying to better the view on the unstable slope. A gap in the tree cover frames the second falls, which is broad and short, spilling over a bulging reddish-brown rock face.

Approaching the crest and cliff of the headwater bowl, edge a pristine meadow basin, textured by grasses, low shrubs, wildflowers, ferns, and berry bushes. Some big trees still suggest an appreciative pause. At 1.1 miles a wildflower slope suggests a stop to overlook the meadow basin and headwall amphitheater and to study the multicolor floral

View from Middle Pyramid summit, Willamette National Forest

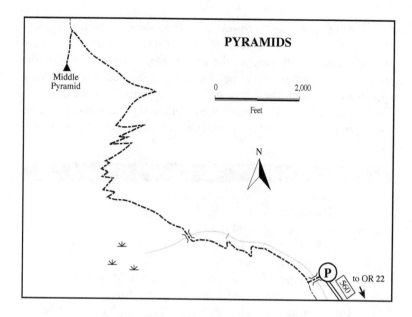

PYRAMIDS

Middle Pyramid

clusters adorning the rocky slope. Paintbrush, stonecrop, larkspur, Oregon sunshine, and yellow monkeyflower contribute to the array.

Ahead, the climb remains unrelenting. An upper-elevation forest of mountain hemlock and true fir hosts travel. At 1.9 miles, top a ridge, arriving at a lovely wildflower point and a gratifying view of Three Sisters, Mount Washington, and the first image of the lofty crags of the Pyramids. This site marks a possible turnaround; for the full hike trace the ridge skyward.

As the trail drifts onto the northeast face, find open looks at Mount Jefferson and the looming crest cliff above the trail. At the switchback at 2.25 miles, find a junction, along with a view of Coffin Mountain. For this hike, you'll head left, taking the switchback to Middle Pyramid. To the right is North Pyramid.

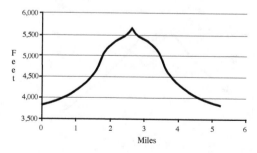

Travel flips to the northwest side of the slope, changing perspective, and then switchbacks to a saddle for another fine view. The final 0.1-mile climb south reaches the former lookout site, with only the small flat and a couple metal poles remaining as clues. A striking view of Mount Jefferson, the Cascade Crest, the South Santiam drainage, Coffin and Bachelor Mountains, the Pyramids skyline, and the western valleys and ridges reward the effort. Catch your breath and backtrack.

61. DUFFY LAKE

Features ▪	Wilderness lake
Distance ▪	6.5 miles round trip
Elevation change ▪	800 feet
Difficulty ▪	Moderate
Season ▪	Late spring into fall
Maps ▪	USFS Mount Jefferson Wilderness, Willamette National Forest
Information ▪	Detroit Ranger District; Northwest Forest Pass, wilderness permit

When urban life is spinning out of control, this hike provides a great wilderness touchstone. This southern entry to Mount Jefferson Wilderness Area is among the easiest and leads to a picturesque mountain lake where mother ducks choose to rear their young. Duffy is a gateway to the acclaimed Eight Lakes Basin. Following the upper waters of the North Fork Santiam upstream, this trail's gradual, comfortable climb helps lull hikers into a state of tranquility. The old-growth Douglas and true fir and dispersed hemlocks above a profusion of Cascade greenery complete the hypnotic spell.

To access this trail, about 11 miles south of Marion Forks and 5.6 miles northwest of Santiam Junction (the junction of US 20

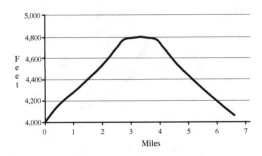

Falls on North Santiam River, Mount Jefferson Wilderness, Willamette National Forest

and OR 22), turn east off OR 22 onto FR 2267 and follow it 3 miles to the trailhead on the loop at road's end.

After the arrival of the spur from Big Meadow Horse Camp (0.1 mile), the trail passes below a talus slope, where pikas sound from hiding. Woodpecker, grouse, junco, and squirrel enliven the forest. A side stream and springs can dampen the trail in late spring and early summer. At 1.5 miles, pass the Turpentine Trail, which heads left to cross the river, either via fording or a rock-hopping crossing.

With the climb, Douglas firs wane from the mix replaced by lodgepole and white pines, along with an entourage of beargrass, huckleberry, and lupine. The trees are less thick allowing more sun to dapple the trail, but it is still a wonderful multistory forest. By 2 miles, overlook the river. It can show quite a different personality, depending on season. Early in the hiking season, it can be racing and noisy; by fall, it may be dry or merely trickling. At 2.5 miles reach the river crossing, a fording early in the season.

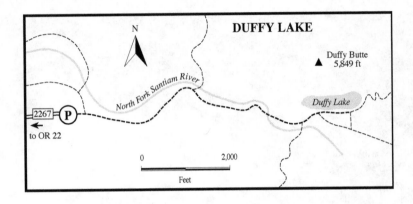

At 2.9 miles, bypass the trail on the right; it leads to Maxwell trailhead. At the junction at 3.2 miles, the path straight ahead rounds Duffy Lake en route to Eight Lakes Basin, a right leads to Santiam Pass, and a left leads to the lakeshore. Duffy Lake is a long blue-green scalloped lake rimmed by forest and prairie meadow with a sentinel rocky watchman to its north—Duffy Butte. The forest shows a mottled color with the olive needles of the lodgepole pine, green needles of the fir, and blue needles of the spruce. Along the lake, camping is restricted to designated sites, so day visitors have ample shore to enjoy.

You may choose to explore along the south shore for another 0.25 mile either on the trail to Eight Lakes Basin or a thin secondary path closer to the lake. The latter offers a glimpse at Three Fingered Jack. Either way, find the next lake access at the bridge over the outlet, the head of the Santiam River. Gather new perspectives; including a view of the swayback of Duffy Ridge. Admire its rocky crest, talus slopes, and a red cinder patch sitting like an epaulet on the east shoulder. Return as you came.

McKENZIE RIVER AREA

(ACCESS ROUTES OR 126, US 20, OR 242)

Clear Lake, Willamette National Forest

62. LOWER SODA CREEK FALLS

Features ■	150-foot waterfall
Distance ■	1.5 miles round trip
Elevation change ■	500 feet
Difficulty ■	Easy to moderate
Season ■	Year-round
Map ■	Cascadia State Park brochure
Information ■	Oregon State Parks; fees are required for camping but not for trail or day use

In Cascadia State Park, this hike is short but oh so sweet. It journeys up the cool, lush old-growth canyon setting of Soda Creek to its stunning waterfall—a white ribbon squeezing through a fissure in the steep mossy cliff. Side paths at the trail's end lead to better viewpoints. Soda Creek is a natural mineral spring.

Ideally suited for families, this waterfall trail and Cascadia State Park are reached north off US 20 about 14 miles east of Sweet Home. Locate the trailhead at the lower parking area for the park's extensive picnic ground.

The wide cinderbed trail follows skinny Soda Creek upstream, passing in the shadow of bigleaf maple, Pacific yew, and giant Douglas fir. The understory array is vibrant, showing a mosaic of leaf shapes and shades. Mosses coat the tree trunks and forest floor; snags in the forest may attract the tapping probes of woodpeckers.

Cross back-to-back bridges and hike past the side trail leading left toward the campground. The greenery literally cascades down the flanks of the narrow canyon. An earthen path replaces

Trail in autumn, Cascadia State Park

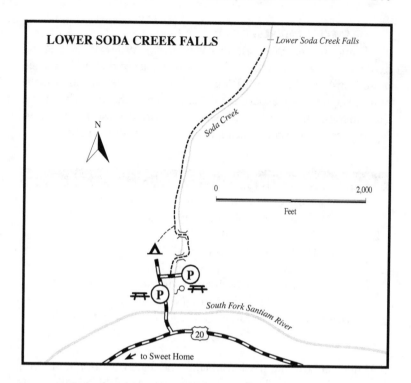

LOWER SODA CREEK FALLS

Lower Soda Creek Falls

Soda Creek

N

0   2,000

Feet

South Fork Santiam River

20

to Sweet Home

the cinder trail about midway, with a few steep segments following. Overlooks of the cascading creek encourage hikers onward.

    Where the trail actually ends, the view of the falls is blocked, but side paths both above and below the trail lead to vantages. Be careful on rocks and tree roots, which can be slippery when wet. The time of year will influence the impact of the watery plummet. Springtime's new leaves or autumn's palette compound the appeal. The return is back the way you came. The South Fork Santiam River, which captures the water of Soda Creek, and the attractive picnic area and campground offer reasons to linger at the park.

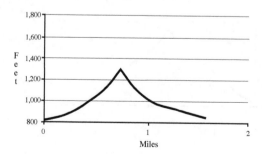

OF SPECIAL INTEREST

Emigrants on the Cascadia–Willamette Valley Wagon Road, better known as the Santiam Wagon Road, part of the Oregon Trail, passed through this South Fork Santiam River area. In places, the telltale wagon ruts are locked in the land. Before the days of the park, the mineral-rich waters of Soda Creek supported a resort hotel catering to guests who came to drink the water for health benefits.

63. IRON MOUNTAIN

Features ▪	Summit vantage, wildflowers
Distance ▪	3.4 miles round trip
Elevation change ▪	1,500 feet
Difficulty ▪	Moderate to difficult
Season ▪	Spring through fall
Maps ▪	USGS Echo Mountain 15' series; USFS Willamette National Forest
Information ▪	Sweet Home Ranger District; Northwest Forest Pass

If wildflowers are your passion and lofty vantages your aspiration, Iron Mountain is your destination. It represents one of the premier wildflower showcases in Oregon, bringing together ancient forest, alpine meadow, and rock ledge floral species. On July 4, the historical date marking the peak of the bloom calendar, wildflower enthusiasts from across the state travel to Iron Mountain. The summit (elevation 5,455 feet) extends a grand 360-degree view that includes the Cascade Crest, much of the Central Cascade neighborhood, and the mountain's own rugged volcanic cliffs. A fire lookout sits atop the mountain.

To reach this trail, from US 20, 35.6 miles east of Sweet Home and 8.6 miles west of the US 20–OR 126 junction, turn south onto

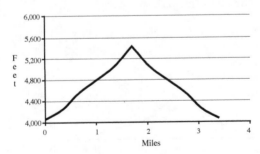

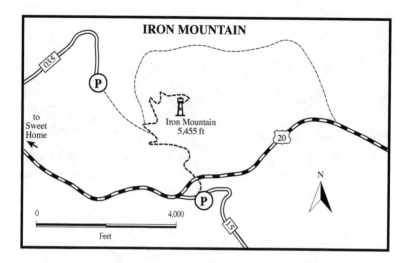

Deer Creek Road/FR 15 at the sign for Iron Mountain trailhead. In 0.3 mile, an ample trailhead parking area serves hikers. The trail begins across FR 15 from the parking area and ascends through forest to cross US 20; be careful at the highway crossing.

A forest of hemlock and true and Douglas fir with a diverse understory of bunchberry, false Solomon's seal, vanilla leaf, lupine, and huckleberry frames the well-graded ascending route. The old-growth setting captivates with its big trees, jagged snags, and midstory vine maples. Together with nearby Echo Mountain, this significant botanical area houses seventeen species of conifer and several rare plants. Listen for the signature voices of woodpecker, hummingbird, and grouse.

As the trail switchbacks uphill, it leaves behind many of the big trees. At the clearing at 0.7 mile, view the summit cliffs and lookout; the layered cliffs show a distinct red band. The trail then enters a steep meadow with bracken fern and tall floral species measuring 18 to 24 inches high and showing a rainbow of color. At 0.9 mile, the Cut-off Trail arrives from FR 035 (seen below and reached north off US 20 west of the main trailhead). It offers a shorter hike to the summit.

At the 1-mile junction, the Cone Peak Trail heads left; Iron Mountain Trail heads right. Each switchback builds upon the view, first introducing Diamond Peak and Browder Ridge, then Cone Peak and Mount Jefferson. The slope grows rockier displaying larkspur, Indian paintbrush, wallflower, star tulip, lupine, columbine, and waterleaf. Islands of trees spot the rock and meadow slope. The sighting of each new volcano urges hikers upward.

Three Sisters view from Iron Mountain Trail, Willamette National Forest

Atop the summit ridge, a detour left out onto a small point unfolds a sweeping vista of the Cascade volcano chain from Mount Adams to Diamond Peak, along with the immediate peaks and ridges and extensive Tombstone Prairie, another wildflower mecca. Ground squirrels beg for handouts, while swallows circle the summit. The lookout affords a different perspective on the setting and the finest look at Iron Mountain's volcanic cliffs. Return as you came.

Tip: For more wildflower viewing, Tombstone Prairie, off US 20 at Tombstone Pass, 0.7 mile east of Iron Mountain, has a 1-mile nature trail through a prairie wildflower meadow. Its circuit visits the settler youth's grave that suggested the name—Tombstone. The rolling prairie shows bracken fern, berry bushes, and skirted spruce, along with a host of wildflowers.

64. CLEAR LAKE

Features ▪	Outstanding lake, lava flow, old growth
Distance ▪	4.9-mile loop, unless eagle nesting closure is in effect
Elevation change ▪	100 feet
Difficulty ▪	Moderate
Season ▪	Spring through fall
Maps ▪	USFS Willamette National Forest; Clear Lake brochure
Information ▪	McKenzie River Ranger District

Clear Lake is one of the prettiest drive-to lakes anywhere. Rimmed by lava flow and old-growth forest, it is a deep 141-acre shimmering blue

208

gem of amazing clarity—the headwater of the McKenzie Wild and Scenic River. Submerged in Clear Lake are the well-preserved trees from the ancient forest swallowed when the lake was formed 3,000 years ago. Bald eagles and ospreys nest along shore, while mergansers and Canada geese lead their broods around the natural lake. Fed by Great Spring, Clear Lake's temperature is a constant 43 degrees, so forget swimming! The lake image, though, more than compensates.

This hike starts either from the day-use area beside rustic Clear Lake Resort or from Coldwater Cove Campground; reach both off OR 126. You will find the turnoff for both the resort and day-use east

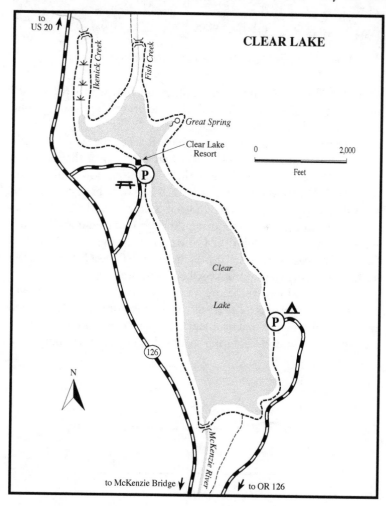

Clear Lake with Three Sisters, Willamette National Forest

off OR 126 about 3.5 miles south of its junction with US 20 or 19 miles north of the community of McKenzie Bridge. The campground turnoff is about another mile south.

Clear Lake formed some 3,000 years ago when the Sand Mountain crater erupted, releasing molten lava that flowed over the terrain to the McKenzie River. Once there, the edge of the flow cooled upon meeting the chill river water. This caused it to stop, back up, and dam the valley, capturing the waters of what is now Clear Lake. The lake clarity traces to the icy underground springs that feed it and by their mere temperature prohibit the growth of most organic matter. The submerged trees in the crystal depths more than 100 feet below the lake's surface are easily viewed from rowboat or shore.

On the lake loop, west shore travel is primarily in rich old-growth Douglas fir forest; east shore travel traces the crusted lava flow dotted by vine maple, juniper, and manzanita. The vine maple become particularly showy in autumn, exploring shades of orange, red, and burgundy.

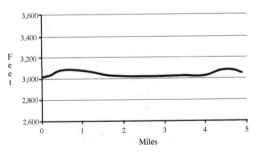

210

Photographers beam at the sight. An osprey clutching a fish in its talons and dripping with water, rowboats, and still-water reflections also suggest snapping a picture.

Beginning clockwise from the day-use area, at the northwest corner of the lake, hikers can glimpse Three Sisters in the distance. At the north end of the lake, the trail crosses Fish Creek bridge. This outlet of Fish Lake is empty in late summer when the shallow upstream lake with the porous volcanic bottom turns to meadow. The lake trail now shares the path of the McKenzie River National Recreation Trail, traversing the east shore. Pass Great Spring, a mesmerizing deep pool which can appear violet or blue-green, depending on cloud cover and the time of day. Ospreys nest above the east shore.

Southwest of Coldwater Cove Campground, keep to the lake loop as the McKenzie River Trail heads left. At the south end of the lake, cross the Clear Lake outlet—the lovely McKenzie River. Here, the river appears aquamarine because of the reflecting sunlight on the white silica at the bottom of the river. Along the southwest shore sits the eagle nesting site that can cause seasonal closures along the trail. Heed signs.

65. UPPER McKENZIE RIVER

Features	▪	Superb river and waterfalls
Distance	▪	3-mile loop
Elevation change	▪	400 feet
Difficulty	▪	Moderate
Season	▪	Spring through fall
Maps	▪	USFS Willamette National Forest; McKenzie River National Recreation Trail brochure
Information	▪	McKenzie River Ranger District

This hike is magical, stealing the hearts of all who tour it. The loop samples part of the 26.5-mile McKenzie National Recreation Trail (NRT), touring along the upper McKenzie Wild and Scenic River. It presents bubbling pools, exciting river falls, ancient forest, and lava flow. Eruptions of Nash Crater 3,500 years ago and Sand Mountain 3,000 years ago sculpted the river corridor as seen today. A major tributary of the Willamette River, the McKenzie River is one of the most beautiful waters in the state. The 100-foot Sahalie Falls and 63-foot

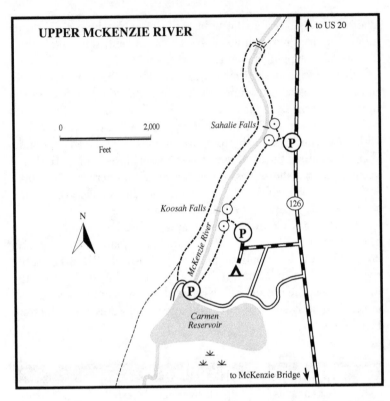

UPPER McKENZIE RIVER

↑ to US 20

Sahalie Falls

Ⓟ

0   2,000

Feet

126

Koosah Falls

Ⓟ

N

McKenzie River

Ⓟ

Carmen
Reservoir

to McKenzie Bridge ↓

Koosah Falls punctuate the hike's middle, but the river has no dull
moments.

Locate trailheads west off OR 126 at the Sahalie and Koosah Falls
Viewpoints. Sahalie Falls Viewpoint is about 5 miles south of the US
20–OR 126 junction or 18 miles north of the village of McKenzie
Bridge. Koosah Falls Viewpoint shares a turnoff with Ice Cap Campground about 0.5 mile farther south.

The loop swings between the upper McKenzie River bridge (above

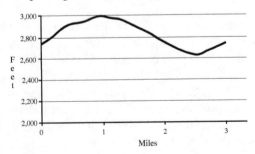

Koosah Falls, McKenzie Wild and Scenic River, Willamette National Forest

Sahalie Falls) and Carmen Reservoir, where a second bridge allows passage between the east and west shores. Starting at the Sahalie Falls Viewpoint parking, descend to the attractive stone-and-wood observation area for open viewing of the forceful 100-foot waterfall thundering over a lava dam and racing away in cascades. Mosses, logs, and flapping cedar bows add to viewing. Observation is also available at the head of the misting falls before you follow the river upstream to the upper bridge and cross to the west shore.

The west shore tour traces the river rim and slope touring mainly in forest of fir, cedar, and hemlock. Vine maple, dogwood, rhododendron, and huckleberry add accent. Vertical distance between the river and trail vary. Evidence of the volcanic past is exposed in the mossy-capped basalt and tree casts, if you are lucky enough to spy one. Tree casts are hollow lava molds of the standing trees at the time of eruption. The tour serves up inspiring river images of black pools, blue-ice cascades, and bubbling swirls. Downstream glimpse Koosah Falls with its parted waters; better falls viewing is from the east shore return.

The trail descends to Carmen Reservoir and the bridge crossing for the loop's continuation. Dippers bob and dive into the river, while otters sometimes glide across the small reservoir. Ospreys or eagles can draw eyes skyward. Head back upstream, gaining new perspective on the wild and scenic river.

The east shore trail traces the forested slope well above the river but still allows overlooks. Pass below Ice Cap Campground before reaching the serial viewpoints for Koosah Falls. The name is Chinook

Indian, roughly meaning heaven. This falls is a broad white water beauty in an attractive amphitheater bowl. Springs arrive through crevices at the base of the falls, complementing the mossy cliff. Sunlight can create rainbow spectrums in the mist. Serial cascades, pools, and a closer pairing of river and trail cap the journey back to Sahalie Falls.

66. CARPENTER MOUNTAIN

Features ▪	Summit lookout and vantage
Distance ▪	2 miles round trip
Elevation change ▪	900 feet
Difficulty ▪	Moderate
Season ▪	Spring through fall, daylight hours
Maps ▪	H. J. Andrews Experimental Forest brochure; USFS Willamette National Forest
Information ▪	McKenzie River Ranger District

The road does much of the work in getting you to this mile-high lookout station atop Carpenter Mountain in H. J. Andrews Experimental Forest, but you'll still have to do your share of puffing. The summit and lookout catwalk offer 360-degree viewing that takes in the Cascade volcano line-up from Mount Hood to Diamond Peak. Below the lookout to the north is Wolf Rock, the largest monolith in Oregon, and it's a show-stopper. The forest mosaic reveals the evolution of the research forest, which has gone from an emphasis on logging in the 1960s to the study of ecosystems and the ways to ensure their health from the 1990s until now. The lookout is staffed during fire season; visitors are welcome.

To reach this outpost, from OR 126, about 3 miles east of the Blue River Junction, turn north onto FR 15 heading toward Blue River

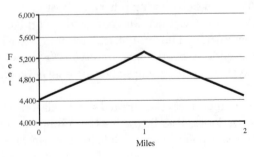

Reservoir. Go 3.5 miles and turn right onto FR 1506, opposite the Lookout boating site. Trail brochures are often stocked at the kiosk after the turn. Stay on FR 1506 to its junction with FR 350 in 6.6 miles; its paved surface ends after 2 miles. Turn left on FR 350 following it another 6 miles to the trailhead parking at a quarried site on the right. The trail begins above the parking.

Although conquering a sizable elevation gain in just a mile, the steady grade of the trail makes the task reasonable. A Douglas and true fir forest cloaks the lower peak. Beargrass and huckleberry dominate the understory. After a quick view of the Three Sisters followed by tree-gap peeks at Mount Washington and Three Fingered Jack, the trail then secrets far-ranging views until the summit.

Wildflower and bracken fern meadow gaps along the upper slope interrupt forest passage. Grouse commonly spook at the approach of boots. Do not disturb any vegetation or markers; remember this is a research forest. The hike is amazingly quiet, interrupted only by the hiker's heartbeat and breathing.

At 0.8 mile, the trail begins to round the prominent columnar basalt perch of the lookout aerie. Where the rocks abut the trail find shrubby vegetation. The last stretch of trail zigzags up the rock to the single-story lookout. Its catwalk is the actual rock of the summit, fenced

Carpenter Mountain Lookout, H. J. Andrews Experimental Forest, Willamette National Forest

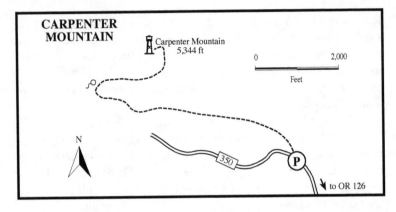

for safety. Nonetheless, keep little ones close in hand. Views sweep 360 degrees with bold images of Three Sisters, Mount Washington, and Mount Jefferson, along with Wolf Rock. Pikas sound from a broad talus slope on the peak's northwestern side. Return as you came, being careful on the first rocky descent.

OF SPECIAL INTEREST

Wolf Rock is a large volcanic plug rising 1,000 feet above the surrounding terrain. It is the largest monolith in Oregon and the third largest in the world. It formed 2 to 4 million years ago when molten rock welled up underground eventually forming a plug that cooled. It became exposed as the surrounding soil eroded away.

67. LOOKOUT CREEK OLD-GROWTH GROVE

Features ■	Outstanding old-growth drainage
Distance ■	7 miles round trip or 3.7-mile shuttle
Elevation change ■	1,500 feet
Difficulty ■	Difficult
Season ■	Spring through fall, daylight hours
Maps ■	H. J. Andrews Experimental Forest brochure; USFS Willamette National Forest
Information ■	McKenzie River Ranger District

This is one of the most challenging trails in the book. It has a modestly improved trail to blend with its setting and may require detective work to find the bypasses that go around downed trees and other obstacles.

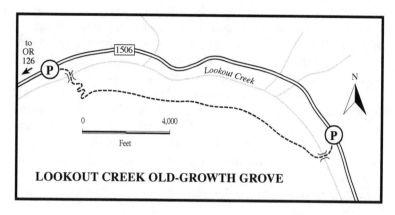

LOOKOUT CREEK OLD-GROWTH GROVE

But whether near the creek or high up the slope, the magnificent big trees enchant. In this unbroken old-growth forest at the foot of Lookout Mountain, Douglas fir, western red cedar, and western hemlock are dominant, adding noble and Pacific silver fir farther upslope. Most of the trees are more than 400 years old; a few top the 800-year mark. The sheer number of big trees and the extensiveness of the grove dazzle. This trail is worth a look, even if you only make it a short distance past the gateways.

To reach this spectacular old-growth stage, from OR 126, about 3 miles east of the Blue River Junction, turn north onto FR 15 heading toward Blue River Reservoir. Go 3.5 miles and turn right onto FR 1506, opposite the Lookout boating site. Trail brochures are often stocked at the kiosk after the turn. Stay on FR 1506 for 6.8 miles, reaching the first trailhead with road shoulder parking for a handful of vehicles. The second trailhead is about 3 miles farther; it has a similar parking situation. Turnaround space is limited at both. FR 1506 is not paved after the first 2 miles.

Starting from the first (the lower) trailhead, enter the magical grove with its big trees, multilayered canopy, snags, logs, and lush

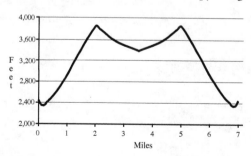

vegetation. Dogwood, vine maple, yew, and young trees fill out the midstory. The trail descends to cross Lookout Creek atop an old-growth log with handrails. A stair-cut log then ascends the south slope, where the trail will remain for most of the journey.

The trail rolls and switchbacks, traveling well above the creek bottom. Lovely big cedars grow along the creek and add to the upper-level forest, as well. Where the trail attains a ridge, trade neck-craning views for eye-level ones. At reroutes, small ribbons can help point out the trail. Remember switchbacks, too, can be used to skirt obstacles. So look around you for your options and if you are uncomfortable with how to proceed, turn back.

Log steps along Lookout Creek Trail, H. J. Andrews Experimental Forest, Willamette National Forest

The dynamic area supports life forms from tiny microorganisms to towering centuries-old trees. Rhododendrons appear on the upper slope. The trail's surges of ascent provide a workout. Although most of the logs have cut passages, a few may have escaped the trail crew's maintenance and require a scramble. You will pass a few false high points before encountering the genuine deal and the start of the descent at 2 miles.

Sounds of rushing water precede the trail's dip through a side creek drainage. The crossing is accomplished atop logs. Switchback up the opposite slope, drawing out of the drainage coolness. Fabulous big cedars greet hikers, but throughout the journey the old-growth reward is nonstop. Here, too, rhododendrons are plentiful and some woodpecker-drilled snags may capture attention.

Encounter the grove's big hemlocks after 2.7 miles. Wind gusts can release a shower of needles. Rollercoaster travel then carries the trail back to Lookout Creek (3.5 miles), where a plank spans the upper creek, which is marked by big boulders and a small pool. Round-trip hikers will likely want to turn around here. Shuttle hikers proceed 0.2 mile farther to the upper trailhead.

OF SPECIAL INTEREST

The sheer weight of plant material in Lookout Creek Old-Growth Grove exceeds that in a tropical rainforest by twice as much. Only the California old-growth redwood forests contain more biomass. In this research forest, studies have been done on spotted owl habitat, the role of fire in the forest, and climatic changes.

68. LITTLE BELKNAP CRATER

Features ▪	Crater, lava flow, vistas
Distance ▪	5 miles round trip
Elevation change ▪	1,000 feet
Difficulty ▪	Moderate
Season ▪	July through September
Map ▪	USFS Mount Washington Wilderness
Information ▪	McKenzie River Ranger District; Northwest Forest Pass, wilderness permit

Otherworldly, lunarlike—maybe, but definitely fascinating, this hike tours a stretch of the Pacific Crest National Scenic Trail (PCT), traversing a young lava flow before spurring off to wriggle up Little

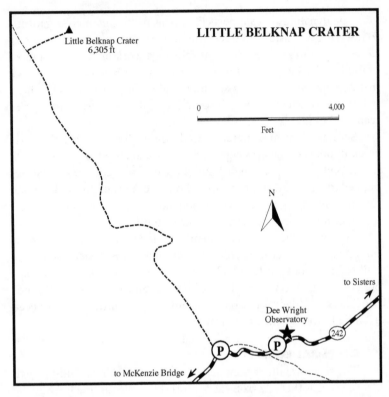

Belknap Crater (elevation 6,305 feet). It's a forbidding yet enticing landscape that normally is inaccessible. The crusty flow shows minimal vegetation save for a few picturesque silver snags. Merely a nubbin, Little Belknap is a parasitic cone on the flank of Belknap Crater and from a distance, appears but a small black dome. Its red cinders and broken top are revealed on closer inspection. Vistas are prime sweeping two wilderness areas: Mount Washington and Three Sisters. The volcanoes in their glacial finery contrast the lava plain or "Black Wilderness."

The trailhead is on McKenzie Pass Highway (OR 242), part of the McKenzie-Santiam National Scenic Byway. From the OR 126–OR 242 junction, 4.4 miles east of the community of McKenzie Bridge, follow OR 242 northeast for 21.3 miles and turn west for the trailhead. When arriving from Sisters, the turnoff is 0.4 mile south of Dee Wright Observatory.

The hike follows the well-maintained PCT north through Mount Washington Wilderness toward Little Belknap Crater. Carry plenty

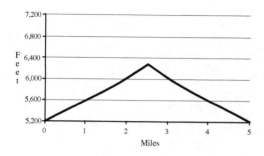

of water, wear heavy-sole boots (much of the trail is on cinders), and be cautious of the glass-sharp ragged basalt. Animals are best left at home. You'll begin by tracing a broad sandy aisle to top a tree island isolated by the 1,500-year-old flow. The light-colored dirt is the volcanic ash from Belknap Crater. Lodgepole pine, mountain hemlock, and true fir find footing here. At 0.3 mile the trail crosses a once fiery tongue of lava to skirt the next island. View Black Crater, Dee Wright Observatory, and Three Sisters.

The jumbled flow conjures up a wealth of impressions. At 0.5 mile capture the first glimpse of your destination, Little Belknap, with Belknap Crater just beyond. Despite the size difference, Little Belknap is the culprit behind all this lava. Ground squirrels race across the flow. After 0.7 mile, the trail commits solely to lava flow travel. From the flow, viewing is 360 degrees with dramatic images in all directions. Among the snags, a few live trees dot the flow, individually or in tiny clusters.

At 2.2 miles a cairn with a protruding stick marks the turnoff

Little Belknap Crater and Pacific Crest Trail, Mount Washington Wilderness, Willamette National Forest

Compass on Dee Wright Observatory, Willamette National Forest

for Little Belknap Crater. The spur traces the spine of a thin ridge. To its sides, look for collapsed lava tubes or their gaping mouths. Upon reaching the crater saddle gain expansive two-wilderness views with Mount Jefferson spied to the north. The trail then twists up the lava fortress dipping into the crater bowl before ascending to the red top (2.5 miles), where the views all come together. Clear-day views stretch from Mount Hood to Three Sisters, but it's the immediate neighborhood that spellbinds. Return when ready.

Tip: While in the vicinity, be sure to check out Dee Wright Observatory, a worthwhile stop just northeast along the scenic byway. This dark fortress atop the flow was constructed of lava and named for an early-day packer with the forest service. It has a series of windows of differing size and heights pinpointing the landmarks of the area; its roof gives an elevated vantage and has an attractive compass dial.

69. SCOTT MOUNTAIN

Features ■	Summit view, wilderness lakes
Distance ■	8 miles round trip
Elevation change ■	1,300 feet
Difficulty ■	Moderate to difficult
Season ■	July through September
Map ■	USFS Mount Washington Wilderness
Information ■	McKenzie River Ranger District; Northwest Forest Pass, wilderness permit

Ideal for individuals and families ready to advance to longer and more challenging trails and greater heights, this popular wilderness trail journeys away from broad, shallow Scott Lake to top cinder-crowned

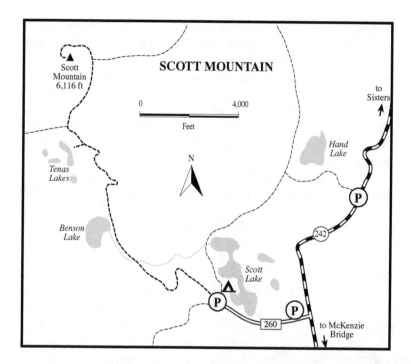

Scott Mountain (elevation 6,116 feet). En route it visits wilderness lakes and gathers images of Mount Washington, Mount Jefferson, and Three Sisters, with their respective wilderness areas. Roaming the meadow and cinder summit, hikers gather a 360-degree panoramic view of the spectacular neighborhood. It's an altogether satisfying journey with moments of quiet, wilderness, and beauty.

Snow on McKenzie Pass and OR 242 keeps the window of recreation here narrow, typically July 1 to October 1, when the road is passable. From the OR 126–OR 242 junction, 4.4 miles east of the community of McKenzie Bridge, go 15.8 miles northeast on OR 242

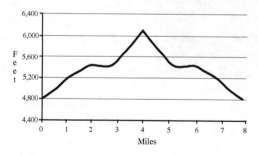

and turn west for Scott Lake. Or you may take OR 242 southwest out of Sisters to the Scott Lake turnoff. Proceed straight for the Benson trailhead at road's end in 1 mile.

Follow the well-trampled Benson Trail as it climbs away from the Scott Lake area. The trail passes through settings of open-cathedral forest, full forest, and meadow and vernal pool. Lichens drip from the fir, lodgepole pine, and mountain hemlock. True and dwarf huckleberry, beargrass, and lupine dress the forest floor. The ascent comes with a comfortable grade.

At 1.1 miles, spurs break away to Benson Lake, an attractive, good-size mountain lake and good short hike option. It is ringed by forest, has a scenic rock-and-log brim, and tosses back stunning morning reflections. Beyond Benson Lake, the trail advances via a drunken course through forest. A few auxiliary ponds and vernal pools are passed before the trail swings up a bouldery slope to travel a meadow-pond plateau at 2 miles. Mosquitoes can annoy.

Tenas Lake, Mount Washington Wilderness, Willamette National Forest

A rustic signpost in 0.2 mile shows Tenas Lakes to the left. Before continuing on to the summit, a 0.1-mile detour here leads to the main water body of Tenas Lakes. It's a captivating batwing-shaped lake rimmed by outcrop and a logjam. Smaller ponds pepper the surrounding forest but require cross-country travel and a bit of luck to find them, so return to the Benson Trail.

Beyond a reflection pond sits the next junction. The Benson Trail now heads left, while summit hikers continue forward to Scott Mountain. Before long, the mountain comes into view; its summit is mostly bald and reddish with cinder. Islands of trees and exposed rock contribute to its character. Where the summit trail arcs left at a large boulder, ignore side trails to the right.

Ahead, a forest gap offers looks at Three Fingered Jack, Mount Jefferson, and just the tip of Mount Hood with Hayrick and Hoodoo Buttes in the foreground. On the mountain's north flank, a brief beltway of big-diameter trees precedes the steep climb into a tight runty forest. Mount Washington and Belknap Crater next add to views. On the shoulder of Scott Mountain is a cinder–wildflower meadow where the frantic burst of grouse can stop hearts.

The summit meadow then grows the view west, south, east, and north before the trail tops out at 4 miles. Views span three wildernesses: Mount Washington, Mount Jefferson, and Three Sisters and encompass forest, lava flow, high peaks, and wilderness-dotting lakes. The return is by backtracking.

70. PROXY FALLS

Features ▪	Intriguing waterfall duo
Distance ▪	1.25-mile loop
Elevation change ▪	100 feet
Difficulty ▪	Easy, with some steeper pitches in the first 0.5 mile
Season ▪	Summer through fall
Map ▪	USFS Three Sisters Wilderness
Information ▪	McKenzie River Ranger District; Northwest Forest Pass, wilderness permit

If you've ever doubted nature has tricks up her sleeve, you might want to check out this hike, a popular stop on the McKenzie-Santiam

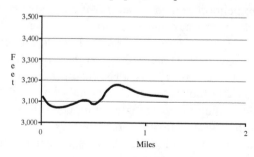

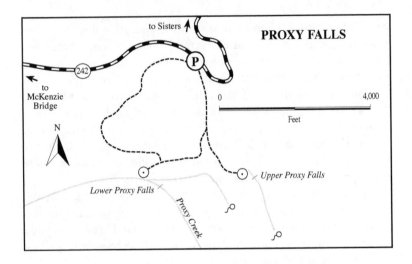

PROXY FALLS

to Sisters

to
McKenzie
Bridge

N

0   4,000

Feet

Lower Proxy Falls

Upper Proxy Falls

Proxy Creek

National Scenic Byway. It serves up a visual antithesis to the spring-launched rivers for which this area of Oregon is famous. Here, the waterfalls seemingly dead-end. In truth, the porous lava at the base of the falls draws the water underground save for tiny remnant pools that never overflow. The Collier Crater lava flow formed the two basalt dams on Proxy Creek over which the waterfalls plunge. It also deposited the basin lava, which creates the spectacle of the disappearing water. The trail may be short, but it is sweet.

From the OR 126–OR 242 junction, 4.4 miles east of the village of McKenzie Bridge, go northeast on OR 242 for 8.5 miles to find Proxy Falls Trail and its parking. Lots can fill on summer weekends.

This trail mounts a lava flow to enter the Three Sisters Wilderness. It travels a forest and flow transition habitat with vine maple, alder, hemlock, yew, red huckleberry, and salal. Fall is a favorite time to tour, when the vine maple blushes red. Mornings and midweek visits promise to be more tranquil. Because of the trail's popularity, the loop is signed for one-way counterclockwise travel to prevent traffic clogs. Start by taking the indicated right fork. The first falls encountered is Lower Proxy Falls. About midway on the loop, find its spur heading right. At Lower Proxy Falls, a vista platform offers a cross-canyon view of the 200-foot waterfall, elegant and white, spilling over a mossy cliff and coming to a seemingly abrupt end. At its base, the porous rock diverts the water's flow underground for a mystifying sight. Cedars fill the canyon, and hemlock and rhododendron frame the vista.

On return to the loop, continue counterclockwise travel, soon

Lower Proxy Falls, Three Sisters Wilderness, Willamette National Forest

coming to the next waterfall spur. Follow it right to arrive at the base pool of Upper Proxy Falls and a good look at this second 200-foot beauty. A mossy delta separates the white, lacy streamers of this falls as it spills down the steep mountainside. The pool has no outlet, yet never overflows—it's truly nature's version of the magician's bottomless glass.

When ready to surrender the view, resume the loop, coming out near the start on OR 242.

71. OLALLIE MOUNTAIN

Features	■	Summit vantage, old lookout, big tree
Distance	■	6.8 miles round trip
Elevation change	■	1,200 feet
Difficulty	■	Moderate to difficult
Season	■	Late spring through fall
Maps	■	USFS Three Sisters Wilderness, Willamette National Forest
Information	■	McKenzie River Ranger District; Northwest Forest Pass, wilderness permit

With wilderness, beauty, solitude, and a sense of accomplishment, this mountain hike fulfills hiker desire. A historic lookout in disrepair sits atop Olallie Mountain (elevation 5,700 feet), adding to the summit character. Views sweep 360 degrees and stretch from Mount Hood south past Diamond Peak. Three Sisters, Mount Jefferson, and Three Fingered Jack cast particularly strong images. En route to the summit, hikers stroll through the high-elevation forest and meadows of Three Sisters Wilderness.

Reach this tucked-away prize from the east end of the village of McKenzie Bridge. On the east side of the river bridge, turn south onto Horse Creek Road and remain on it for 1.7 miles. There turn right heading uphill on FR 1993, a winding single-lane paved route, which changes to gravel for the last 5 miles; be alert for falling rock. Reach the Pat Saddle trailhead after driving 19.8 miles on FR 1993 and descend left into the trail parking lot.

From parking, be sure to follow the marked Olallie Trail to Olallie Mountain Trail; do not take the French Pete Trail, which begins at the wilderness register. The hike to Olallie Mountain begins in a high-elevation forest with Douglas fir in the mix; beargrass and huckleberry

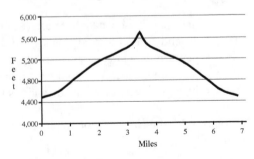

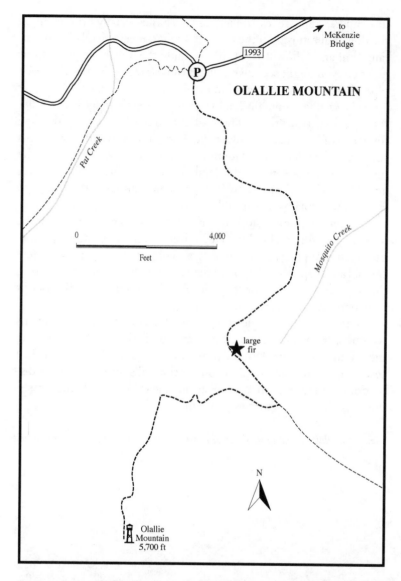

dominate the understory. Drainages show alder and salmonberry. Deer, grouse, and woodpecker can be spied. The trail maintains a comfortable climb the entire way, even as the terrain changes from gentle slope to ridge to a steeply dropping forest slope.

At about 1.5 miles, just before the crossing of the Mosquito Creek headwaters, a gigantic Douglas fir tree sits on the left side of the trail—

its diameter approaches 10 feet! The tree is especially prominent on the downhill return. On the ridge at 2 miles, meet the Olallie Mountain Trail and follow it right. If you study the lodgepole pine at this junction, you might see the markings of bear claws. Notice the reach of the bear stretches above adult eye-level.

The Olallie Mountain Trail ascends, tracing the ridge with a fuller forest of low, stout trees. The trail is channel-like passing through fountains of beargrass. Meadow openings allow outward views across the forested wilderness to Mount Bachelor and associated peaks. The blue haze of a hot summer day lends an ethereal quality. Coneflower and lupine adorn the meadow. The gradient steps up a bit nearing the summit but remains manageable.

Travel the summit slope before taking a switchback to reach the lookout structure (3.4 miles). Views overlook the vast untouched forest expanse of plateaus and drainages. Volcano viewing is top notch. Behold an exceptional view of Three Sisters with the Separation Creek drainage. Hawks soar past at eye-level and epitomize the spirit of this lofty outpost—wild, free, and inspiring.

The lookout is a single-story structure, with shutters guarding its windows. It has been adopted by a group of friends who are raising money for its repair. Do not disturb the historic structure. A final restoration plan is not in place; one option calls for the lookout's dismantling and relocation to a site outside the wilderness. When chased down by the wind, return as you came.

View from Olallie Mountain, Three Sisters Wilderness, Willamette National Forest

72. ERMA BELL LAKES

Features ▪	Wilderness lakes, waterfall, rhododendron
Distance ▪	5.8 miles round trip
Elevation change ▪	250 feet
Difficulty ▪	Moderate
Season ▪	Summer through fall
Maps ▪	USFS Three Sisters Wilderness, Willamette National Forest
Information ▪	Middle Fork Ranger District; Northwest Forest Pass, wilderness permit

This family hike rounds up a series of three attractive lakes tucked away in the southwest corner of the Three Sisters Wilderness. The trail passes through changing forest and meadow settings. In early summer, the rhododendron blooms endorse travel. A secluded waterfall adds to the discovery. After taking this hike, you will drip with contentment.

From OR 126 about 5 miles east of the Blue River Junction, turn south onto FR 19 (Aufderheide Forest Drive) toward Cougar Reservoir and go 25.7 miles. There, just past Box Canyon Horse Camp, turn left on FR 1957 and proceed another 3.6 miles to Skookum Creek Campground and the trailhead at road's end.

Cross Skookum Creek below camp and briefly pursue its crystal-line stair-stepping waters downstream. The trail then arcs into the drainage of the North Fork Middle Fork Willamette River, which flows far below. This river originates at Waldo Lake. En route to Lower Erma Bell Lake, the trail is wide, leveled, and groomed with an easy grade and few roots or rocks. It is intended to be a challenging barrier-free trail for wheelchair athletes. Tall Douglas firs shade the way.

Keep right at 0.6 mile, where the Irish Mountain Trail heads left

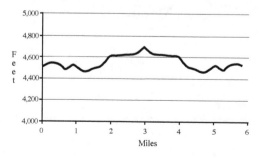

to Otter Lake. Beyond a vibrant area of vine maple, the trail descends to cross the footbridge over the outlet water of Otter Lake. It's a steep approach to the bridge for wheelchairs. Alders and out-of-place cottonwoods line the creek.

A steady climb and a profusion of rhododendron precede the left spur to Lower Erma Bell Lake (1.5 miles). The trail emerges at the rocky lake ring—one last difficult approach for wheelchair users. With a rounded valentine shape, Lower Erma Bell occupies a picturesque basin shaped by steep forested slopes and areas of talus. Its waters are deep and a stunning blue. The rush of an inlet waterfall hidden from view contributes to the setting.

The trail then skirts the lake, crossing the outlet to climb the west ridge. Rhododendron bushes create a lovely travel aisle. At 2 miles, a 30-foot side path leads left to an overlook of the falls on the watery link between Middle and Lower Erma Bell Lakes. A forest window fanned by evergreen boughs presents this terraced, white-icing wedding-cake falls and its shiny black basalt cliff.

The side spur to Middle Erma Bell Lake is 100 feet farther on the

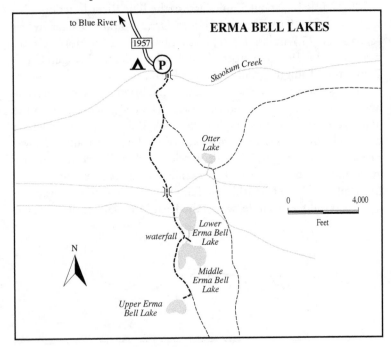

Lower Erma Bell Lake, Three Sisters Wilderness, Willamette National Forest

primary trail. Middle Erma is a larger, comma-shaped lake with a rolling forested basin, exposed walls of rock and shrub, and sun-gilded grassy points. Pollen seasonally glints on the surface, while logs criss-cross the lake bottom. Chinquapin, beargrass, and lovely big firs grace the camp area.

As you resume the hike south, travel the western outskirts of Middle Erma Bell, touring in forest and traversing a low ridge showered in rhododendron. Hike past a serene pond ringed by shrubs and chosen as a stopover by ducks. At 2.8 miles look to your right for the 0.1-mile spur to Upper Erma Bell Lake—the smallest of the three related lakes. Its tree rim semi-secludes the oval water from the main trail. Aquatic plants color the lake ring, while wildflowers accent its shore. Its tranquil image suggests a supine admiration, using your day pack for a pillow. When ready, return as you came, revisiting your favorite waters.

WALDO LAKE–MIDDLE FORK WILLAMETTE RIVER AREA

(ACCESS ROUTES OR 58 AND ROW RIVER ROAD)

Diamond Creek Falls, Willamette National Forest

73. CONSTITUTION GROVE

Features ▪	Old-growth grandeur
Distance ▪	0.2-mile loop
Elevation change ▪	Minimal
Difficulty ▪	Easy
Season ▪	Spring through fall
Maps ▪	USFS Willamette National Forest, Waldo Lake Wilderness
Information ▪	Middle Fork Ranger District; Northwest Forest Pass

This hike travels a grove dedicated on the 200th anniversary of the signing of the Constitution. The towering Douglas firs and western red cedars wear attractive name plaques honoring the document's signers, so a stroll through the grove is also a stroll through history. The grove occupies a sloped plateau above the North Fork Middle Fork Willamette Wild and Scenic River, which has a growing trail system that may one day span its length. Presently only pieces are in place.

This lovely out-of-the-way grove is reached from Westfir, off OR 58 west of Oakridge. Starting at the Westfir Covered Bridge junction, proceed north on FR 19, Aufderheide Scenic Drive, for 26.7 miles. The grove's turnout parking and access are on the right. Wooden signs and memorial plaques announce the grove. If you take FR 19 south off OR 126, reach the grove in about 30 miles.

Where the trail descends into the gallery of big trees, the George Washington tree heads up the tour. Benjamin Franklin, James Madison, and Alexander Hamilton are other familiar names seen in the grove. At the time the Constitution was signed, these trees were still young but more than 200 years of growth have changed all that.

Many big trees within the grove go unnamed, so there's plenty to

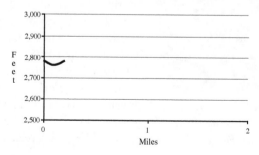

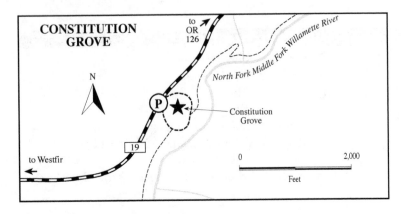

see. Small hemlock, vine maple, rhododendron, dogwood, and a varied understory mosaic complement the tall, straight trunks. The grove trail swings a 0.2-mile counterclockwise loop, twice meeting the undeveloped North Fork Trail.

North Fork of the Middle Fork Willamette Wild and Scenic River, Willamette National Forest

The North Fork Middle Fork Willamette Wild and Scenic River remains mostly a secret, flowing through its richly vegetated canyon, but its voice can be heard. Rhododendron favor the slope toward the river. After the second meeting with the signed North Fork Trail, the loop swings back up through the grove to the trailhead.

Tip: While in the neighborhood, you might like to continue the old-growth discovery on the Shale Ridge Trail, a pleasant, lightly traveled trail. Find its trailhead 2.8 miles upstream from (northeast of) Constitution Grove. This groomed trail extends a comfortable walk through more of the North Fork old growth, traveling in Waldo Lake Wilderness. Waldo Lake is the river's source. The trail is relatively flat and easy until the North Fork fording at just over 2.5 miles. Solitude abounds. A Northwest Forest Pass and a wilderness permit are required for the Shale Ridge Trail.

74. WALDO MOUNTAIN

Features	▪	Challenging hike, summit lookout and vistas
Distance	▪	6.2 miles round trip
Elevation change	▪	1,900 feet
Difficulty	▪	Difficult
Season	▪	Summer through fall
Maps	▪	USFS Waldo Lake Wilderness, Willamette National Forest
Information	▪	Middle Fork Ranger District; Northwest Forest Pass, wilderness permit

This trail will give your cardiovascular system a workout, taking you to the top of Waldo Mountain, which rises above the northwest shore of Waldo Lake. Its summit and lookout catwalk unfold a gratifying 360-degree view that aptly rewards the effort. Admire the Cascade Crest and Waldo Lake Wilderness. On this trail, solitude can be found even on summer weekends. During fire season, the lookout is generally staffed.

At the east side of Oakridge, turn north off OR 58 onto Fish Hatchery Road following it 1.3 miles to Salmon Creek Road/FR 24. Turn right on Salmon Creek Road and stay on it to its junction with FR 2417 in about 10 miles. Bear left on FR 2417, which later changes to gravel, and proceed 6.1 miles. There turn right on FR 2424 to find the trailhead in another 3.6 miles; it jointly serves the Waldo Mountain and Salmon Lakes Trails.

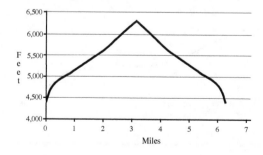

Waldo Mountain Lookout, Waldo Lake Wilderness, Willamette National Forest

Ascend from the trailhead, bearing left at the fork in 300 feet for Waldo Mountain. The scenery is spectacular with old-growth hemlock and true and Douglas fir. The trail ascends in Jekyll and Hyde fashion, with Mr. Hyde showing up at the start. This steep climbing segment continues to 0.7 mile. There the trail begins contouring the slope, leaving behind the biggest trees—the Douglas firs.

An attractive rhododendron aisle heads up the next half mile. Beargrass grows among the radial leaves and lodgepole pines appear. The low stature forest means sunnier trekking. At 1.4 miles, cross into Waldo Lake Wilderness. Where runoff traces the trail, rocks rear up in the bed. Tighter forest precedes the ridge and trail junction at 2.1 miles. Here, meet the Waldo Meadows Trail, and follow it left to pick up the next leg of the mountain trail in 200 feet. Turn right for the summit.

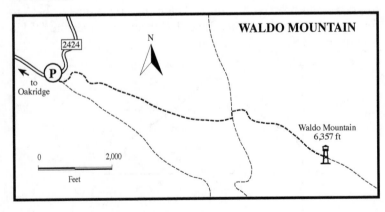

The fountains of beargrass provide an attractive edge to the trail. At 2.5 miles, top the ridge and follow it east as it gains height. Where the ridge narrows, obtain your first look at the world beyond the trail. Grouse can startle you from your reverie. Reach the summit lookout at 3.1 miles, finding the long-withheld view. Volcano views stretch from Diamond Peak north to Mount Hood. To the east is the big view of Waldo Lake and its associated wilderness; to the west are Salmon Lakes. North of Waldo Lake, you can count the waters of Six Lakes Basin. When ready, retrace your steps to the trailhead.

75. SHORELINE TRAIL, WALDO LAKE

Features ■	One of the clearest lakes in the world
Distance ■	4 miles round trip
Elevation change ■	Minimal
Difficulty ■	Easy
Season ■	Summer through fall
Maps ■	USFS Waldo Lake Wilderness, Willamette National Forest
Information ■	Middle Fork Ranger District; Northwest Forest Pass

Cobalt blue and highly photogenic, Waldo Lake, at an elevation of 5,414 feet, has a short hiking season but is well worth clearing your calendar to see. Some 12,000 years ago, a glacial cap gouged out Waldo Lake along with hundreds of potholes and other lake depressions. With no permanent inlet, the 10-square-mile Waldo Lake lacks organic material, making it one of the four clearest lakes in the world. Crater Lake, Lake Tahoe in the Sierra Nevada, and Lake Baikal in Siberia complete the list. Rocky spits, islands and bays, picturesque black rocks stringing off shore, and still morning reflections captivate. Cross-lake views feature Waldo Mountain, Mount Fuji, and often, graceful sailboats.

To get to this lake from Oakridge, travel 23 miles southeast on OR 58 and turn left onto FR 5897 toward Waldo Lake. Continue north on FR 5897 and 5898 for 12.7 miles, following the signs to North Waldo Campground. Find the trailhead in the upper parking lot of the North Waldo Day-Use Area.

This sampling of the Shoreline Trail strings south along the lakeshore from the North Waldo area past Islet Campground, ending at a beach a mile south of Islet. Although the hike tours the developed

Waldo Lake along Shoreline Trail, Willamette National Forest

shore of the lake, the viewing is all wilderness. When looking toward the north end of the lake, you'll probably notice the bronze, black, and silver snags from a massive burn, the Charlton Fire of 1996. This fire scorched 10,400 acres. Its heat was so intense that it left behind a landscape slow to recover. Nonetheless, a few pioneer species—wildflowers and woodpeckers—are coming back. To get a closer look at the burn, at some point during your stay you might want to hike north a short distance on either the Shoreline Trail or the Waldo Lake Trail. Start each at the North Waldo Day-Use Area.

Southbound, the Shoreline Trail journeys through high-elevation forest with a huckleberry–beargrass understory. The lake is close for

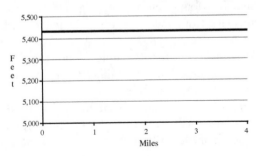

viewing and easy access. Benches dot the way. If you are staying in one of the developed campgrounds along the trail, this shoreline path is ideal for your morning wake-up stroll or sunset viewing. At 1 mile find Islet Peninsula, a narrow point, traveled by a 0.1-mile spur.

Cross the Islet boat launch and continue south in forest and winter blowdown. Pass tiny pocket beaches, coves, and rocky points before the trail dead-ends at a crescent sandy beach. Drift logs add to the beach's character; views extend to Waldo Mountain and Mount Fuji. For trip planning, beware: mosquitoes pester from early to midsummer. By mid-August, though, travel is generally carefree.

Tip: You may also want to sample part of the 21-mile Waldo Lake Trail, which totally encircles this beautiful blue lake that reaches a maximum depth of 427 feet. The trail traces the wilderness boundary much of the way. Travel is in settings of forest, burn, meadow, and pond. The west shore is more rugged, while the east-shore segment is completely removed from Waldo Lake. A Northwest Forest Pass is required for trail parking for the Waldo Lake Trail.

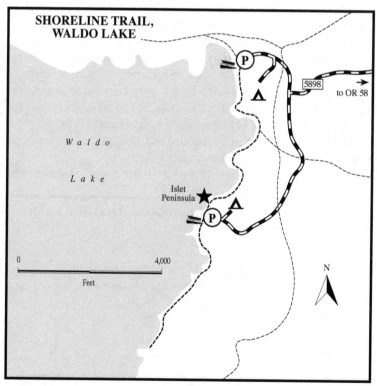

76. JOE GODDARD NATURE TRAIL

Features	▪	Magical old-growth grove
Distance	▪	0.5 mile round trip
Elevation change	▪	Minimal
Difficulty	▪	Easy
Season	▪	Spring through fall
Maps	▪	USFS Waldo Lake Wilderness, Willamette National Forest
Information	▪	Middle Fork Ranger District; Northwest Forest Pass

This trail is both short and out-of-the-way, a combination that usually means most people don't bother to go. But sometimes, the natural offering is worth the extra effort and that's true here. In this fanciful multistory old-growth setting along Black Creek, the trees range from 450 to 700 years old and reach jaw-dropping size, humbling onlookers. Forest Ranger Joe Goddard, for whom the trail is named, stumbled upon the grove while building fire trails in the 1950s. He was so impressed that he campaigned for the grove's preservation.

Your journey to this special place begins at the east side of Oakridge. There turn north off OR 58 onto Fish Hatchery Road, following it 1.3 miles to Salmon Creek Road/FR 24. Turn right on Salmon Creek Road and stay on it to its end at a junction in 13.1 miles. Now proceed forward on gravel FR 2421, reaching the right turn (FR 2421.393) to Goddard trailhead in 6.6 miles. Parking is 0.1 mile ahead alongside the narrow 2-track road. Turnaround space is limited.

The bridge in place over Black Creek is a historic log vehicular

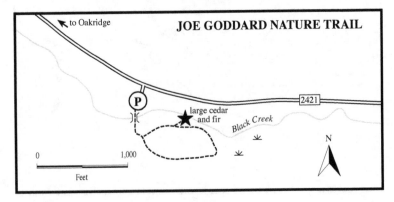

Douglas fir on Joe Goddard Nature Trail, Willamette National Forest

bridge, the last of its kind in the Middle Fork District. Built in 1959, it consists of four massive side-by-side logs but it is missing its cross-boards. Below the bridge, Black Creek is an attractive clear-flowing stream draped by alders.

Ahead, the grove loop swings left off the old road grade. A panel listing the area flora and fauna shows how vital and wild the site is. Besides the record-size Douglas fir, western red cedar, and western hemlock, discover some of the largest Pacific yew in the district. The thick mosses and lush riparian vegetation reinforce the magical image. The grove's tallest tree measures 251 feet high. Tree diameters can exceed 9 feet and grooves in the thick bark are as deep as an adult's hand. Many of the grove's trees have lost their tops in windstorms—all part of the life cycle. Shafts of light penetrate the grove and contribute to its aura.

Side spurs and signs listing the trees' statistics point out the truly big guys. While the big Douglas firs are common in many groves, the enormous cedars here are particularly pleasing, since so often they were the first trees harvested. Mossy stumps and nurse logs nurture the next generation of forest. Where the trail passes through a cut-log

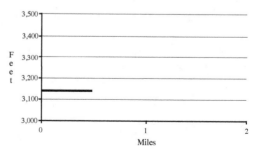

and timeline, note the tree's beginning back in 1340, as well as Joe Goddard's birthday. The restful lullaby of the creek and the rustic picnic tables fashioned from blown-down trees complement the grove and provide yet another excuse to linger. Cone harvest middens reveal that squirrels, too, use the tables.

77. BRICE CREEK–TRESTLE FALLS

Features	■	Historic area, scenic creek, waterfalls
Distance	■	5.5 miles round trip
Elevation change	■	900 feet
Difficulty	■	Moderate to difficult
Season	■	Year-round, except during low-elevation snows
Map	■	USFS Umpqua National Forest
Information	■	Cottage Grove Ranger District; Northwest Forest Pass, hikers-only on spur to Lower Trestle Creek Falls and Upper Trestle Creek Trail

In this place of natural beauty at the foot of the Calapooya Mountains, you'll journey back in time tracing the shores of clear-flowing Brice Creek before looping up the Trestle Creek side drainage, which houses a pair of box canyon waterfalls. The Brice Creek section of the hike follows the historic Frank Bryce Trail, which led to the Bohemia Mining District in the early 1900s, when gold not nature was the intoxicant. The hike begins at the treed flat of what was Lund Park, a bustling mining and freight warehouse site and an overnight wayside en route to the mining district. The ditch along Brice Creek brought water to power both Lund Park and the electric tram that linked the mines.

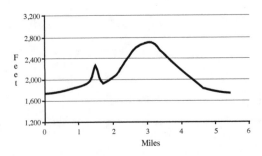

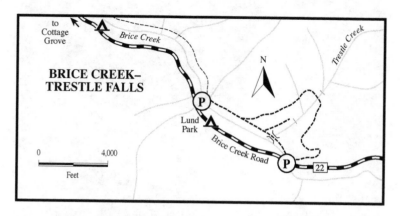

To get there from exit 174 off I-5 at Cottage Grove, head east on Row River Road for 19 miles to the Layng Junction and then continue straight on Brice Creek Road/FR 22 for another 6.8 miles to Lund Park, the selected trailhead, past Cedar Creek Campground.

Hike across the bridge and turn right on the Brice Creek Trail. On this trail, mountain bikes share the way. Charismatic Brice Creek engages with cascades, pools, and picturesque swirls. Cedar, fir, and hemlock shade the path. Hazel, dogwood, and rhododendron lend complement.

The trail contours the slope between 25 and 100 feet above alder-lined Brice Creek. Admire the creek's clarity and its colorful rock-and-boulder bed; riffles add excitement. Above the trail, view extensive outcrops with fern shelves and moss-rounded ledges. At 0.8 mile, cross a thin tributary and come to a junction. Proceed forward remaining along Brice Creek for a counterclockwise loop, now tracing the levee to the ditch that brought water to Lund Park.

Before the Trestle Creek footbridge (1.2 miles), take the 0.3-mile spur left up Trestle Creek drainage to view the lower falls. Parts of the spur can be steep and uneven. Cliffs precede the box canyon, where the 50- to 60-foot Lower Trestle Creek Falls pours over a ledge to skip down the jagged rock of the cliff to a log-jammed pool.

Resuming the loop, cross Trestle Creek Bridge. The confluence here may call you aside with its union of bedrock outcrops, a small gorge on Brice Creek, and the cascading arrival of Trestle Creek. Where Brice Creek Trail emerges at FR 22 (2.1 miles); look for contemporary claim markers.

To visit Upper Trestle Creek Falls and continue the loop, turn left on FR 22, walk 50 feet, and head left at the Upper Trestle Creek

Upper Trestle Creek Falls, Umpqua National Forest

trailhead. A steady ascent of Brice Creek's northern slope follows. Where the climb levels off, pass below a massive outcrop and encounter magnificent old-growth trees and rhododendron showings. At 3.1 miles, the trail crosses the nose of a ridge.

A slow descent then arcs into the Trestle Creek drainage. Weeping cliffs precede the upper falls. This split-level falls plummets some 80 feet from a sidewall of its box canyon. The top part shows a droplet veil; the lower part broadens and skips over ledges of the jet black cliff. Nearby stands an exceptional cedar, and the cliffs compound the drama.

The trail continues by passing behind the droplet veil of the top section of Upper Trestle Creek Falls. Where the trail draws away from the main drainage, descend and round the folded, forested slope. Side drainages seclude tiny charming waterfalls and skipping cascades. Return to Brice Creek Trail at 4.7 miles and backtrack to Lund Park.

78. BOBBY LAKE

Features	■	Huge natural mountain lake
Distance	■	4.5 miles round trip
Elevation change	■	100 feet
Difficulty	■	Easy to moderate
Season	■	Summer into fall
Maps	■	USFS Waldo Lake Wilderness, Willamette National Forest
Information	■	Middle Fork Ranger District; Northwest Forest Pass

A great ramble for foot and mind, this easy trail opens the west door to Bobby Lake. It travels in mountain hemlock and crosses over the Cascade Crest to reach Bobby Lake on the eastern side of the crest. Bobby Lake is a large mountain lake. It cannot be seen in its entirety from one place, so most likely you will want to roam once you get there. The trail along the north shore passes through Deschutes National Forest to emerge at the eastern gateway near Davis Lake. Hiking to the right leads to a popular outcrop for admiring the scenic water.

To reach this lake trail from Oakridge, travel 23 miles southeast on OR 58 and turn left onto FR 5897 toward Waldo Lake. At 5.4 miles, reach the Bobby and Betty Lake trailheads on opposite sides of the road. There is an ample parking lot on the left; when using it, cross carefully to the Bobby Lake Trail on the right side of FR 5897.

Follow the wide needlemat trail into a mature mountain hemlock forest dripping with lichen. A few lodgepole pines, big western white pines, and dwarf huckleberry add to the forest walk. The terrain is gentle, despite being so near the crest. This trail is part of the Eugene to (Pacific) Crest Trail; you might notice the markers. At the junction at 0.3 mile continue forward; to the right is the Gold Lake Trail.

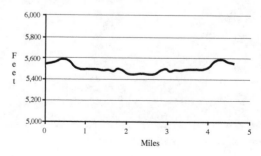

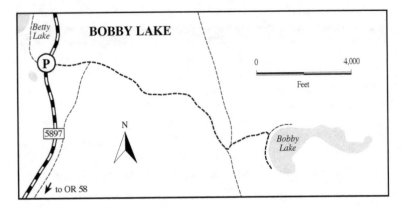

The trail mildly undulates on its forest meander. A blowdown site with uprooted trees and snags varies viewing at 0.9 mile. At 1.75 miles, meet the Pacific Crest Trail and follow it left 0.1 mile before bearing right to resume the journey to Bobby Lake.

Here the trail crosses over the crest, where it becomes the Moore Creek Trail in Deschutes National Forest. The trail forks upon arriving at the lake (2 miles). Left continues the Moore Creek Trail; a right leads to a large forest opening for lake viewing before rounding to the outcrop vantage (2.25 miles).

Bobby Lake, Deschutes National Forest

At 86 acres in size, Bobby Lake is an engaging natural lake with a vast open water, quiet coves, and plenty of room for hikers to disperse. The lake is rimmed by forest, with Maiden Peak rising above its rolling skyline to the south. Sunken logs lace across the ashy lakebed. With no inlet, the spring-fed lake is remarkably clear and reaches 70 feet in depth. The rock outcrop, the turnaround for this hike, slopes into the blue water and adds views of The Twins to the north. When ready, return west.

79. DIAMOND CREEK FALLS

Features ■	90-foot waterfall, rhododendrons
Distance ■	3.7 miles round trip
Elevation change ■	300 feet
Difficulty ■	Easy to moderate
Season ■	Late spring through fall
Maps ■	USFS Diamond Peak Wilderness, Willamette National Forest
Information ■	Middle Fork Ranger District; Northwest Forest Pass

This hike starts at the Salt Creek Falls Observation Area and offers a loop trip to Diamond Creek Falls tucked away on the forest slope. The watery plummet of Diamond Creek Falls spills as a broad fan of white lace. It is especially lovely in late spring to early summer, when it is accessible yet full and exuberant. The trail extends a couple of different perspectives on the waterfall. Attractive mid-elevation forest and rhododendron usher hikers to the watery delight.

Look for the Salt Creek Falls viewpoint turnoff south off OR 58, about 21 miles east of Oakridge and 5 miles west of Willamette Pass. Follow the paved access road to the viewpoint and trailhead parking

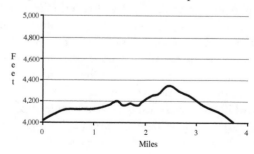

Diamond Creek Falls, Willamette National Forest

area. A kiosk, restroom, and picnic area serve visitors. You will find the viewing for Salt Creek Falls 100 feet behind the kiosk. The trail to Diamond Creek Falls begins upstream at the picnic area, with a footbridge crossing of Salt Creek. A trail sign greets you once across.

Head toward Diamond Creek Falls and Vivian Lake, passing through hemlock-fir forest, coming to the loop junction in 0.2 mile. Now, head right (counterclockwise) toward Too Much Bear Lake and the falls. The trail ascends parallel to Salt Creek, reaching the rim of the basalt cliffs that shape the canyon. At 0.4 mile, a left spur leads to Too Much Bear Lake in a matter of strides. This large oval pool is ringed by rhododendron, mountain ash, and vine maple, with forest marching to its shore. In early summer, pink pompoms add to the reflection; in fall the adorning hues are red and gold.

Upon return to the loop trail, spurs lead to overlooks of Salt Creek and Diamond Creek Canyons. The spur at 0.8 mile offers a glimpse at a lower falls on Diamond Creek. At 1.5 miles reach the actual Diamond Creek Falls spur. It switchbacks and descends via stair-cut log, ramp, and boardwalk (be careful when wet) to cross the bridge over Diamond Creek. Proceed upstream to the base-of-the-falls view (1.7 miles). The falls spills in white streamers tracing the gentle angle of the cliff. The creek's race away from the falls' base, picturesque boulders, logs, and moss contribute to the setting, making this site a winner.

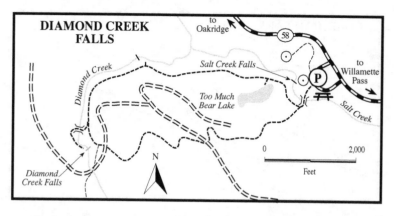

DIAMOND CREEK FALLS

Back on the primary trail, find an upper, side-angle view of the falls before coming to the loop junction at 2.1 miles; head left. The trail twice crosses forest roads and travels in tranquil forest lush with rhododendron. The rhododendron bushes stretch shoulder- to head-high and provide a showy escort back to the trailhead.

Tip: You couldn't ask for a better trailhead than the one here at Salt Creek Falls. Salt Creek Falls, viewed from the rim observation railing and lower deck, is the second tallest waterfall in Oregon. It measures in at 286 feet high and spills at a rate of 50,000 gallons per minute. A natural extension to an area visit is the 0.5-mile Salt Creek Falls Trail. A stairway links the viewpoints, and interpretive signs explain the area's natural history.

80. CORRIGAN LAKE

Features ■	Wonderful wilderness lake, Diamond Peak views
Distance ■	3.2 miles round trip
Elevation change ■	500 feet
Difficulty ■	Moderate
Season ■	Summer into fall
Maps ■	USFS Diamond Peak Wilderness, Willamette National Forest
Information ■	Middle Fork Ranger District; Northwest Forest Pass, wilderness permit

An artery to Diamond Peak, this trail offers a pleasing wilderness experience in alpine forest with a shimmery prize at the hike's end. Ideal

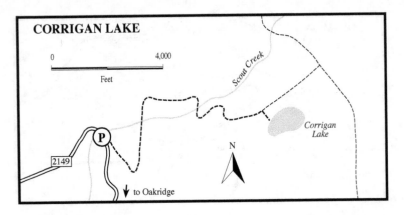

for families, the trip rolls out a fairly easy climb while still providing a sense of accomplishment. En route gather a view of Diamond Peak and the Calapooya ridge. A lakeshore view of Diamond Peak is available from the western shoreline. Because the spur to Corrigan Lake is unmarked, watch for it at 1.5 miles.

To reach this lake trail, from OR 58 at the eastern outskirts of Oakridge, turn south on Kitson Springs Road and in 0.5 mile bear right onto FR 21. Follow it about 29 miles to its junction with FR 2149 (Pioneer Gulch Road). Turn left and remain on FR 2149 for 4.6 miles to find the trailhead on the right and ample parking on the left beside a creek.

The trail ascends into wilderness, touring a high-elevation forest of mountain hemlock and true firs (noble, Pacific silver, and grand) with a huckleberry understory. A few larger Douglas-fir trees punctuate the lower slope. The design of the trail with switchbacks and long angled traverses eases the climb. Prince's pine, orchids, and bride's bonnet add delicate bloom in season. Sunlight dances from the lichen tresses on the trees.

At 1.2 miles the trail crosses the steep upper drainage of Scout

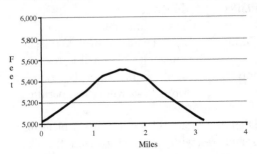

Corrigan Lake and Diamond Peak, Diamond Peak Wilderness, Willamette National Forest

Creek that flows past trail parking. Soon after the trail wraps around the ridge, gathering its first impression of Diamond Peak. The ridge holds a drier, more open forest. At 1.5 miles, where the Corrigan Lake Trail turns left toward the Diamond Peak Trail, bear right (straight) to arrive at the west shore of lovely oval Corrigan Lake (1.6 miles).

This lake is truly a high-mountain charmer. The bold look at Diamond Peak and its flanking east and west ridges at the point of arrival is just frosting. The hypnotic blue-green or emerald lake, depending on lighting, is forest-rimmed. The west shore has an open spacing of big pines that eases lake viewing and welcomes you to sit a spell. The knocking of a woodpecker or the raucous call of a raven alone breaks the still. Backtrack when ready to give up the lake serenity.

81. ROCKPILE AND MARIE LAKES

Features	Wilderness lakes
Distance	5.2 miles round trip
Elevation change	1,100 feet
Difficulty	Moderate
Season	Summer into fall
Maps	USFS Diamond Peak Wilderness, Willamette National Forest
Information	Middle Fork Ranger District; Northwest Forest Pass, wilderness permit

This hike follows the lightly used Rockpile Trail into Diamond Peak Wilderness and leads to a pair of high lakes, approaching the Cascade

253

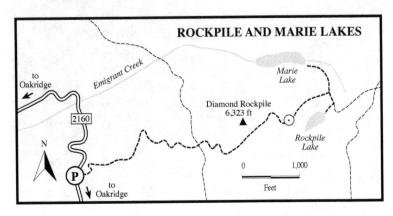

ROCKPILE AND MARIE LAKES

Crest. Hikers ascend through high-elevation forest, snaring views south-southeast where the trail reveals Sawtooth Mountain, Cowhorn Peak, and Mount Thielsen. Marie Lake is the larger of the two lakes; Rockpile is the more secluded lake. Alpine meadow spreads between forest in the lakes area.

To reach this trail from OR 58 at the eastern outskirts of Oakridge, turn south on Kitson Springs Road and in 0.5 mile bear right onto FR 21. Follow it about 29 miles to its junction with FR 2149 (Pioneer Gulch Road). Turn left (north) on FR 2149, following it 3.5 miles. There turn right on FR 2160 (Rockpile Road) and proceed 2.4 miles, finding the trailhead on the left. There is parking on the side of the road both before and after the trailhead.

The trail ascends through a true fir–mountain hemlock–mixed pine forest with an understory of huckleberry, kinnikinnick, manzanita, and a few rhododendrons. It ascends the broad fanning base of Diamond Peak, maintaining a fairly comfortable gradient briefly broken by a few steeper segments. At 0.9 mile reach the four-way junction with Diamond Peak Trail and proceed forward.

As the trail traces a long contour across the south slope, look above you to view the rocky ridge crest of Diamond Rockpile (elevation 6,323

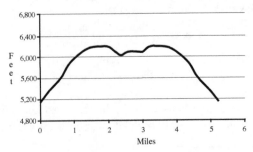

feet). Dwarf huckleberry becomes the lone remaining ground cover and its presence is only patchy. A few mushrooms poke through the needlemat. After the trail reaches the height of the ridge, find the first view with boulder seating at 1.8 miles. Overlook the headwaters of the Middle Fork Willamette River toward Sawtooth Mountain and Cowhorn Peak. Later, Mount Thielsen comes into view. A fog band sometimes lays in the river valley.

After 2 miles the descent to the lakes basin begins. Spy the blue-green water of Rockpile Lake at the base of the slope. To the left glimpse the south face of Diamond Peak. At the headwater of Emigrant Creek (2.2 miles), find the lakes trail junction. Left leads to Marie Lake; right leads to the Pacific Crest Trail (PCT) and Rockpile Lake.

Reach Marie Lake in 0.2 mile. Marie is a long narrow lake preceded by alpine flora and tiny mountain hemlocks. Cinders along shore betray the site's volcanic origin. The forest rim closes out views of Diamond Peak, but hikers are treated to a fine length-of-the-lake view. Boulders and logs edge the shallows.

Proceeding toward the PCT from the headwater of Emigrant Creek adds an open view of Diamond Peak and a visit to Rockpile Lake. Skirt and cross the meadow. You will locate a secondary footpath heading right where the primary trail mounts a low pumiceous sand mound. Follow the footpath right to reach Rockpile Lake in 0.1 mile; the top of the mound near the junction offers the open view of Diamond Peak with its ragged-rock side ridge. Pretty Rockpile Lake is a round serene lake guarded by forest. Its snug location adds to its charm. After visiting both the lake and the Diamond Peak view, return to the 2.2-mile junction (3 miles), and backtrack to the trailhead (5.2 miles).

Diamond Peak, Diamond Peak Wilderness, Willamette National Forest

82. INDIGO LAKE

Features ■	Picturesque lake, Sawtooth Mountain
Distance ■	4.5 miles round trip
Elevation change ■	600 feet
Difficulty ■	Moderate
Season ■	Summer into fall
Maps ■	USFS Rogue–Umpqua Divide, Boulder Creek, and Mount Thielsen Wildernesses; Willamette National Forest
Information ■	Middle Fork Ranger District; Northwest Forest Pass

At the remote southeast corner of Willamette National Forest, mile-high Timpanogas Lake is the hub to a fine trail system offering short hikes to mountain lakes. The selected hike travels to the most captivating of the lakes, Indigo Lake, so named for its brilliant deep-blue color. It sits at the northern foot of Sawtooth Mountain, which is equally well named and the perfect complement. Although the lake is a popular destination, it is still wild enough for pine marten to slip about the rocks in search for pikas. In early to midsummer, mosquitoes help curb visitor numbers and the length of visitor stays; come prepared with spray and netting. Later in the hiking season, you can linger for a more relaxed appreciation.

To reach Timpanogas Lake, its campground, and the trailhead for Indigo Lake, from OR 58 at the eastern outskirts of Oakridge, turn south on Kitson Springs Road toward Hills Creek Reservoir. Go 0.5 mile, and turn right on FR 21, following it for about 32 miles. There turn left on FR 2154 and continue another 11 miles or so to enter this camp on the left. It is a paved and good gravel route. Find the trailhead in camp.

Timpanogas and Lower Timpanogas Lakes abut the campground and provide a scenic start and stop for the hike. Locate the start for the

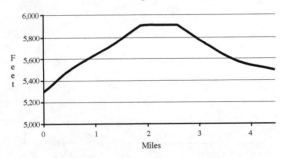

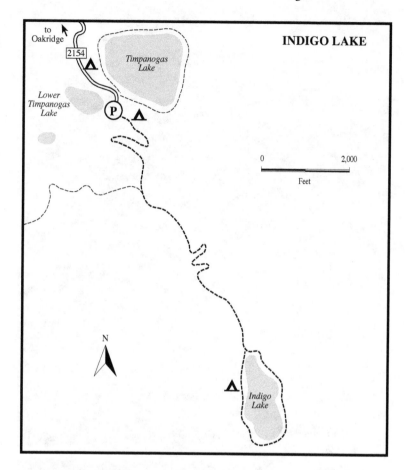

Indigo Lake Trail at the end of the trailhead turnout above Lower Timpanogas Lake. Ascend in a mid-elevation forest of Pacific silver fir and Engelmann spruce with ground-hugging huckleberry and later, showings of heather.

At the 0.75-mile junction, the path ahead continues to Indigo Lake, the middle fork leads to Sawtooth Mountain in 3.5 miles, and the right fork is the 0.5-mile tie trail linking this hike with the June Lake Trail. On the Indigo Lake Trail follow a sparkling tributary upstream, tracing a bench above the water. Then cross the tributary on stones, still chasing it upstream. Where the trail leaves this trickle of water, it weaves through forest, stringing together small meadows and views of Sawtooth Mountain. Cooper's hawks and tiny, neatly camouflaged frogs may compel pauses for better appreciation.

At 1.9 miles arrive at Indigo Lake (elevation 5,900 feet). Sawtooth

Indigo Lake and Sawtooth Mountain, Cascade Lakes Recreation Area, Willamette National Forest

Mountain (elevation 7,302 feet), with its light gray rock, scree slopes, and vertical broken cliffs, looms above the lake setting. A 0.7-mile trail rings the lake in all its blue brilliance, touring in mixed conifer forest and crossing a scree slope where the tread disappears. Pikas scold hikers who invade the rocky complex. The lake is deepest below the scree slope, offering a hole for swimming or fishing. Water-soaked logs from long ago lie at the lake bottom and are visible through the clear water. Five primitive campsites dot the forested shore. The return is as you came.

APPENDIX A
CAMPGROUNDS NEAR TRAILS

HIKE 1

Fort Stevens State Park. This year-round full-service campground has more than 500 campsites, with hookups, tent sites, and hike/bike sites available along with 15 yurts. At the park, discover Oregon's northernmost coastal beach, the Columbia River mouth, an historic military site, and the shipwreck—*Peter Iredale*.

HIKES 3 and 4

Oswald West State Park. This seasonal 28-site walk-in campground sits in an old-growth Sitka spruce setting just inland from the sea. Find a self-service pay station, wheelbarrows to haul gear, restrooms, and water. In summer, sites fill quickly. RVers visiting these trails should go to **Nehalem Bay State Park.** This year-round, full-service park campground is west off US 101 about 7 miles south of Oswald West. It has more than 280 family campsites, plus horse sites and yurts.

HIKES 5, 6, and 7

Cape Lookout State Park. This year-round, full-service family campground strings behind the coastal dune offering open and tree-shaded sites. Campers have convenient access to the beach and headland hikes. It has 39 hookup sites, 176 basic sites, and 10 yurts.

HIKE 9

Beverly Beach State Park. This year-round full-service park campground off US 101 about 7 miles north of Newport (3.6 miles north of Yaquina Head) offers a convenient base for exploring the BLM Outstanding Natural Area. It has 258 sites, about half with hookups, and 21 yurts. Besides beach and coastal access, it has a short nature trail.

HIKES 10 and 11

Cape Perpetua Campground. South of Yachats, this forest service campground along Cape Creek in Cape Perpetua Special Interest Area occupies a lovely grassy drainage bottom between the wooded rises of Cooks Ridge and Cape Perpetua. The campground offers 38 basic sites, and its season runs from Memorial Day weekend into October. The scenic headland has a number of short trails; the interpretive center has exhibits introducing the natural history.

HIKES 12 and 13

Carl G. Washburne State Park. Along the prized Heceta Head coastline, 14 miles north of Florence, this full-service, year-round park campground offers 58 hookup sites, 7 walk-in tent sites, and 2 yurts for overnight lodging. Other park offerings include hiking trails, an ocean beach, and a trail link to Heceta Head Lighthouse.

HIKE 13

Baker Beach Campground. At the beach trailhead, this small forest service campground offers 5 primitive fee sites with hitching posts for horses. A vault toilet is the lone amenity; bring water.

HIKE 14

Jessie M. Honeyman Memorial State Park. Just a couple of miles south of the South Jetty turnoff, this full-service, year-round campground has 360 sites and 10 yurts, offering a convenient place to base when you are exploring Oregon Dunes National Recreation Area. The park provides access to three freshwater lakes and 500-foot dunes. But with direct off-road vehicle access to the dunes from camp, it can get noisy.

HIKE 15

Saddle Mountain State Park. This state park offers 10 seasonal primitive walk-in tent sites at the trailhead.

HIKE 16

Nestucca River Campgrounds. On Nestucca River Road (part of the route to Niagara Falls), a string of four BLM recreation sites between 14 miles and 25 miles east of Beaver offer 38 basic tree-shaded riverside campsites. Most are open April through November, with Rocky Bend open year-round. Find vault toilets. Water is available at the larger seasonal campgrounds.

HIKE 18

Marys Peak Campground. In a scenic patch of small noble firs below the summit, the 6 basic tent sites of this forest service campground are open May through October. The camp sits along the Marys Peak Auto Tour route and is passed by the Meadow Edge Trail. It is within convenient reach of summit views and the other peak trails.

HIKE 19

North Fork Siuslaw Campground. En route to Pawn Old Growth (2.5 miles south of the trailhead), you will find this primitive no-frills 7-site forest service campground. It is best suited for tents; no water.

HIKES 25 and 26
Silver Falls State Park. This year-round full-service developed park campground offers quick access to the Silver Creek Canyon Trail (also known as "Trail of Ten Falls"), a bike trail, and horse trails. It has 100 sites, half with electricity, as well as 14 cabins. The park's historic lodge invites visitors inside with its small food service, gift shop, and few exhibits. On showery days, it offers a chance to duck out of the raindrops.

HIKE 27
Waterloo (Linn) County Park. Reached north off US 20, 0.7 mile west of the turnoff to McDowell Creek Park, this large relaxing county park alongside the South Santiam River offers 60 hookup sites and room to roam. Beware of poison oak in your rambles. River sports also occupy guests.

HIKES 30 through 34
Ainsworth State Park. This fully developed 49-site seasonal campground on the Columbia River Scenic Highway (exit 35 off I-84) provides a convenient base for Gorge discovery. The long-distance Gorge Trail, tracing the front wall of the Oregon side of the Gorge, passes above camp and stitches together many area attractions.

HIKES 36 and 37
Eagle Creek Campground. Reached via I-84 eastbound, exit 41, this seasonal U.S. Forest Service campground offers 19 basic forested sites with running-water facilities. It sits on a slope above Eagle Creek, providing a base for area hiking. In fall, salmon struggle upstream to spawn in the clean gravels.

HIKE 38
Wahtum Lake Campground. This primitive U.S. Forest Service campground at the trailhead offers a handful of forest rim sites. No camping is allowed within 200 feet of the lakeshore. Picnic tables and toilet are the lone amenities.

HIKES 39 and 40
Lost Lake Campground. Part of the Lost Lake recreation complex, this attractive forest service campground, open May into October, sits back from the lake edge in a glorious mixed-conifer forest with a rhododendron complement. It has 80 basic sites, 31 walk-in tent sites, 6 horse sites, and some cabins.

HIKE 41
Cloud Cap Saddle Campground. This seasonal forest service campground offers a handful of sites along the Timberline Trail. Find tables, vault toilet, and piped water (when temperatures are warm enough). The high-elevation camp enjoys a grand neighborhood.

HIKE 42

Sherwood Campground. This seasonal forest service campground nestled among the big trees between the East Fork Hood River and OR 35 offers a convenient base for discovering the hike to Tamanawas Falls and other area trails. It has 14 basic sites and vault toilets; bring water.

HIKE 43

Lost Creek Campground. This seasonal forest service campground is designed for the wheelchair public and offers 10 wheelchair-accessible basic sites and 5 walk-in/roll-in sites. It sits in an engaging setting of mountain hemlock and rhododendron near Lost Creek. Other visitors to the area should camp at McNeil Campground (see following entry).

HIKES 43 and 44

McNeil Campground. Above the deep-cut Sandy River course, in the open forest of Old Maid Flat, this seasonal forest service campground is reached off FR 1825 en route to the featured trailheads. It offers 34 basic sites with vault toilets but no water.

HIKE 45

Tollgate Campground. East of the Wildwood BLM Recreation Site, you will find this seasonal forest service campground south off US 26, 0.4 mile east of Rhododendron. It is tucked among the big trees along Zigzag River. The campground has 15 basic sites and sits beside the historic site of a toll station on Old Barlow Road—part of the Oregon Trail.

HIKE 46

Alpine Campground. Reached via Timberline Road on Mount Hood, this forest service campground (open July through September) offers 16 basic tent sites, serving hiker and snowboarder. RVers can find an overnight base at either Camp Creek or Trillium Lake Campgrounds. You'll find both of these on US 26 (see their listings that follow).

HIKES 46, 47, and 49

Camp Creek Campground. This attractive seasonal forest service campground offers 25 basic sites nestled among the big trees along Camp Creek. It is south off US 26, 2.6 miles east of Rhododendron.

HIKE 48

Green Canyon Campground. At this campground on Salmon River Road, 4.5 miles south off US 26, picturesque centuries-old trees and the Salmon River complement stays. It is open late May through September and offers 15 basic sites and quiet.

HIKES 46, 49, and 50

Trillium Lake Campground. Beside a picturesque lake with a popular Mount Hood view, this seasonal forest service campground offers 57 basic sites. Find the marked turn for the campground south off US 26, 1.7 miles east of Government Camp and west of the US 26–OR 35 intersection.

HIKE 51

Ripplebrook or Rainbow Campground. Both are seasonal forest service campgrounds near the OR 224–FR 46–FR 57 junction, 0.5 mile south of the Alder Flat trailhead. Both offer family camping along the Oak Grove Fork of the Clackamas River. Ripplebrook has 13 sites; Rainbow, 17 sites.

HIKE 52

Kingfisher Campground. This seasonal forest service campground on FR 70 en route to Bagby Hot Springs has 23 basic sites in old-growth forest along the Hot Springs Fork of the Collawash River.

HIKE 53

Elkhorn Valley Recreation Site. Along the Little North Santiam River en route to Opal Creek, this seasonal BLM campground offers 23 basic sites in old growth. The river is one of the most engaging in the state, with deep pools drawing summertime swimmers.

HIKE 54

Lower Lake Campground. Away from the bustle found at the core of Olallie Lake Scenic Area, this quiet, rustic forest service campground offers 8 forested sites. It is open seasonally and has no water. The camp's namesake lake sits just a short hike away.

HIKE 55

Olallie Lake Campgrounds. Paul Dennis, Camp Ten, and Peninsula Campgrounds offer convenient overnight bases for exploring the Olallie and Monon Lakes area. Together, they offer dozens of sites, with water available at Paul Dennis and Peninsula. They are seasonal, forested, and sit beside Olallie Lake.

HIKE 56

Breitenbush Campground. En route to the trailhead on FR 46 (9.1 miles north of Detroit), find this seasonal forest service campground tucked in a picturesque forest along the Breitenbush River. The campground has 29 basic sites.

HIKE 59

Marion Forks Campground. Off OR 22 in Marion Forks (0.1 mile south of the Marion Lake trailhead turnoff), this attractive, lightly used seasonal forest service campground offers 15 basic sites on the south shore of pretty Marion Creek. Its neighbor is the Marion Forks Fish Hatchery.

HIKE 62

Cascadia State Park. In the South Santiam River Valley, this seasonally open state park offers 25 basic campsites. Besides the campground, the park rolls out a relaxing riverside setting of lawn and shade trees for day use and pic-nicking. Park visitors divide their time between Lower Soda Creek Falls and the river.

HIKE 63

Lost Prairie Campground. About 4.5 miles east of the Iron Mountain trailhead turnoff, this seasonal forest service campground has 4 basic and 6 walk-in tent sites. It also provides easy access to both Tombstone Prairie and the Hackleman old-growth grove.

HIKES 64 and 65

Coldwater Cove Campground. On the east shore of Clear Lake, this seasonal forest service campground offers 35 basic sites in the shadow of firs. From camp, find convenient shoreline and lake trail access. The east shore segment of the lake loop is part of the McKenzie River National Recreation Trail.

Ice Cap Campground. In a forest setting downstream from Clear Lake, this seasonal forest service campground on the McKenzie River at Koosah Falls offers 14 basic sites and 8 tent sites. Sahalie and Koosah Falls and the McKenzie River Trail lie within easy reach of camp.

HIKES 68 and 69

Scott Lake Campground. Off McKenzie Pass Scenic Byway in the forest along Scott Lake (5.5 miles south of the Little Belknap Crater/PCT trailhead), find 20 tent sites with toilets but no water. This is a seasonal forest service campground. Overnighters can explore Scott Mountain, Little Belknap Crater, and other area trails.

HIKE 70

Limberlost Campground. This seasonal forest service campground on OR 242, 1.4 miles northeast of its junction with OR 126 and 7.1 miles south of Proxy trailhead, offers 12 forested sites above Lost Creek and has easy access to McKenzie Pass Scenic Byway and its many trail offerings.

HIKE 72
Skookum Creek Campground. At the gateway to Erma Bell Lakes, this forested walk-in campground along Skookum Creek has a large central parking area and offers 8 tent sites.

HIKE 73
Kiahanie Campground. About 7 miles southwest of Constitution Grove, this forest service campground offers 19 basic sites in uncut forest along the North Fork Middle Fork Willamette Wild and Scenic River. It is open seasonally.

HIKES 75 and 78
Waldo Lake Campgrounds. Three seasonal forest service campgrounds along Waldo Lake's shore—North Waldo, Islet, and Shadow Bay—offer convenient access to the featured Shoreline and Bobby Lake Trails, as well as others. Altogether they offer 177 basic sites. North Waldo and Islet sit alongside the described section of the Shoreline Trail.

HIKE 77
Cedar Creek Campground. This quiet, shady campground along Brice Creek offers 8 basic sites but has no drinking water; bring what you will need from home. It's a forest service campground, generally open year-round.

HIKE 79
Gold Lake Campground. North off OR 58 east of the Salt Creek Falls viewpoint, this serene campground sits in forest along a pristine alpine lake—the headwater of Salt Creek. This forest service campground has 20 basic sites and is usually open June through September.

HIKES 80 and 81
Indigo Springs Campground. On FR 21 just before its junction with FR 2149, find this tiny forest service campground with just 3 sites and no drinking water. Nonetheless, it enjoys a rich forest setting along Indigo Springs and Creek and sits next to the historic Oregon Central Military Wagon Road. The campground is open spring through fall. Larger Sacandaga Campground (sixteen sites) sits a few miles farther west.

HIKE 82
Timpanogas Lake Campground. This forest service campground below the Cascade Crest provides a base for lake discovery, with Timpanogas and Lower Timpanogas Lakes right in camp. It is typically open July to mid-October and has 10 basic sites. Mosquitoes can chase campers away in early to midsummer.

APPENDIX B
CONTACTS, RESOURCES, AND MAPS

MAP SOURCES

Green Trails, Inc.
  P.O. Box 77734
  Seattle, WA 98177
  (206) 546-6277 (MAPS)
  www.greentrails.com/ormap.shtml

USGS Information Services
  P.O. Box 25286
  Denver, CO 80225
  1-888-ASK-USGS
  mac.usgs.gov/

NORTHWEST FOREST PASS

For a current listing of Northwest Forest Pass trails or to purchase a
  Northwest Forest Pass online: *www.fs.fed.us/r6/rec.htm*

PERTINENT AGENCIES

Bureau of Land Management: *www.or.blm.gov/directory.htm*
Nature of the Northwest (information center for nature and
  outdoor recreation in Oregon and Washington):
  www.naturenw.org/
Oregon Department of Fish and Wildlife: *www.dfw.state.or.us/*
Oregon State Parks: *www.prd.state.or.us/*
Portland City Parks: *www.parks.ci.portland.or.us/*
U.S. Fish and Wildlife Service: *www.fws.gov*
U.S. National Forests, Pacific Northwest Region: *www.fs.fed.us/r6/*

HIKING ORGANIZATIONS
Chemeketans:
   www.chemeketans.org/

Mazamas:
   909 NW 19th Avenue
   Portland, OR 97209
   (503) 227-2345
   www.mazamas.org/

Obsidians:
   P.O. Box 322
   Eugene, OR, 97440
   www.obsidians.org/

Leave No Trace:
   www.LNT.org

WEATHER
The Weather Station's forecast: *www.weather.com/*
Local television station weather forecasts:
   KATU: *www.katu.com/weather/*
   KGW: *www.kgw.com/weather/*
   KOIN: *www.koin.com/weather/cgi-bin/weather.cgi*

ROAD REPORTS
Oregon Department of Transportation:
   1-800-977-ODOT (1-800-977-6368)
   www.tripcheck.com/

APPENDIX C
TRAIL COMPARISON GRID

Water. Because some sources are seasonal and systems can fail, always bring a safe quantity.

Area Camping. This heading indicates developed campgrounds at or near trails. Cross-reference Appendix A.

Family. Most trails are suitable for family use. Parents must match trails to interest, age, and ability of youngsters.

Hike Name	Hike #	Agency Trail #	Feature	Round-Trip Distance (miles)	Pass/Fee	Permits	Hiker	Horse	Mountain Bike	Leashed Pets	Toilet	Water	Area Camping	Family
BARRIER-FREE TRAILS														
Bridal Veil Falls and Overlook	31		waterfall and wildflowers	0.5-mile Overlook Trail only			•			•	•	•	•	•
Historic 804 Trail	10		rocky coast	1.5			•			•	•	•	•	•
Lakeshore Trail, Lost Lake	39	656	tucked-away lake	part of its 3 miles	•		•			•	•	•	•	•
Lost Creek	43	776	scenic creek, buried forest	0.5	•		•			•	•	•	•	•
Powell Butte	23		urban natural area	0.6-mile Mountain View Trail only			•			•	•	•		•
Wildwood Wetland	45		rare habitat and wildlife viewing	0.9	•		•				•	•	•	•
Willamette Mission State Park	24		Willamette River	up to 4.2	•		•		•	•	•	•		•

EASY TRAILS

Hike Name	Hike #	Agency Trail #	Feature	Round-Trip Distance (miles)	Pass/Fee	Permits	Hiker	Horse	Mountain Bike	Leashed Pets	Toilet	Water	Area Camping	Family
Alder Flat	51	574	old growth, wild and scenic river	1.8	•		•			•			•	•
Bridal Veil Falls and Overlook	31		waterfall and wildflowers	1.2			•			•			•	•
Coffenbury Lake	1		coastal lake	2.4	•		•			•	•	•	•	•
Constitution Grove	73	3675	old growth	0.2	•		•			•	•	•	•	•
Joe Goddard Nature Trail	76	3690	fabulous old growth	0.5	•		•							•
Lakeshore Trail, Lost Lake	39	656	tucked-away lake	3	•		•			•	•		•	•
Little Zigzag Falls	47	795C	picturesque falls and creek	0.6	•		•			•			•	•
Oak Island	21		birdwatching	up to 3.4	•		•			•				•
Pawn Old Growth	19		500-year-old trees	0.9			•			•	•			•
Powell Butte	23		urban natural area	2			•			•				•
Proxy Falls	70	3932	waterfall duo	1.4	•	•	•			•	•	•	•	•
Restless Waters–Cooks Chasm	11		rocky coast	1.8	•		•			•	•		•	•
Salal Hill	9		lighthouse and coastal views	0.7			•				•		•	•
Shoreline Trail, Waldo Lake	75	3590.2	one of clearest lakes in the world	4	•		•		•	•	•		•	•
Wahclella Falls	36	438	50-foot waterfall	2	•		•			•	•		•	•
Woodpecker Loop	28		wildlife refuge, birding	1.2			•			•	•			•

Hike Name	Hike #	Agency Trail #	Feature	Round-Trip Distance (miles)	Pass/Fee	Permits	Hiker	Horse	Mountain Bike	Leashed Pets	Toilet	Water	Area Camping	Family
EASY TO MODERATE TRAILS														
Bagby Hot Springs	52	544	rustic hot springs tubs, old growth	3	•		•			•	•		•	
Baker Beach	13		lightly traveled beach	up to 6.2	•		•			•			•	•
Bobby Lake	78	3663	lovely, big mountain lake	4.5	•		•	•	•	•	•		•	•
Diamond Creek Falls	79	3598	90-foot waterfall	3.7	•		•	•	•	•	•	•	•	•
Lower Soda Creek Falls	62		150-foot waterfall	1.5			•			•	•		•	•
McDowell Creek Falls	27		scenic creek canyon, 3 waterfalls	2.2			•			•	•		•	•
South Breitenbush Gorge	56	3366	old growth, gorge	4 or a 2 or 2.5-mile shuttle	•		•	•	•	•			•	•
South Jetty Beach	14		Oregon Dunes NRA beach	up to 7.4	•		•			•	•		•	•
Sweet Creek	20		falls and cascades	5.2	•		•			•	•			•
EASY UP TO DIFFICULT TRAILS (depends on distance walked)														
Bayocean Peninsula	5		spit, ocean, bay	up to 7.4			•			•	•		•	•
Netarts Spit	6		ocean spit, Three Arch views, harbor seals	up to 10	•		•			•	•	•	•	•
Wildwood, Germantown Road	22		urban wilderness forest	up to 10			•			•				•

MODERATE TRAILS

Hike Name	Hike #	Agency Trail #	Feature	Round-Trip Distance (miles)	Pass/Fee	Permits	Hiker	Horse	Mountain Bike	Leashed Pets	Toilet	Water	Area Camping	Family
Buried Forest	46	600/2000	Mount Hood views and volcanic legacy	1.2	•		•	•		•	•	•	•	•
Cape Falcon	3		coastal views	4.5			•			•	•	•	•	
Cape Lookout	7		coastal headland	4.8	•		•			•			•	•
Carpenter Mountain	66	3302	summit lookout and vantage	2			•			•				•
Clear Lake	64	3507	icy natural lake, lava flow	4.9	•		•		•	•	•	•	•	•
Corrigan Lake	80	3654	wilderness lake, Diamond Peak views	3.2		•	•	•		•			•	•
Drift Creek Falls	17	1378	suspension bridge, falls	3	•		•			•				•
Duffy Lake	61	3427	wilderness lake	6.5	•	•	•	•		•	•			•
Elowah and Upper McCord Creek Falls	35		pair of waterfall destinations	3.2			•			•	•		•	•
Erma Bell Lakes	72	3563	wilderness lakes	5.8	•	•	•			•			•	•
Heceta Head	12		lighthouse, costal views	4	•		•			•	•	•	•	
Indigo Lake	82	3649	fantastic high lake	4.5	•		•	•		•		•	•	•
Latourell Falls	30		250-foot waterfall, 100-foot upper falls	2.5			•			•		•	•	•

MODERATE TRAILS (continued)

Hike Name	Hike #	Agency Trail #	Feature	Round-Trip Distance (miles)	Pass/Fee	Permits	Hiker	Horse	Mountain Bike	Leashed Pets	Toilet	Water	Area Camping	Family
Little Belknap Crater	68	2000	crater, lava flow	5	•	•	•			•			•	
Lower Lake–Fish Lake	54	717	mountain lakes, berries	3.2			•	•		•	•		•	•
Marion Lake	59	3436	mountain lake and vistas	5.2	•	•	•	•	•	•	•		•	•
Meadow Edge–Marys Peak Summit	18		summit meadows	3	•		•	•		•			•	•
Mirror Lake	49	664	mountain lake, Mount Hood view	3.2	•		•			•			•	•
Mount Pisgah	29		panorama, oak-prairie hillside, wildflowers	3.2			•			•			•	•
Multnomah Falls	33	441	fourth tallest falls in nation	2.4			•			•	•	•		•
Neahkahnie Mountain	4		coastal views	3			•							
Niagara Falls	16	1379	waterfalls	2			•			•	•	•	•	•
"Old" Salmon River Trail	48	742A	Wild and Scenic River, ancient forest	5.2	•		•			•		•	•	•
Rockpile and Marie Lakes	81	3632	wilderness lakes	5.2		•	•		•	•			•	•
Silver Creek Canyon, South Loop	25		waterfalls	2.1	•		•	•		•	•	•	•	•
Triple Falls	34	438 and 424	trio of side-by-side falls	4.2			•			•			•	•

Hike Name	Hike #	Agency Trail #	Feature	Round-Trip Distance (miles)	Pass/Fee	Permits	Hiker	Horse	Mountain Bike	Leashed Pets	Toilet	Water	Area Camping	Family
MODERATE TRAILS (continued)														
Upper McKenzie River	65	3507	superb river and waterfalls	3			•		•	•	•	•	•	•
Wahtum Lake–Chinidere Mountain	38	406H and 2000	wilderness lake and view	4.7	•	•	•	•		•	•		•	•
MODERATE TO DIFFICULT TRAILS														
Brice Creek–Trestle Falls	77	1403 and 1403C	lovely creek and waterfalls	5.5	•		•		•	•	•		•	•
Coffin Mountain	58	3425	summit lookout, views, beargrass	3	•		•			•				•
Eagle Creek	37	440	premier creek canyon and falls	7.1	•		•			•	•	•	•	•
Harts Cove	8	1303	headland vista and falls	5.4	•		•			•				•
Iron Mountain	63	3389	summit views, wildflowers	3.4	•		•			•	•		•	•
Lost Lake Butte	40	616	summit views	4.5	•		•			•	•	•	•	•
Olallie Lake–Monon Lake	55	731, 732, and 729	mountain lakes, berries	up to 8.4	•		•	•		•	•	•	•	•
Olallie Mountain	71	3529 and 3530	summit views, old lookout	6.8	•	•	•	•		•				
Opal Creek	53	3338	critical old-growth, drainage	7	•		•		•	•			•	•

Hike Name	Hike #	Agency Trail #	Feature	Round-Trip Distance (miles)	Pass/Fee	Permits	Hiker	Horse	Mountain Bike	Leashed Pets	Toilet	Water	Area Camping	Family
MODERATE TO DIFFICULT TRAILS (continued)														
Scott Mountain	69	3531	summit views, wilderness lakes	8	•	•	•	•		•	•		•	•
Silver Creek Canyon, North Loop	26		waterfalls	3	•		•				•		•	•
Tamanawas Falls	42	650 and 650A	100-foot waterfall	4	•		•			•			•	
DIFFICULT TRAILS														
Angels Rest	32	415	gorge views	4.5	•		•			•			•	
Lookout Creek Old-Growth Grove	67	4105	extensive old-growth drainage	7 or 3.7-mile shuttle			•			•				
Old Barlow Road	50		part of the Oregon Trail	2			•			•			•	
Pyramids	60	3380	vistas, wildflowers	5.2	•		•			•			•	
Ramona Falls	44	797	waterfall and mudflow	7.3	•	•	•	•		•			•	•
Saddle Mountain	15		summit	5.9	•		•			•	•	•	•	
Tillamook Head	2		coastal views	5.4	•		•			•	•	•		
Timberline Trail: Cooper Spur Shelter Segment	41	600	Mount Hood, Eliot Glacier	2.8 or 3.2	•	•	•			•	•	•	•	
Triangulation Peak	57	3373 and 3374	volcano views	4.4	•	•	•	•		•				•
Waldo Mountain	74	3592	summit lookout and views	6.2	•	•	•	•		•				

APPENDIX D
TRAIL PICKS: AUTHORS' FAVORITES– FAMILY FAVORITES

AUTHORS' FAVORITES

Asking us to choose favorites among trails is a little like asking parents to choose favorites among their children. Too, on any given day, our list of trail picks may vary. Different habitats bring different rewards and challenges; different days bring different discoveries. With that said, this is our list (in alphabetical order).

Bayocean Peninsula (Hike 5). Even though it's becoming better known, this peninsular offering keeps its sense of an isolated wild. We still have times when the beach is our own, save for the wildlife. Because of the option of exploring the ocean beach, the bay shore path, or a loop linking the two, we can vary our outings here, and the birding is usually good.

Indigo Lake (Hike 82). Despite—or perhaps because of—the mosquitoes and limited window of access, we've fallen in love with this lightly visited out-of-the-way lake. Its truly indigo waters coupled with the chiseled ridge of Sawtooth Mountain create a stunning destination. Pikas and even a pine marten can be spied.

Little Belknap Crater (Hike 68). This lava flow and crater trek inspires marvel with its crusty jumbled expanse, its few pioneering species, and its silver ghosts of former trees. Views are unforgettable with the Three Sisters and Mount Washington Wildernesses facing off here. It's a fun, short adventure into a nether land that chews at the boot leather and draws a striking contrast to the signature green of Northwest Oregon.

Opal Creek (Hike 53). This hike seduces with its towering old-growth trees, crystalline blue-green waters, refreshing falls and pools, and its mining past. An environmental battlefield that was saved, Opal Creek is a touchstone to what is important.

Silver Creek Canyon, North Loop (Hike 26). You could hardly go wrong with any loop in Silver Falls State Park, but this one's our favorite. It receives a bit lighter traffic and visits some superb falls, including our favorite—Middle North Falls—by way of a spur. The picturesque canyon is itself engaging.

Timberline Trail, Cooper Spur Shelter Segment (Hike 41). Awakening the senses, this hike at or above tree line on Mount Hood provides an up-close look at the mountain's majesty and power. The peak and its terrain-bulldozing Eliot Glacier have a spellbinding presence. Weather changes and wind only heighten the drama.

Wahtum Lake–Chinidere Mountain (Hike 38). This hike into the Mark O. Hatfield Wilderness inspires with the beauty of Wahtum Lake and the brief but challenging assault on rocky-topped Chinidere Mountain. The summit vantage presents views of the untouched forest and up to seven volcanoes on clear days. The duo aptly satisfies our wilderness cravings.

FAMILY FAVORITES

Selecting a trail that's right for your family is best done by you, the reader. But these trails appeal to all ages and are sorted by their difficulty rating: barrier-free, easy, moderate, or moderate to difficult. As your youngsters' skill and confidence improves, you can introduce them to more difficult trails. Those seniors who are scaling back from long distances, uneven surfaces, or sharp changes in elevation will find suitable offerings within this list as well.

BARRIER-FREE TRAILS

Willamette Mission State Park (Hike 24). This park gushes with valley charm, and the interlocking loops of the paved hiking trail system are ideal, allowing families to shorten or lengthen their walks as needed or desired. Riverside spurs, rich woodland tangles, filbert groves, mission history, a champion cottonwood, and inviting picnic grounds combine for a fun family outing. Just beware of poison oak when reaching for blackberries or fallen nuts.

EASY TRAILS

Lakeshore Trail, Lost Lake (Hike 39). This shoreline loop advanced by long stretches of barrier-free trail on the eastern half rounds a gorgeous triangular-shaped mountain lake with a panoramic view of Mount Hood. It has a short but satisfying length, with old-growth, marsh, and lake discoveries. Families can extend the outing with a picnic, a stroll of the site's fine Old-Growth Barrier-free Trail, or a row across the lake.

Restless Waters–Cooks Chasm (Hike 11). The clash of sea and land is a spectacle to thrill all ages, and few places show it as well as this trail in Cape Perpetua Special Interest Area. The thunder, spray, and power are felt from the tips of your fingers to the toes of your boots. The views come nonstop. But parents, keep a close eye on your children where spurs lead either to shore or the edge of high-spouting attractions. Watch footing on any wet stretches of trail and steps.

MODERATE TRAILS

Drift Creek Falls (Hike 17). This hike selection has enough elevation change and distance to provide a sense of accomplishment for all. The towering suspension bridge tucked away in the canyon, the elegant waterfall, and some record-size trees help etch the trail in everyone's memory.

Upper McKenzie River (Hike 65). With two superb waterfalls, Sahalie and Koosah; a stunningly beautiful river of bubbling pools, aqua stretches, and blackwater deeps; and an engaging forest to house it all, this loop can't miss. Dippers dive into the icy waters, kingfishers make noisy passes through the canyon, and ospreys soar overhead.

MODERATE TO DIFFICULT TRAILS

Olallie Lake–Monon Lake (Hike 55). Two big wondrous mountain lakes, forest and burn, and meadow, marsh, and huckleberry patch shape discovery. Berry-stained faces are a good endorsement of the trail. Fortunately, berry season arrives after the mosquito numbers have dramatically reduced. The trail is mostly flat, and the hike's length, which determines difficulty, can be adjusted for your needs. Views include Mount Jefferson and Olallie Butte.

Scott Mountain (Hike 69). This one is ideal for youngsters' first "big" hike. It offers challenging and changing scenery, passing vernal ponds and wilderness lakes en route to the summit. These satisfying interim stops are nice if you need to shorten the hike before attaining the summit; flexibility is important when you're a parent. A vantage extending northern views prior to reaching the top likewise can signal a stop or help encourage youngsters up the final distance.

APPENDIX E
BASIC EQUIPMENT FOR DAY HIKING

The amount and type of gear required on a trip will depend on the particulars of the hike, how far you are from help, season, weather, and your personal comfort level. A good fanny pack or day pack to transport the gear is necessary. Be sure your choice carries comfortably when full and has pockets for water bottles. Safe drinking water is always a necessity.

TEN ESSENTIALS

This list compiled by The Mountaineers is the cornerstone to safe outdoor travel. For short hikes in well-traveled areas, you probably can hike safely with only some of these items, but review the list carefully. For longer trips, unfamiliar and lightly traveled areas, and/or foul conditions, play it safe and go for all ten:

1. Extra food
2. Extra clothing
3. Sunglasses
4. Knife
5. Firestarter
6. Matches in waterproof container
7. First-aid kit and manual
8. Flashlight with extra batteries and bulb
9. Map(s) for the trail
10. Compass

FOOD

Because hiking expends energy, bring plenty of food. Be sure to pack smart; choose items you like and will eat; be sure choices won't crush, leak, or spoil in the pack; and repackage items in plastic zip-seal bags when conditions are wet. High-energy food such as cookies, candy bars, protein bars, dried fruit, crackers, and nuts (already shelled) are good choices. Sandwiches (no mayonnaise), hard-boiled eggs, apples, carrot and celery sticks, and the like are other possibilities. Avoid bananas because they continue to ripen in the pack and can bruise and smash, leaving you with an icky mess. Pack extra food in case of delay, either because of an emergency or because you're having a good time.

CLOTHING

Besides a pair of well-fitting hiking boots (with a double sock layer of a light undersock and a wool outer sock), you will need comfortable clothes that you can move in and soil without concern. The following are some of the items to consider for wearing or carrying with you:

- ❑ Longjohns
- ❑ Convertible pants
- ❑ Long-sleeved shirt
- ❑ Wool sweater
- ❑ Wool hat and gloves
- ❑ Visor or cap
- ❑ Rainwear
- ❑ Extra socks
- ❑ Warm coat
- ❑ Belt
- ❑ Swimsuit/trunks
- ❑ Wading shoes

OTHER GEAR
Personal items:
- ❑ Prescriptions
- ❑ Allergy pills
- ❑ Watch
- ❑ Wallet and keys
- ❑ Emergency medical information
- ❑ Toilet paper (and trowel)
- ❑ Diapers and a bag to carry out soiled diapers
- ❑ Biodegradable soap/towelettes

Safety items:
- ❑ Emergency blanket
- ❑ Water pump or purification tablets
- ❑ Whistle
- ❑ Pencil and paper
- ❑ Picture wire for emergency repairs

Miscellaneous:

- ❏ Permits
- ❏ Sunscreen and lip balm
- ❏ Insect repellent/netting
- ❏ Leash
- ❏ Binoculars
- ❏ Camera and film
- ❏ Guidebooks
- ❏ Identification books
- ❏ Foam pad for sitting
- ❏ Large trash bags for emergency shelter for self or gear
- ❏ Zip-seal plastic bags for soiled tissue and trash

APPENDIX F
FURTHER READING

CAMPING

Ostertag, Rhonda and George. *Camping Oregon*. Guilford, CT: FalconGuide/Globe Pequot Press, 1999.

CULTURAL HISTORY

DeVoto, Bernard, ed. *The Journals of Lewis and Clark*. Boston: Houghton Mifflin Company, 1953.

HIKING AND SAFETY

Manning, Harvey. *Backpacking: One Step at a Time*. New York: Vintage Books, 1986.

Preston, Gilbert, M.D. *Wilderness First Aid: When You Can't Call 911*. Guilford, CT: FalconGuide/Globe Pequot Press, 1997.

NATURAL HISTORY

Jolley, Russ. *Wildflowers of the Columbia Gorge: A Comprehensive Field Guide*. Portland, OR: Oregon Historical Society Press, 1988.

Little, Elbert L. *The Audubon Society Field Guide to North American Trees (Western Region)*. New York: Alfred A. Knopf, 1980.

Scott, Shirley L., ed. *National Geographic Society Field Guide to the Birds of North America*. Washington, D.C.: National Geographic Society, 1996.

Spellenberg, Richard. *The Audubon Society Field Guide to North American Wildflowers*. New York: Alfred A. Knopf, 2001.

OTHER

McArthur, Lewis A. *Oregon Geographic Names*. 6th ed. Portland, OR: Oregon Historical Society Press, 1992.

APPENDIX G
AGENCY LISTINGS

**Cape Perpetua
Interpretive Center**
2400 Highway 101 South
Yachats, OR 97498
(541) 547-3289

**Clackamas River
Ranger District**
595 Northwest Industrial Way
Estacada, OR 97023
(503) 630-6861

**Columbia River Gorge
National Scenic Area**
902 Wasco Avenue, Suite 200
Hood River, OR 97031
(541) 386-2333

**Cottage Grove
Ranger District**
78405 Cedar Park Road
Cottage Grove, OR 97424
(541) 767-5000

Detroit Ranger District
HC 73, Box 320
Mill City, OR 97360
(503) 854-3366

Hebo Ranger District
P.O. Box 235
Hebo, OR 97122
(503) 392-3161

Hood River Ranger District
6780 Highway 35
Mt. Hood–Parkdale, OR 97041
(541) 352-6002

Lane County Parks Division
90064 Coburg Road
Eugene, OR 97408
(541) 682-2000

**Linn County Parks and
Recreation Department**
3010 Ferry Street Southwest
Albany, OR 97321
(541) 967-3917

Mapleton Ranger District
4480 Highway 101, Building G
Florence, OR 97439
(541) 902-8526

**McKenzie River
Ranger District**
57600 McKenzie Highway
McKenzie Bridge, OR 97413
(541) 822-3381

Middle Fork Ranger District
46375 Highway 58
Westfir, OR 97492
(541) 782-2291

Mount Hood Information Center
65000 East Highway 26
Welches, OR 97067
(503) 622-4822

Oregon Dunes National Recreation Area
855 Highway Avenue
Reedsport, OR 97467
(541) 271-3611

Oregon State Parks
Oregon Parks and Recreation Department
1115 Commercial Street Northeast
Salem, OR 97301
(503) 378-6305
Park information line:
  1-800-551-6949
www.prd.state.or.us/

Portland Parks and Recreation Department
Hoyt Arboretum
4000 Southwest Fairview Boulevard
Portland, OR 97221
(503) 228-8733

Powell Butte Nature Park
Portland Parks and Recreation, East Field Office
5701 Southeast 86th
Portland, OR 97266
(503) 823-6131

Salem District, BLM
1717 Fabry Road Southeast
Salem, OR 97306
(503) 375-5646

Sauvie Island Wildlife Area
18330 Northwest Sauvie Island Road
Portland, OR 97231
(503) 621-3488

Sweet Home Ranger District
3225 Highway 20
Sweet Home, OR 97386
(541) 367-5168

Tillamook County Parks
P.O. Box 633
Garibaldi, OR 97118
(503) 322-3477

Waldport Ranger District
1049 Southwest Pacific Highway
Waldport, OR 97394
(541) 563-3211

William L. Finley National Wildlife Refuge
26208 Finley Refuge Road
Corvallis, OR 97333
(541) 757-7236

Yaquina Head Outstanding Natural Area
P.O. Box 936
Newport, OR 97365
(541) 574-3100

INDEX

ABOUT THE AUTHORS

RHONDA and GEORGE OSTERTAG have been wearing out hiking boots over the past twenty years, uncovering Oregon's prized haunts in nature. They have more than a dozen outdoor guidebooks to their credit, as well as hundreds of articles, calendars, and postcards. While they prefer to be outdoors, they do find their way back to the computer to share their discoveries with readers. This book gathers the finest short hikes in the northwest part of the state of Oregon, coaxing even the couch potato onto the trail.

THE MOUNTAINEERS, founded in 1906, is a nonprofit outdoor activity and conservation club, whose mission is "to explore, study, preserve, and enjoy the natural beauty of the outdoors. . . . " Based in Seattle, Washington, the club is now one of the largest such organizations in the United States, with seven branches throughout Washington State.

The Mountaineers sponsors both classes and year-round outdoor activities in the Pacific Northwest, which include hiking, mountain climbing, ski-touring, snowshoeing, bicycling, camping, kayaking and canoeing, nature study, sailing, and adventure travel. The club's conservation division supports environmental causes through educational activities, sponsoring legislation, and presenting informational programs. All club activities are led by skilled, experienced volunteers, who are dedicated to promoting safe and responsible enjoyment and preservation of the outdoors.

If you would like to participate in these organized outdoor activities or the club's programs, consider a membership in The Mountaineers. For information and an application, write or call The Mountaineers, Program Center, 7700 Sand Point Way NE, Seattle, WA 98115; 206-521-6001.

The Mountaineers Books, an active, nonprofit publishing program of the club, produces guidebooks, instructional texts, historical works, natural history guides, and works on environmental conservation. All books produced by The Mountaineers Books fulfill the club's mission.

Send or call for our catalog of more than 500 outdoor titles:

The Mountaineers Books
1001 SW Klickitat Way, Suite 201
Seattle, WA 98134
800-553-4453
mbooks@mountaineersbooks.org
www.mountaineersbooks.org

The Mountaineers Books is proud to be a corporate sponsor of Leave No Trace, whose mission is to promote and inspire responsible outdoor recreation through education, research, and partnerships. The Leave No Trace program is focused specifically on human-powered (nonmotorized) recreation.

Leave No Trace strives to educate visitors about the nature of their recreational impacts, as well as offer techniques to prevent and minimize such impacts. Leave No Trace is best understood as an educational and ethical program, not as a set of rules and regulations.

For more information, visit *www.LNT.org*, or call 800-332-4100.

CPSIA information can be obtained
at www.ICGtesting.com
Printed in the USA
HW010939011218
85999-54135FF